I0340895

Cover image: *Norterma, Yellow Tara, destroyer of material , social and spiritual poverty.* Painted by Ruth Perini (Srimukti) 2020

Śāṇḍilya Upaniṣad

Timeless Teachings on the Eightfold Path of Yoga

Original Sanskrit text with Transliteration, Translation and Commentary

by Ruth Perini (Śrimukti)

Dedication

In love and gratitude to my friend

and mentor

Swami Satyadharma Saraswati

(1946-2019)

CONTENTS

Introduction 1
Invocation 8
CHAPTER 1
First Section
Verse
1. Eight Limbs; Yama 10
Second Section
Verse
1. Niyama 23
Third Section
Eight Āsanas
Verse
1-3. Svastikāsana, Gomukhāsana, Padmāsana 31
4-7. Vīrāsana, Siṃhāsana, Siddhāsana 36
8-12. Bhadrāsana, Muktāsana, Māyūrāsana 39
13-15. Mastery of Āsana 43
Fourth Section
The Subtle Body
Verse
1. Śāṇḍilya Inquires 45
2-5a. Pranic Body 47
5b-7. Maṇipura Cakra 50
8. Kuṇḍalinī 52
9-11. Fourteen Nāḍīs 55
12-14. Ten Vāyus 61
Fifth Section
Verse
1. Preparation for Yoga Practice 68
2-3. Meditating on Agni Maṇḍala 71
Sixth Section
Verse
1-2. Prāṇāyāma 74
3-4. Gāyatrī Sāvitrī Sarasvatī 75
5. Prāṇāyāma with Om 77
Seventh Section
Verse
1. Nāḍī Śodhana Prāṇāyāma 79
2-6. Kumbhaka 82
7-13. Effects of Nāḍī Śodhana Prāṇāyāma 85
13.1-13.4. Destruction of Disease (1) 90
13.5-13.6. Sahita and Kevala Kumbhaka 93

14-16. Vaiṣṇavī and Khecarī Mudrā 97
17-23. Dissolution of Mind 100
24-27. Yoga and Jñāna 104
28-36. Control of Prāṇa 107
36kha-38. Awakening Kuṇḍalinī 112
39-42gha. Khecarī Mudrā (2) 115
43-51. Destruction of Disease (2) 119
52a. Knowledge of All Worlds 124
52b. Effects of Constraint 129
Eighth Section
Verse
1-2. Pratyāhāraḥ 133
Ninth Section
Verse
1. Dhāraṇā 136
Tenth Section
Verse
1. Dhyāna 139
Eleventh Section
Verse
1. Samādhi 141
CHAPTER 2
Verse
1-6. Knowledge of Brahman 142
CHAPTER 3
First Section
Verse
1-6. Creation of the Universe 147
Second Section
Verse
1-10. Names of Brahman 153
11-15. Dattātreya 157

APPENDICES
A.End Notes 160
B.References 162
C.Pronunciation Guide 163
D.Sanskrit Text 165
E.Continuous Translation 187
F.Swami Satyadharma 208
G.Author's Note 212

Introduction

Veda is a Sanskrit word meaning 'knowledge'. In the context of the Vedas, it means 'revealed knowledge which is *śruti*, 'heard' from within, not taught. These ancient spiritual texts or hymns, through which we can learn much of the perceptions and insights of the early vedic seers, are grouped into four *samhitas* or collections: *Rig Veda, Yajur Veda, Sāma Veda* and *Atharva Veda*. They were revealed to enlightened beings 3,000 to 4,500 years ago or more (the Rig-Veda contains astronomical references describing occurrences in 5,000 to 3,000 BCE), and transmitted orally by the sages from generation to generation within brahmin families.

The four Vedas were considered to be divine revelations, and each word was carefully memorised. This was to ensure accurate transmission, but also because each syllable was considered to have spiritual power, its source being the supreme, eternal sound. This was a mammoth task, as there are 20,358 verses in the four Vedas, approximately two thousand printed pages. They were composed in fifteen different metres, which demanded perfect control of the breath. Georg Feuerstein describes them as 'a composite of symbol, metaphor, allegory, myth and story, as well as paradox and riddle' and their composers as 'recipients and revealers of the invisible order of the cosmos [with] inspired insights or illumined visions'[1].

Rig Veda

The Rig Veda is the oldest spiritual text in the world and still regarded as sacred, containing 1,028 hymns or songs of 10,589 verses in praise of the divine (*rig* or *ric* meaning 'praise'). Each hymn is recognised as a *mantra*, a sacred sound vibration, which releases energy from limited material awareness, thus expanding the consciousness. It is also the earliest surviving form of Sanskrit. The illumined seers composed the hymns while established in the highest consciousness, thus able to commune with luminous beings of the higher realms. There are about 250 hymns in praise of *Indra*, the divine force behind the ocean, heavens, thunder, lightning, rain and the light of the sun; 200 of *Agni*, born of the Sun, becoming the god of sacrificial fire, and over 100 of *Soma*, who gives immortality, and who is connected to the Sun, Moon, mountains, rivers and oceans. Others are dedicated to *Varuna*, who protects cosmic order; the *Ashvins*, supreme healers; *Ushas*, goddess of the dawn; *Aditi*, goddess of eternity; and *Saraswati*, goddess of the Vedas and of music and the arts.

Yajur Veda

The hymns of the Yajur-Veda, Veda of Sacrifice, consist of sacrificial formulas or prayers, including those of an internal or spiritual nature, which are chanted by the *adhvaryu* (priest), who performs the sacrifice. About a third of its 1,975 verses are taken from the Rig Veda. The rest are original and in prose form.

Sāma Veda

The Sāma Veda,Veda of Chants, gives instructions on the chanting of vedic hymns. The majority of its 1,875 verses are from the Rig Veda; only 75 verses are original. Many of the hymns were sung by special priests during sacrificial rites. Some are still sung today.

Atharva Veda

The Atharva Veda, named after the seer Atharvan, whose family were great seers in vedic times, contains 731 hymns of 5,977 verses, about one fifth of which are from the RigVeda. It is significant because it combines the essence of both tantric and vedic traditions, and also contains many chants and prayers for overcoming disease and adversity. Lord Atharvan is the Rishi in the Śāṇḍilya Upaniṣad who instructs his disciple Śāṇḍilya in the eightfold path of yoga.

The vedic people and their culture

The vedic people lived for over 2,500 years mainly along the banks of the Saraswati River, which was located in Northern India between the modern Ravi and Yamuna Rivers down to what is now the desert of Rajasthan. The Saraswati River dried up in about 1,900 BCE due to tectonic upheavals. Other areas of habitation included the Ganges River and its tributaries, rivers in Afghanistan (previously called Gandhara), the Himalayas and Mount Kailash in Tibet.The vedic people had a complex multi-tiered view of the universe, in which humankind, nature and the divine are intertwined and interrelated. They had a deep knowledge of the oceans, mountains, deserts and forests of the physical world, as well as of the subtle worlds of deities and different levels of consciousness. People lived in cities or villages or were nomads, and were fully engaged in worldly life. They were an agrarian people, yet also had herds of cattle, horses and camels. Cities were constructed of stone, bricks and metal. They built chariots and ships. They were skilled workers in gold, metal, clay, stone, wood, leather and wool, and showed a very high standard in arts, crafts, astrology, medicine, music, dance and poetry.

After the Vedas

The Vedas were the foundation for the later revelations (*śruti*) in the *Brāhmaṇas* (ritual texts), the *Āraṇyakas* (texts on rituals and meditation for forest-dwelling ascetics) and the *Upaniṣads* (esoteric texts). Later still, the Vedas were the basis for numerous works of remembered or traditional knowledge, known as *smṛti,* including the epics: i.e. the *Mahābhārata, Rāmāyaṇa* and *Purāṇas,* and the *Sūtras,* or threads of knowledge, e.g. *Yoga Sūtras.* All these texts contain many concepts and practices, which come directly from the four Vedas.

Upanişads

The word *upanişad* is comprised of three roots: *upa* or 'near', *ni* or 'attentively', and *sad,* 'to sit'. The term describes the situation in which these unique texts were transmitted. The students or disciples sat near the realised master and listened attentively, as he expounded his experiences and understanding of the ultimate reality. These teachings are said to destroy the ignorance or illusion of the spiritual aspirant in regard to what is self and non-self, what is real and unreal, in relation to the absolute and relative reality. Only disciples were chosen, who had persevered in *sādhana catuṣṭaya*, the four kinds of spiritual effort, viz. *viveka* (discrimination between the permanent and impermanent), *vairagya* (non-attachment), *ṣadsampatti* (six virtues of serenity, self-control, withdrawal of the senses, endurance, perfect concentration and strong faith) and *mumukṣutva* (intense desire for liberation).

The Upaniṣads are derived from the Āranyakas, because they were chanted in the forest (*āranya*) after the aspirant had retired from worldly life. They are recorded in the later form of Sanskrit used in the Brāhmaṇas, and considered the last phase of *śruti*, vedic revelation. The Upaniṣads are regarded as *vedānta*, the end of the Vedas, inferring that *vedānta* is the end or completion of all perceivable knowledge, as they guide the aspirant beyond the limited mind to the *ātman* (spiritual self) and thus to *mokṣa* (liberation). Each upaniṣad reflected the teachings and tradition of a realized master, and was connected with a specific Veda and vedic school. It is estimated that there are over 200 Upaniṣads, which have been divided into seven groups: *Major*, *Vedānta*, *Śaiva, Śakta, Vaiśnava, Sannyasa* and *Yoga.*

Yoga Upaniṣads

The twenty one Yoga Upaniṣads give an understanding of the hidden forces in nature and human beings, and describe esoteric yogic practices by which these forces can be manipulated and controlled. They emphasise that the inner journey to the one permanent reality, the *ātman*, is the essential one. Journeys to external places, such as holy sites and temples, as well as rituals and ceremonies, are not given importance. Their teachings give important information on the subtle body (*cakras, koṣas, prāṇa, kuṇḍalinī,* meditative states), and the tantric and yogic techniques, not given in the earlier upaniṣads, to attain them. Therefore, they are regarded as a significant integration of Vedānta and Tantra, which were previously considered incompatible. They are classified as 'minor' only because they postdate Adi Shankara.

Although their teachings actually predate Patañjali, the Yoga Upaniṣads were codified after the *Yoga Sūtras of Patañjali,* and form an important part of the classical yoga literature. However, they contain no references to Patañjali or his *Yoga Sūtras*. So, although the compilation of the Yoga Upaniṣads is post-Patañjali, the *vidyās*, or meditative disciplines, contained within them are pre-Patañjali. The Yoga Upaniṣads emerged at a time when the vedic and tantric cultures were coming together to share their knowledge. The wise thinkers from each culture sat down together and discussed how their insights and teachings could be combined in order to benefit humanity. Thus these upanisads combine the teachings of both tantra and yoga. It is evident in them that yoga leads to vedānta, and vedānta leads to yoga. However, they were written down by vedantic scholars and practitioners in order to show that these *vidyās* and related practices were not borrowed from Patañjali, but were known and practised from the ancient period.

Within the twenty-one Yoga Upaniṣads are six sub-groups which have their own main focus. The *Bindu Upaniṣads*, which include the *Amṛta-Bindu* (also known as the *Brahma-Bindu-Upaniṣad*), *Amṛta-Nada-Bindu*, *Nada-Bindu*, *Dhyāna-Bindu* and *Tejo-Bindu-Upaniṣads*, all concentrate on the bindu, the source or origin of all sound, and hence of creation. Bindu represents the transcendental sound manifested in the mantra *Aum*. The *Hamsa-Mantra, Soham*, is the main practice of the *Hamsa, Brahma-Vidya, Mahavakya* and *Paśupata-Brahma-Upaniṣads*. Concentration on *prāṇa*, the life force related to the process of inhalation and exhalation, brings the yogin to the knowledge of the transcendental self. The light of pure consciousness, which the enlightened irradiate is the theme of the *Advaya-Taraka* and *Maṅḍala-Brahmana-Upaniṣads*. The *Kṣurika-Upaniṣad* (*kṣurika* meaning 'dagger') emphasises non-attachment as a means to liberation. The sixth group, comprised of eight late Yoga Upaniṣads from 1200 to 1300 A.D., covers teachings related to hatha and kundalini yogas. They are the *Yoga-Kuṅḍalī, Yoga-Tattwa, Yoga-Śikhā, Varāha, Śāṇḍilya, Tri-Śikhi-Brahmana, Yoga-Darśana* and *Yoga-Cūdāmani Upaniṣads.*

Śāṇḍilya Upaniṣad

The Śāṇḍilya Upaniṣad is connected with the Atharva Veda. It commences with the yogin invoking Rāma to guide him along the eightfold path of yoga to liberation.

In the first verse of chapter one, Śāṇḍilya asks Atharvan to instruct him in the eight limbed path of yoga, with the aim of reaching the true Self. Śāṇḍilya himself was a Rishi with many disciples, and was the progenitor of the Śāṇḍilya lineage. Atharvan was a Vedic rishi, who, together with Angiras, is said to have revealed the Atharva Veda, and was the first to perform *yagña*, fire oblations.

The first two sections describe the foundations of yoga, *yama* and *niyama,* external and internal restraints. Section three describes the eight āsanas, which, as well as having physical, mental and energic benefits, prepare the body for sitting still for a long time in meditation without discomfort.
Later sections describe the fourteen main *nāḍīs,* ten *vāyus, maṇipura cakra* and *kuṇḍalinī* of the subtle or pranic body.

The methods of purification of the nāḍīs are described in great detail, as purification is considered necessary for the higher stages of concentration (*dhāraṇā*) and meditation (*dhyāna*). The prerequisites for yoga practice are listed. A meditation on *agni maṇḍala* is given. Prāṇāyāma is defined as AUM, and the practice of *nāḍī śodhana prāṇāyāma* with emphasis on *kumbhaka* and the effects of the practice are described in detail.

Teachings are then given on *khecarī* and *vaiṣṇavī mudrā*, control of *prāṇa*, awakening *kuṇḍalinī*, *saṃyama, pratyāhāraḥ, dhāraṇā, dhyāna* and *samādhi.* The necessity of both yoga and *jñāna* for liberation is emphasised.

Chapter two has sections on knowledge of Brahman, creation of the universe, the names of Brahman, and Dattātreya.

शाण्डिल्योपनिषत्

śāṇḍilyopaniṣat

Śāṇḍilya Upaniṣad

Opening Invocation

शाण्डिल्योपनिषत्प्रोक्तयमाद्यष्टाङ्गयोगिनः ।यद्वाधाद्यान्ति कैवल्यं स रामो मे पर गतिः ।।ॐ भद्रं कर्णेभिः शान्तिः ।।

śāṇḍilyopaniṣatproktayamādyaṣṭāṅgayoginaḥyadvādhād-yānti kaivalyaṃ sa rāmo me para gatiḥom bhadraṃ karṇebhiḥ śāntiḥ

Anvay

śāṇḍilyopaniṣat: Śāṇḍilya Upaniṣad; *prokta*: describes; *aṣṭa-aṅga*: eight limbs; *yoginaḥ*: of the yogin; *yama-ādi*: beginning with *yama* (rules of conduct); *yadvā*: just as; *yānti adhāt*: they move up to; *kaivalyam*: liberation; *sa rāmaḥ*: Rāma; *me para gatiḥ*: my supreme refuge; *karṇebhiḥ*: may we hear; *bhadram*: auspicious; *śāntiḥ*: peace.

Translation

Śāṇḍilya Upaniṣad describes the eightfold path of the yogins, beginning with *yama.* Just as they ascend to liberation, so Rāma is my supreme refuge. Om, may we hear [that which is] auspicious. Peace.

Commentary

Just as the yogins follow the eightfold path of yoga to wisdom and liberation, so is the worship of Rāma the path to liberation and renunciation. The aspirant invokes Rāma to guide him through the eightfold path of yoga. Rāma's life was a model for the *yamas* and *niyamas,* the foundation of the eightfold path. Rāma was an incarnation (*avātara*) of the god Viṣṇu, having the qualities of renunciation, equanimity and self-discipline.

CHAPTER ONE

First Section

Verse 1: Eight Limbs of Yoga; Yama

ह वा अथर्वाणं पप्रच्छात्मलाभोपायभूतमष्टाङ्गयोगमनुब्रूहीति ।स होवाचाथर्वा यमनियमासनप्राणायामप्रत्याहारधारणाधानसमधयोऽष्टाङ्गानि ।तत्र दश यमाः । तथा नियमाः । असनानयष्टौ । त्रयः प्राणायामाः । पञ्च प्रत्याहाराः ।तथा धारणा । द्विप्रकारं ध्यानम् । समाधिस्त्वेकरूपः ।तत्राहिंसासत्यास्तयब्रह्मचर्यदयार्जवक्षामाधृतिमिताहारशौचानि चेति यमा दश ।तत्राहिंसा नाम मनोवाक्कायकर्मभिः सर्वभूतेषु सर्वदाऽक्लेशजननम् ।सत्यं नाम मनोवाक्कायकर्मभिर्भूतहितयथर्थाभिभाषणम् । अस्तेयं नाम मनोवाक्कायवर्मभिः परद्रव्येषु निःस्पृहता ।ब्रह्मचर्य नाम सर्वावस्थासु मनोवाक्कायवर्मभिः सर्वत्र मैथुनत्यागः ।दया नाम सर्वभूतेषु सर्वत्रानुग्रहः ।आर्जवं नाम मनोवाक्कायकर्मणां विहिताविहितेषु जनेषु निवृत्तौ वा एकरूपत्वम् ।क्षमा नाम प्रियाप्रियेषु सर्वेषु ताडनपूजनेषु सहनम् ।धृतिर्नामार्थहानौ स्वेष्टबन्धुवियोगे तत्प्राप्तौ सर्वत्र चेतःस्थापनम् ।मिताहारो नाम चतुर्थांशावशेषकसुस्निग्धमधुराहारः ।शौचं नाम द्विविधं बाह्मान्तरं चेति । तत्र मृच्चलाभ्यां बाह्म् ।मनःशुद्धिरान्तरम् । तदध्यात्मविद्यया लभ्यम् ।।१।।

śāṇḍilyo ha vā atharvāṇaṃ papracchātmalābhopāyabhūtamaṣṭāṅgayogamanubrūhītisa hovācātharvā yamaniyamāsanaprāṇāyāmapratyāhāradhāraṇādhyānasama dhayo'ṣṭāṅgānitatra daśa yamāḥ tathā niyamāḥ āsanānyaṣṭau trayaḥ prāṇāyāmāḥ pañca pratyāhārāḥtathā dhāraṇā dviprakāraṃ dhyānam samādhistvekarūpaḥtatrāhiṃsāsatyāsteyabrahmacaryadayārj avakṣāmādhṛtimitāhāraśaucāni ceti yamā daśatatrāhiṃsā nāma manovākkāyakarmabhiḥ sarvabhūteṣu sarvadā'kleśajananamsatyaṃ nāma manovākkāyakarmabhirbhūtahitayatharthābhibhāṣaṇamaste yaṃ nāma manovākkāyavarmabhiḥ paradravyeṣu niḥspṛhatābrahmacarya nāma sarvāvasthāsu manovākkāyavarmabhiḥ sarvatra maithunatyāgaḥdayā nāma sarvabhūteṣu sarvatrānugrahaḥārjavaṃ nāma manovākkāyakarmaṇāṃ vihitāvihiteṣu janeṣu nivṛttau vā ekarūpatvamkṣamā nāma priyāpriyeṣu sarveṣu tāḍanapūjaneṣu sahanamdhṛtirnāmārthahānau sveṣṭabandhuviyoge tatprāptau sarvatra cetaḥsthāpanammitāhāro nāma caturthāṃśāvaśeṣakasusnigdhamadhurāhāraḥśaucaṃ nāma dvividhaṃ bāhṛmāntaraṃ ceti tatra mṛccalābhyāṃ bāhṛmmanaḥśuddhirāntaram tadadhyātmavidyayā labhyam (1)

Vocabulary

śāṇḍilyo ha: Śāṇḍilya himself; *papraccha atharvāṇam*: did ask Atharvan; *brūhi*: impart; *aṣṭa-aṅga-yogam*: eight limbs [of] yoga; *bhūtam*: being; *lābha-upāya ātma*: means of attaining the ātma; *sa atharvā ha āvaca*: Atharvan did respond thus; *aṣṭa-aṅgāni*: eight limbs; *tatra*: there; *daśa yamāḥ*: ten yamas; *tathā*: likewise; *niyamāḥ*: niyamas; *aṣṭau āsanāni*: eight āsanas; *trayaḥ prāṇāyāmāḥ*: three kinds of prāṇāyama; *pañca pratyāhārāḥ*: five [of] pratyāhāra; *tathā dhāraṇā*: also [of] dhāraṇā; *dhyānam dviprakāram*: dhyāna [has] two kinds; *tu samādhiḥ eka-rūpaḥ*: but samādhi [has only] one kind; *tatra daśa yama*: there [are] ten yamas; *ahiṃsā*: non-violence; *nāma*: called; *sarvadā*: always;

jananam: cause; *akleśa*: non-suffering; *karmabhiḥ*: through the actions of; *manaḥ-vāk-kāya*: mind, speech [or] body; *satyam*: truth; *abhibhāṣaṇam*: speaking; *hita-yathārtha*: beneficial [and] suitable for; *bhūta*: living beings; *karmabhiḥ*: through the actions of; *manaḥ-vāk-kāya*: mind, speech [or] body; *asteyam*: honesty; *niḥspṛhatā*: not craving; *paradravyeṣu*: for the goods of others; *karmabhiḥ*: through the actions of; *manaḥ-vāk-kāya*: mind, speech [or] body; *brahmacarya*: continence; *sarvatra*: always; *tyāgaḥ*: forsaking; *maithuna*: sexual intercourse; *sarva-avasthāsu*: in all conditions; *dayā*: compassion; *anugrahaḥ*: treating kindly; *sarva-bhūteṣu*: all creatures; *sarvatra*: everywhere; *ārjava*: straightforwardness; *janeṣu*: maintaining; *nivṛttau vā ekarūpatvam*: steadiness and equanimity; *manaḥ-vāk-kāya*: mind, speech [and] body; *vihita-avihiteṣu*: in the accomplishment or non-accomplishment; *karmaṇām*: of actions; *kṣamā*: patience; *sahanam*: enduring; *sarveṣu*: everything; *priya-apriyeṣu*: pleasant [and] unpleasant; *tāḍana-pūjaneṣu*: respect [or] insult; *dhṛti*: firmness; *sarvatra*: always; *sthāpanam*: preserving; *prāptau*: whether one has got; *artha-hānau*: wealth [or] poverty; *viyoge*: separated from; *sva-iṣṭa*: dear ones; *bandhu*: relatives; *mitāhāra*: moderate, balanced diet; *āhāraḥ*: taking of food; *su-snigdha-madhura*: good oily {and] sweet; *avaśeṣaka*: leaving empty; *caturtha-aṃśa*: quarter; *ca iti*: and it is said; *śauca*: cleanliness; *dvividham*: of two kinds: *bāhṛm*: external; *āntaram*: internal; *tatra*: of these; *bāhṛm*: external; *mṛj*: cleaning; *jalābhyām*: with water; *āntaram*: internal; *śuddhiḥ*: purification; *manaḥ*: mind; *tat*: this; *labhyam*: to be obtained; *ātma-vidyayā*: through knowledge of the inner self.

Translation

Śāṇḍilya himself did ask Atharvan: "[Please] impart [to me] the eight limbs [of] yoga, being the means of attaining the ātmā."Atharvan did respond thus: "The eight limbs [of yoga are] *yama, niyama, āsana, prāṇāyama, pratyāhāra, dhāraṇā, dhyāna* [and] *samādhi.* There [are] ten yamas, likewise [ten] niyamas, eight āsanas, three kinds of prāṇāyama, five [of] pratyāhāra, [and] also [of] dhāraṇā. Dhyāna [has] two kinds, but samādhi [has only] one.There [are] ten yamas: *ahiṃsā, satya, asteya, brahmacarya, dayā, ārjava, kṣamā, dhṛti, mitāhāra* and *śauca.*Non-violence (called *ahiṃsā*) [is] always the cause [of] non-suffering to all living beings through the actions of mind, speech [or] body. Truth (called *satya*) [is] speaking [that which is] beneficial and suitable for living beings through the actions of mind, speech [or] body. Honesty (called *asteyam*) [is] not craving for the goods of others through the actions of mind, speech [or] body. Continence (called *brahmacarya*) [is] always forsaking sexual intercourse in all conditions through the actions of mind, speech [or] body. Compassion (called *dayā*) [is] treating kindly all creatures everywhere. Straightforwardness (called *ārjava*) [is] maintaining steadiness and equanimity of mind, speech [and] body in the accomplishment or non-accomplishment of actions. Patience (called *kṣamā*) [is] enduring everything pleasant [and] unpleasant, [such as] respect [or] insult. Firmness (called *dhṛti*) is always preserving (firmness of mind) whether one has wealth or poverty, or separated from dear ones or relatives. A moderate, balanced diet (called *mitāhāra*) [is] the taking of good, [naturally] oily [and] sweet food, leaving a quarter [of the stomach] empty. And it is said cleanliness (called *śauca*) [is] of two kinds: external [and] internal. Of these, external is cleaning with water; internal [is] purification [of] the mind. This [is] to be obtained through knowledge of the inner self.

Commentary

Atharvan acknowledges Rishi Śāṇḍilya, himself a realised sage, and begins by naming the eight limbs of yoga: (i) yama, external observances, moral interaction with others, (ii) niyama, internal disciplines, (iii) āsana, postures, (iv) prāṇāyāma, breath control, (v) pratyāhāra, introversion of the senses, (vi) dhāraṇā, concentration, (vii) dhyāna, meditation, and (viii) samādhi, transcendental consciousness. The ten yamas recommended here are: (i) ahiṃsā, non-violence, (ii) satya, truthfulness in speech, (iii) asteya, honesty in action, (iv) brahmacarya, abstinence or moderation in sexual conduct, (v) daya, kindness or compassion, (vi) ārjava, straightforwardness, (vii) kṣamā, patience, (viii) dhṛti, equanimity, (ix) mitāhāra, moderate and balanced diet, and (x) śauca, cleanliness of body and mind. These are qualities we want to see in our nearest and dearest, be they family members, friends, or those we place our trust in to do their best for our community or country. By taking care of our own needs first, food, shelter and so on, we are our own nearest and dearest, even though we might like to see ourselves as unselfish and altruistic. So it is in our own interest to develop the qualities of the yamas. It is only then that we are able to help others.

In our life there may be more moments of discomfort and unhappiness than of joy and ecstasy. The yamas and niyamas are the foundation of a system which gives endless joy and ecstasy, as it takes us back to our true nature. This system of yoga works on the ocean of the mind, the citta, which contains all our saṃskaras, subtle impressions and past actions, stopping the fluctuations created by violence in all its forms, so that we can see our true nature deep within ourselves. Like the surface of the ocean, citta is easily influenced by externals. There is stillness in the depths of the ocean, unruffled by externals. So we need to go deep in our mind to access the stillness and peace, unaffected by externals.

We are all beings of nature, having the qualities of tamas (inertia), rajas (dynamism) and sattwa (harmony). These qualities are called guṇas. The difference between humans and other sentient beings, is that we have a mind, which is capable of thinking, expansion of awareness and evolution.

The Bhagavad Gita says, in Chapter 14 'The Three Guṇas', 'Sattva, the quality of goodness, will be prominent when the whole being is enlightened with knowledge. O Arjuna, when there is an increase in rajas, the mode of passion, attachment, deep yearning, fruitive activity will develop. When there is an increase in tamas, the mode of ignorance, darkness, madness and delusions are manifested.'[2] If tamas and rajas dominate, we can't concentrate, and therefore can't meditate. Changes to diet and lifestyle are necessary. The yamas and niyamas provide us with a way to implement these changes. With the increase of sattwa, a transparent lucidity develops and we start to see the world with more clarity. When all spiritual practice is based on the strong foundation of yama and niyama, there is freedom from fear, false self-identification and suffering.

Ahiṃsā

Ahiṃsā means non-harming in action, speech and thought. It is an absence of violence from within. It goes beyond mere abstention from harming to positive nurturing, protecting the weak, helping those who have suffered from acts of violence and creating non-destructive ways of living, including our interaction with animals and the environment.

When the mind is focused on violence, it is impossible to think of, practise or develop the higher qualities. Violence has the quality of tamas, darkness and ignorance. Ahiṃsā is sattwic, a positive expression of universal love, recognising and experiencing the divine nature of all creation. Non-violence, the verse says, is active not passive and prevents violence. A person who is established in non-violence creates an atmosphere of peace, which affects all in one's vicinity. The great sage Ramana Maharishi was perfectly established in ahiṃsā, so that even the peacocks and cobra danced together.[3] Georg Feuerstein in 'The Yoga Tradition' says: 'the desire not to harm another being springs from the impulse towards unification and ultimate transcendence of the ego.' [4]

We have qualities and instincts within us, which are seemingly contradictory. So we have aggressive instincts as well as the qualities of empathy and kindness. By developing the positive qualities, we lessen the power of the negative instincts, for the benefit of society and for our spiritual development, in that we become more aware of our unity with all beings.

Mahāvīra, the founder of Jainism, gave extensive rules on non-harming, including wearing a mask so as not to inhale minute creatures.[5] Although we may not be able to comply with that, we can become aware of how many lives are sacrificed for our own. Another example is not eating food that grows under ground, as digging up the root vegetables kills the insects and worms in the earth around them.

Gandhi's non-violent campaign, based on the philosophy of satyāgraha, was successful and has inspired others, such as Martin Luther King and Nelson Mandela. In response to violence, satyāgraha does not accept being a passive victim, which allows injustice to flourish, corrupting both perpetrator and victim. Nor does it accept fighting back with violence, as this creates more violence. Satyāgraha incorporates the values of ahiṃsā, satyam and tapas (self-restraint). Its purpose is to end injustice by awakening the adversary's sense of justice.
'Practice of ahiṃsā develops love. Ahiṃsā is another name for truth or love. Ahiṃsā is universal love. It is pure love. It is divine Prem. Where there is love, there you will find ahiṃsā. Where there is ahiṃsā, there you will find love and selfless service. They all go together. It is positive, cosmic love. It is the development of a mental attitude in which hatred is replaced by love. Ahiṃsā is true sacrifice. Ahiṃsā is forgiveness. Ahiṃsā is Śakti (power). Ahiṃsā is true strength.' Swami Śivānanda[6]

For these reasons, ahiṃsā, or non-violence, is the first yama, upon which all the other yamas are based, and without which the higher stages of aṣṭāṅga yoga cannot be attained.

Satyam

Satyam, truth, is the second yama, meaning truthfulness in speech, with the awareness of that which is correct and true, without distortion by saṃskaras and vrittis. Its deeper meaning is awareness of that which is unchanging and permanent, the True Reality, Brahman.

The content of spoken words is important. It is said that whoever has attained perfection in satyam, their speech will become reality. Silence is preferable to harsh and frivolous speech which has a harmful effect on the mind of both speaker and listener, disturbing the mind with false understandings and desires.

That which is perceived by the senses, i.e., seen through the eyes, heard through the ears, tasted by the tongue, and so on, is said to be true in the worldly sense through one's own perception. In the same way, Brahman, the ever-expanding and luminous consciousness, is the ultimate truth, which can be known through developing one's inner awareness. The ultimate truth is that Brahman, the universal consciousness, is all-pervading; it is the substratum of existence, which pervades everything everywhere. Because Brahman is everywhere, it cannot be elsewhere; it cannot be in one place, but not in another. The understanding of the nature of Brahman leads to the highest truth, satyam.

'Truth can never contradict non-injury. When it does, it is no more a truth, but the selfishness of the man which is on the fore. When truth-speaking leads another to dishonour, injury and pain, it is no longer a virtue. Speak what is true. Speak what is pleasant. Speak no disagreeable truth, speak no agreeable falsehood.' Swami Sivananda[7]

Asteya

The third yama is asteya, the literal meaning of which is not cheating or stealing. It also means honesty with ourselves about our motives, opinions and actions in our life, and in our dealings with others. It is the nature of the mind to wander, perceiving objects through senses. Thus the mind becomes dissatisfied, and preoccupied with satisfying its cravings. 'Over-consumption is a form of theft, by depleting resources which others need. Pollution of the environment is stealing from present and future generations.' [8]

A wise person understands that desire for wealth and possessions by any means has a very disturbing effect on the mind. In order to keep such thoughts at bay, one would be honest in all dealings. This honesty is called asteya, and it is an essential quality for an aspirant of aṣṭaṅga yoga.

Brahmacarya

Brahmacarya, absolute control of sensual impulses, is the fourth yama. This is an important restraint for yogis, and was often understood as total abstinence of sexual interaction. Nowadays brahmacarya refers to moderate and ethical sexual behaviour, rather than total abstinence. In times of old, sexual relations and producing of progeny were duties incumbent on every husband and wife. And most people were obliged to marry from an early age. Total restraint was only considered appropriate for a renunciate, or sannyasi, who did not marry.

The word brahmacarya has two roots: *brahma*,'the ever-expanding luminous consciousness', and *carya*, 'wandering'. Hence, the term brahmacarya means one who moves about in the absolute consciousness, implying that energy is directed to the highest realm, absolute consciousness, and not the lowest realm which contains the genitals. In the sexual act, the most powerful energy is expended, necessary to create a human being. The higher the goal, the more energy is needed to attain it. The mind achieves brahmacarya, when it is absorbed in the absolute consciousness.

We generally associate the highest consciousness with the crown of the head, whereas the sexual act is triggered by the nether regions between the legs. 'Sexual stimulation feeds hungers for sensory experiences and leads to a loss of semen and vital energy (ojas)'.[9] Thus, the yogi who practises moderation and restraint in regard to sexual conduct is able to remain absorbed in the absolute consciousness. One can also avoid arousing lust by not listening to people talk about sex or watching erotic movies, when the awareness is drawn to the sensual, carnal realm of the lower regions. Therefore all energy in thought, word and deed should be directed towards the highest goal, pure consciousness.

Dayā

Dayā, compassion, kindness, is the fifth yama. Kindness is not just an isolated action, but a quality of nature, which can be developed through yogic practice and purification. Kindness is an attribute of *sattwa guṇa*, the balanced or pure quality of nature. Unless this quality is always present in everyday life, acts of kindness will alternate with acts of selfishness and subversion, which are the expressions of *rajas* and *tamas* guṇas.

It is normal for the three guṇas to express themselves in life. This is why the forces of darkness often overcome the force of light. The yogi is a person who strives to live in the light, as far as possible. One method for achieving this is to be kind and merciful to all beings. In this sense, kindness becomes a way of life, a way of thinking, speaking, and acting with awareness and sensitivity towards oneself and others. Such kindness is called dayā, or compassion, by the saints and teachers of all spiritual traditions and religions, including Vedānta.

Ārjavam

Ārjavam means to be straightforward with oneself, and with all of one's associations and dealings in life in thought, speech and behaviour. Such a person has integrity, is honest, not devious and is free from crookedness or deceit.

A straightforward person is able to see and accept things as they are, rather than as they could or should be. In thinking about how things could be, the mind becomes overworked and bent. There is often a very thin line between cleverness and crookedness. The devious mind can never accept or rest in one view or one truth. It seeks to explore and adjust all the possible paths in order to find the best for its own purposes. In this pursuit, the mind deviates from the one and becomes lost in the many.

To be straightforward is an important requisite for the higher practices of yoga, because it enables one to remain in alignment with truth. Ultimately, truth relates with the one underlying substratum of existence, which we are all a part of, the universal unchanging permanent reality free from illusion and delusion. One who makes a habit of cunning and deceit, will be unable to recognise this truth, whether in the relative or absolute sense.

Kṣamā

Kṣamā, patience and endurance, is a quality difficult to develop and maintain in this era of fast food, fast trains and planes, fast communication via internet and smartphone, where opportunities for developing patience are regarded as inconveniences.

A person who is able to remain calm and accept how things unfold, without losing patience, is in control of the mind and senses. As soon as one becomes impatient, irritation sets in. At this moment, one loses control over the speech and mind, and begins to react in ways, which are often detrimental to oneself, and to others as well. Patience is the ability to maintain a calm, steady approach, regardless of what one may hope or expect. In this sense, patience is a yogic quality, which allows one to live in harmony with the present moment, and to deal with what may arise in the best and most appropriate manner.

Patience is also very necessary for the serious practitioner, who undertakes a regular yoga practice, or sādhana. A person who is impatient in daily life, will definitely become impatient with his or her sādhana, and begin to doubt its efficacy. This is a great block in one's progress, because yoga unfolds in its own time. To achieve the long-term goal of *samādhi* and *mokṣa*, patience is an essential quality and a sign of mature character. The practitioner, who becomes impatient, will be unable to continue the practice with a calm and steady mind. Hence the efforts made will ultimately yield no result. In this sense, the quality of patience is like a rock in the midst of a vast and fast flowing river. It allows the practitioner to take hold and remain steady and still, even though the water of life is flowing past all around at a very rapid rate.

Dhṛti

Dhṛti, equanimity, is the ability to maintain a firm, calm and balanced state of mind and to remain true to one's principles, even in the midst of turbulence all around. This state of mind is necessary to achieve any important goal, especially the goal of mokṣa, liberation from the cycle of birth and death. Sri Krishna in the *Bhagavad Gita* compares the mind of a yogi which is controlled and focused to an unflickering lamp in a windless place.10

Mitāhāra

Mitāhāra, moderation in food, is necessary for yoga practice. In the *Bhagavad Gita*, Sri Krishna states that the yogi should neither eat too much nor too little.11 In yoga, balanced diet and practices are like the two wings of a bird. Just as a bird cannot fly on one wing only, a yogic practitioner cannot progress to spiritual heights by performing the practices alone. The yogis who have a *sattwic* diet are able to experience the subtle effects of their yoga practices. A sattwic diet is comprised of fresh fruits, vegetables, whole grains, nuts and legumes. Dairy products were also recommended for yogis, because in ancient times the people kept their own cows and tended them with great care. The milk products produced by these cows were pure and free from harmful chemicals and residues. The food of a yogic diet should be easily and quickly digested. This is because a yogi needs more time for practice, and the stomach needs to be empty during these periods for optimum results. Therefore the stomach should only be three quarters full after a meal, leaving one fourth empty, so that the digestion process is facilitated. The yogi who observes mitāhāra on a regular basis, over years, will be more likely able to delve deeply into the practices of yoga without experiencing imbalance, obstruction or negative effects.

Śauca

Śauca is cleanliness in body and mind. In fact, it is the first of the *niyamas*, or internal disciplines, recommended in *rāja yoga* by the sage Patanjali. This verse clarifies that cleanliness may be external or internal. External cleanliness is easily achieved by washing the physical body regularly. Keeping one's environment clean helps to declutter and purify the mind. The yogi who regularly reflects on the mind, realises the inner purity of the Self. The understanding that 'my inner self, my consciousness,' is inherently pure results in internal cleanliness. This realisation that 'I am innately pure' is the cleanliness of the wise yogis. Georg Feuerstein defines yoga as 'a process of self-purification which strips away all the dross of the mind, so that it can shine forth in its original purity'.[12]

Second Section

Verse 1: Niyama

तपः

सन्तोषास्तिक्यदानेश्वरपूजनसिद्धान्तश्रवणह्रिमतिजपव्रतानि दश नियमाः ।तत्र तपो नाम विध्युक्तकृच्छ्रचान्द्रायणादिभिः शरीरशोषणम् ।संतोषो नाम यदृच्छालाभसंतुष्टिः । आस्तिक्यं नाम वेदोक्तधर्माधर्मेषु विश्वासः ।दानं नाम न्यायार्जितस्य धनधान्यादेः श्रद्धयार्थिभ्यः प्रदानम् ।ईश्वरपूजनं नाम प्रसन्नस्वभावेन यथाशक्ति विष्णुरुद्रादिपूजनम् ।सिद्धान्तश्रवणं नाम वेदान्तार्थविचारः । ह्रीर्नाम वेदलौकिकमार्गकुत्सितकर्मणि लज्जा ।मतिर्नाम वेदविहितकर्ममार्गेषु श्रद्धा । जपो नाम विधिवद्गुरूपदिष्ट वेदाविरुद्धमन्त्राभ्यासः ।तद् द्विविधं वाचिकं मानसं चेति । मानसं तु मनसा ध्यानयुक्तं मे ।वाचिकं द्विविधमुच्चैरुपां शुभेदेन । उच्चैरुच्चारणं यथोक्त फलम् ।उपांशु सहस्रगुणम् । मानसं कोटिगुणम् ।व्रतं नाम वेदोक्तविधिनिषेधानुष्ठाननैयत्यम् ।।१।।

tapaḥ santoṣāstikyadāneśvarapūjanasiddhāntaśravaṇahrīmatijapav ratāni daśa niyamāḥtatra tapo nāma vidhyuktakṛcchracāndrāyaṇādibhiḥ śarīraśoṣaṇamsaṃtoṣo nāma yadṛcchālābhasaṃtuṣṭiḥ āstikyaṃ nāma vedoktadharmādharmeṣu viśvāsaḥdānaṃ nāma nyāyārjitasya dhanadhānyādeḥ śraddhayārthibhyaḥ pradānamīśvarapūjanaṃ nāma prasannasvabhāvena yathāśakti viṣṇurudrādipūjanamsiddhāntaśravaṇaṃ nāma vedāntārthavicāraḥ hrīrnāma vedalaukikamārgakutsitakarmaṇi lajjāmatirnāma vedavihitakarmamārgeṣu śraddhā japo nāma vidhivadgurūpadiṣṭa vedāviruddhamantrābhyāsaḥtad dvividhaṃ vācikaṃ mānasaṃ ceti mānasaṃ tu manasā dhyānayuktaṃ mevācikaṃ dvividhamuccairupāṃ śubhedena uccairuccāraṇaṃ yathokta phalamupāṃśu sahasraguṇam mānasaṃ koṭiguṇamvrataṃ nāma vedoktavidhiniṣedhānuṣṭhānanai yatyam (1)

Vocabulary

daśa niyamāḥ: ten niyamas; *tatra*: of these; *tapaḥ*: austerity; *nāma*: called; *śoṣanam*: destroying; *śarīra*: body; *kṛcchra cāndrāyaṇa*: *kṛcchra cāndrāyaṇa*, special diets (see commentary); *vidhi-ukta*: as expressed in the precepts; *santoṣa*: contentment; *yad-ṛccha*: whatever happens; *alābha*: loss; *saṃtuṣṭiḥ*: acceptance of; *āstikya*: piety; *viśvāsaḥ*: faith; *dharma-adharmeṣu*: in the rules of right and wrong; *veda-ukta*: as described in the Vedas; *dāna*: donation; *pradānam*: giving; *śraddhayā*: with faith; *dhana-dhānyādeḥ*: money [and] corn; *nyāya-arjitasya*: acquired honestly; *arthibhyaḥ*: to those in need; *īśvara-pūjana*: worship of the Lord; *pūjanam*: worshipping; *viṣṇu-rudra-ādi*: Viṣṇu, Rudra etc; *prasanna-sva-bhāvena*: with one's pure inherent nature; *yathāśakti*: to the utmost of one's power; *siddhānta-śravaṇam*: listening to sacred teachings; *vicāraḥ*: reflecting on; *vedānta-artha*: meaning of Vedānta; *hrīḥ*: shame; *lajjā*: ashamed of; *karmaṇi*: actions; *kutsita*: despicable; *laukika*: according to; *veda-mārga*: way of the Vedas; *mati*: understanding; *śraddhā*: faith; *karma-mārgeṣu*: in the paths of action; *veda-vihita*: prescribed by the Vedas; *japa*: mantra repetition; *abhyāsaḥ*: constant practice; *vidhivat*: duly; *guru-upadiṣṭaḥ*: initiated by the guru; *veda-aviruddhaḥ*: not contrary to the Vedas; *tad*: it; *dvividham*: of two kinds; *vācikam*: spoken; *ca*: and; *mānasam*: mental; *tu*: now; *yuktam*: is connected with; *dhyāna*: meditation; *manasā*: by the mind; *vācikam*: spoken; *śubhedena*: different; *dvividham*: two kinds; *uccaiḥ-upām*: loud [and] low; *uccaiḥ-uccāraṇam*: loud pronunciation;

phalam: reward; *yathā-ukta*: as stated; *upāṃśu*: low; *sahasra-guṇam*: thousand kinds; *mānasam*: mental; *koṭi-guṇam*: crore (ten million) kinds; *vrata*: vow; *naiyatyam*: obligatory; *anuṣṭhāna*: practice; *vidhiniṣedha*: precepts and prohibitions; *veda-ukta*: stated in the Vedas.

Translation

The ten niyamas [are]: *tapas, santoṣa, āstikya, dāna, īśvarapūjana, hrīḥ, mati, japa* [and] *vrata.*Of these, austerity (called *tapas*) [is] destroying [attachment to] the body through [penances such as] *kṛcchra* [and] *cāndrāyaṇa* etc as expressed in the precepts. Contentment (called *santoṣa*) [is] acceptance of whatever happens [and] whatever loss. Piety (called *āstikya*) [is] faith in the rules of right [and] wrong as described in the Vedas. Donation (called *dāna*) [is] giving with faith corn [and] money acquired honestly to those in need. Worship of the Lord (called *īśvarapūjana*) [is] worshipping Viṣṇu, Rudra etc with one's pure inherent nature to the utmost of one's power. Listening to sacred teachings (called *siddhāntaśravaṇam*) [is] reflecting on the meaning of Vedānta. Shame (called *hrīḥ*) [is being] ashamed of actions [which are] despicable according to the way of the Vedas. Understanding (called *mati*) [is] faith in the paths of action prescribed by the Vedas. Mantra repetition (called *japa*) [is] constant practice of the mantra [into which one is] duly initiated by the guru, [and which is] not contrary to the Vedas. It [is] of two kinds, spoken and mental. Now the mental is connected with meditation by the mind. The spoken [has] two different kinds, loud and low. The loud pronunciation [gives] the reward as stated [in the Vedas]. The low [gives rewards of] a thousand kinds, the mental ten million kinds. A vow (called *vrata*) [is] the obligatory practice of the precepts [and] prohibitions stated in the Vedas.

Commentary

The ten niyamas are internal disciplines, which allow the

practitioner to gain control over the senses and manage the mind at a deeper level. These ten qualities are given in the following order: (i) *tapas*, austerity, endurance; (ii) *santoṣa*, contentment; (iii) *āstikya*, faith in the highest consciousness; (iv) *dāna*, charity, giving to others; (v) *īśvara pūja*, worship of the highest consciousness; (vi) *siddhānta śravaṇa*, listening to the scriptures; (vii) *hrī*, remorse or shame; (viii) *mati*, desire for humility; (ix) *japa*, repetition of mantra, syllables or words of power; and (x) *vrata*, vow or commitment.

Tapas

Tapas is the practice of self-discipline and austerity (not self-abuse), so that one can bear all difficulties on the spiritual path. This is contrary to the modern mindset accustomed to instant gratification. By strengthening the willpower, the mind and body are strengthened. The practice of tapas teaches us to forebear insult, in the knowledge that those who are violent in speech have twisted bitter minds. Tapas means 'to burn', and is practised for the process of self-transformation, where impurities of the self are burnt so that the true Self is clearly apparent. Through the physical tapas of fasting, excess fat, as well as accumulated toxins, are 'burned' away. Old *saṃskaras* are burned through mental tapas. Through the verbal tapas of *moun*a, silence, speech is controlled. All impurities are removed by fire.

Santoṣa

Santoṣa means that inner contentment where one is satisfied with one's situation, living in the present, thus reducing desires and the craving aspect of the mind. It is the opposite of greed, which is boosted by our consumer mentality. In worldly life people are constantly influenced by their desires. They see or hear about some person, place or thing, and they want that for themselves. They feel happy when their desires are obtained, and unhappy when their desires remain unfulfilled. Therefore, when the same happiness that is experienced from the fulfilment of desire becomes constant, irrespective of whether one's desire is obtained or not, this is known as santoṣa. A wise person, having understood the nature of desire and its influence on the mind, has only one desire, to attain insight into truth.

Āstikya

Āstikya is faith in the higher reality. The vedic tradition is based on two types of knowledge: (i) *śruti*, knowledge that is heard or revealed directly from the source, and (ii) *smṛti*, knowledge based on what has been remembered and passed down. Through these two channels, knowledge of the higher reality has been passed down throughout the ages. The śrutis are comprised of teachings that were heard directly from sages and yogis, who experienced them in their own sādhana and meditation. When the teachings were remembered and passed down from generation to generation orally and then in written form, they were known as smṛti, which also means memory. Because śruti and smṛti comprise the body of vedic knowledge, which relates with the existence of a higher reality, the yogic aspirant must have faith in them. By listening to and studying these texts, one develops an understanding of the higher reality, which leads to āstikya, or faith. In the absence of this faith, the worldly tendencies remain dominant, and the higher stages of yoga are difficult to attain.

Dāna

Dāna means donation, gift, unconditional giving. Giving freely allows one to expand the boundaries of consciousness, which are held tightly in place by the ego. These are the boundaries of my life, my house, my job, my family, my friends, my assets, my expectations. When there is a strong sense of I and mine, it becomes difficult to give anything freely to anybody, without wanting or expecting something in return. Giving with any form of expectation is not dāna, because it further gratifies and expands the ego. Thus, it is necessary to practise giving freely in order to release the sense of ego and pride that arise from attaining wealth and position. Motive or intent is essential on the path to yoga. The yoga aspirant should give without pride or expectation of recognition. Giving freely in order to help others is also a way to balance the karmas, and remove negativity and greed, which obstruct the access to higher yoga.

Īśvara pūja

Īśvara pūja, worship of the highest consciousness, teaches us to remain humble knowing that there is something, whether we call it God, the Source or the Supreme Reality, which is higher than ourselves and to which we can aspire. In rāja yoga there is no mention of God, apart from the term Īśvara, which means the indestructible reality. Īśvara is indestructible, because it is unmanifest. It is the subtle reality behind the manifestation of all existence. Whatever is manifest is destructible, but being unmanifest, Īśvara is indestructible. How then does one worship the unmanifest reality, without giving it some manifest form or association, which is then destructible? The verse says one must worship with one's 'pure inherent nature', that is, which is the embodiment of truth, love, non-violence and free from worldly desires; and 'to the utmost of one's power', that is, with complete sincerity and dedication.

Siddhānta śravaṇa

Siddhānta śravaṇa, listening to sacred teachings: the verse says this means 'reflecting on the meaning and teachings of Vedānta'. 'Vedānta' is composed of two words: Veda is knowledge revealed to the ancient rishis in meditation by Brahman, the Supreme Being; 'anta' is the end or outcome of this revealed knowledge (śruti) expressed in the Upaniṣads.

The first teaching is that there is an ultimate reality, which is permanent, constant and indestructible. This permanent reality is the substratum that supports and sustains the manifest creation. Being uncreated, it is not experienced in the dimension of time, space and object. It can only be experienced and known from within, when the consciousness has transcended the body and mind, and all of the associations of the world.

The second teaching relates to infinite knowledge. Vedānta is an esoteric philosophy, which is based on inner knowledge of the eternal truth of the ever-expanding consciousness. This knowledge is said to be infinite, while all other knowledge is relative and limited to time, space and object.

The third teaching is about supreme bliss. In our worldly life, our emotions are constantly swinging between the dualities of pleasure and pain, success and failure, praise and blame. From the study of Vedānta we learn that we can access the inner happiness, which is permanent and enduring, and does not depend on outer experiences. Paramānanda, supreme bliss, is the quality of experience in the highest consciousness, when the awareness has completely transcended the world of name, form, and ideation. This happiness is absolute, without beginning or end.

Hrī

Hrī means shame in the sense of remorse. When the yoga aspirant regrets that he or she has lapsed in practising any of the yamas or niyamas, he or she will make amends, resolving to maintain a sincere practice.

Mati

Mati is understanding and faith in the paths of action prescribed by the Vedas. Yoga does not advocate blind faith or intellectual understanding. Mati is the faith and understanding that comes from deep intuition and experience.

Japa

Mantra repetition (called *japa*) [is] constant practice of the sacred mantra [into which one is] initiated by the guru, [and which is] not contrary to the Vedas. The Sanskrit word 'mantra' is derived from two words, 'manas' meaning 'mind' and 'trā' meaning 'freed from'. The sacred mantra is always located in the heart, can be practised anywhere and at any time. By repeating it constantly, the mind gradually identifies with it, freed from the attractions and diversions of daily life.

Vrata

No progress can be made on the path of yoga without making a vow, a sincere commitment to adhere to the yamas and niyamas, thereby cultivating one's character, whatever the circumstances.

Developing Yamas and Niyamas

Make a *saṅkalpa* to practise one yama and one niyama every day for a set length of time. Keep a daily journal to record the effects on your mind and actions. Practise them in your relationships, at work, in your thoughts (Patañjali says if you have a negative thought, replace it with a positive one) which lead to actions and can elevate or depress others. At the same time practise courage, be kind to yourself, observe your fears objectively, be authentic with yourself, don't put on a nice mask, appreciate and enjoy what you have now in every aspect of life without being over-indulgent.

Ways of perfecting yama and niyama:

satsang (keeping company with the wise), āsana, prāṇāyama, meditation, making each action an expression of creativity, learning, compassion and wisdom. The aim of the yamas and niyamas is not to deprive ourselves or turn ourselves into ascetics. It is the foundation of the eightfold path of yoga whose aim is to reach and experience the state of absolute freedom.

Third Section

Eight Āsanas
Verses 1 to 3: Svastikāsana, Gomukhāsana and Padmāsana

स्वस्तिकगोमुखपद्मवीरसिंहभद्रमुक्तमयूराख्यान्यासनान्यष्टै । स्वस्तिकं नाम जानूर्वोरन्तरे सम्यक्कृत्वा पादतले उभे । ऋजुकायः समासीनः स्वस्तिकं तत्प्रचक्षते ॥१॥ सव्ये दक्षिणगुल्फं तु पृष्ठपार्श्वे नियोजयेत् । दक्षिणेऽपि तथा सव्यं गोमुखं गोमुखं यथा ॥२॥ अङ्गुष्ठेन निबधिन्याद्धस्ताभ्यां व्युत्क्तमेण च । ऊर्वोरुपरि शाण्डिल्य कृत्वा पादतले उभे । पद्मासनं भवेदेतत्सर्वेषामपि पूजितम्

॥३॥*svastikagomukhapadmavīrasiṃhabhadramuktamayūrākhyānyāsanānyaṣṭai svastikaṃ nāma jānūrvorantare samyakkṛtvā pādatale ubhe ṛjukāyaḥ samāsīnaḥ svastikaṃ tatpracakṣate (1)*
savye dakṣiṇagulphaṃ tu pṛṣṭhapārśve niyojayetdakṣiṇe'pi tathā savyaṃ gomukhaṃ gomukhaṃ yathā (2) aṅguṣṭhena nibadhinyāddhastābhyāṃ vyutktmeṇa ca ūrvorupari śāṇḍilya kṛtvā pādatale ubhe padmāsanaṃ bhavedetatsarveṣāmapi pūjitam (3)

Vocabulary

aṣṭai āsanāni: eight *āsanas* (postures); *ākhyāni:* are called; *svastika:* auspicious; *gomukha:* cow- face*; padma:* lotus; *vīra:* hero; *siṃha:* lion; *bhadra:* gracious; *mukta:* liberated; *mayūra:* peacock; *samāsinaḥ:* sitting with; *kāyaḥ:* body; *ṛju:* straight; *kṛtvā:* placing; *jānūrvoḥ:* both knees; *samyak:* exactly; *antare pādatale ubhe:* parallel with both soles of the feet; *tat pracakṣate svastikam:* this is called *svastika,* the auspicious [pose]; *niyojayet:* placing; *dakṣiṇa-gulpham:* right ankle; *savye:* on the left; *pārśve:* beside; *pṛṣṭha:* back; *api tathā:* and then; *savyam:* left; *dakṣiṇe:* on the right; *yathā:*

thus; *gomukham:* cow-face [pose]; *śāṇḍilya:* O Śāṇḍilya; *padmāsana:* lotus pose; *kṛtvā:* placing; *ubhe pādatale:* both soles of the feet; *ūrvoḥ-upari:* upward on the thighs; *ca:* and; *aṅguṣṭhena vyutktmeṇa:* with big toes turned up; *nibadhinyāt:* held; *hastābhyām:* by the hands; *etat pūjitam:* this is honoured; *sarveṣām:* by all.

Translation

The eight *āsanas* are called *svastika* (auspicious), *gomukha* (cow-face), *padma* (lotus), *vīra* (hero), *siṃha* (lion), *bhadra* (gracious), *mukta* (liberated) [and] *mayūra* (peacock). Sitting with the body straight, placing both knees exactly parallel with both soles of the feet, this is called svastika, the auspicious [pose]. Placing the right ankle on the left beside the back, and then the left on the right is thus gomukha, the cow-face [pose]. O Śāṇḍilya, padmāsana is placing both soles of the feet upward on the thighs, and with big toes turned up, held by the hands. This is honoured by all.

Commentary

The word āsana comes from the verb ās, meaning 'to sit'. Therefore the noun āsana means 'a seat'. In yoga it is used to mean 'posture'. Patañjali used it to mean 'a steady comfortable sitting position' because one has to sit comfortably without moving if one wishes to meditate for any length of time. Later, masters of the Haṭha Yoga school developed a whole system of postures. The postures described here have physical, mental and energic benefits, and many people perform them just for these benefits. However the main purposes of these postures are to enable us to sit longer in meditation without discomfort or having to move. For this reason, the whole progression of yoga āsana developed, including āsanas, for every possible type of bodily movement: forward, backward, sideways, upward, inverted, and balancing.

When the progression of āsana is properly mastered, the

aspirant should be able to remove the toxins, tensions and stiffness from the body, so that sitting in one posture for a long period of time becomes possible for the purpose of meditation. Meditation in all these positions, except gomukhāsana and siṃhāsana, is intensified by placing the hands in *gyān* or *cin mudrā*, where the tip of the first finger touches either the tip or the base of the thumb, creating a seal or lock, preventing *prāṇa* from leaking out of the body. Once the hands are in the mudrā, they are placed on the knees. In gyān mudrā, the palms face downwards. In cin mudrā, they face upwards. Gyān mudrā means 'wisdom seal', and cin mudrā means 'consciousness seal'. You can experiment, first having the hands in any position, and then in each of these two mudrās. Then notice the subtle effects of each, keeping in mind that yoga entails expansion of awareness.

Svastikāsana

'Svasti' means 'auspicious'; the suffix *'ka'* means 'belonging to'. So *svastika* literally means an 'auspicious object'. The svastika, auspicious object, has been portrayed as a cross with arms of equal length bent at right angles, usually in the clockwise direction, imitating the daily course of the Sun (in the Northern Hemisphere). It has been a symbol of prosperity and good fortune for thousands of years in the ancient and modern world. In India it is still widely used by Hindus, Jains and Buddhists. A common analogy of the swastika is that its four limbs represent the four directions of the world, which have one common centre, consciousness. Therefore, this pose can be considered as the one most auspicious for realising the unity of all existence. In Nazi Germany this symbol was distorted both in appearance, the arms of the cross being oblique, and in meaning, a symbol of violence and racism. Svastikāsana helps relieve varicose veins and sore muscles, and diminish fluid retention in the legs.

Suṣumnā nāḍī, the central energy flow in the spine, is

stimulated to move from *mūlādhāra cakra* at the base of the spine towards *sahasrāra cakra* at the crown of the head. This is an easier version of *siddhāsana*, which is why Atharvan describes eight āsanas, not nine. Do not sit in this position if you have sciatica or sacral injury.

Gomukhāsana

'Go' means 'cow' and *'mukha'* means 'face'. This posture bears similarity to the face of a cow. The cow is considered sacred for several reasons. Sri Krishna, the avatār, was a cow herder. The cow gives many benefits without asking for anything in return. She provides nutrition and energy in the form of milk. Her dung is used as a fertiliser, as it is rich in minerals. Cow dung is saved and used for fuel, as it is high in methane, and can generate heat and electricity. Many villagers use a mixture made of mud and cow dung either to make bricks for their homes or as an insulation from extreme hot and cold temperatures by plastering the walls with it. Vedic sacred fire ceremonies, called *yajña* or *agnihotra*, use cow dung and ghee as fuel, which has been found to purify the air, having anti-pollutant and anti-radiation effects on the environment.

If you can hold *gomukhāsana* for at least ten minutes, you will notice all fatigue, tension and anxiety decreasing. This posture also stimulates the kidneys, relieves back pain, and relaxes the shoulders, neck. It removes cramps in the legs, making the muscles malleable. The position of the arms straightens the back and opens up the chest, improving posture. Keep your attention on the natural breath and on *ājña cakra* at the eyebrow centre or *anāhata cakra* at the heart centre. Be careful of the knees when bending and straightening the legs. Legs can be stretched out in front if the knees are weak, injured or stiff.

Padmāsana

Padmāsana is named after the lotus flower, because the lotus has its roots in the mud, and submerges every night into the muddy water, then rises and blooms again the next morning, its petals pristine and unsullied. Like the lotus, we can remain unsullied by obstacles and painful experiences, using them to advance spiritually. If not forced into this posture, the body can be held steady for quite some time, calming the mind, and entering deep states of meditation. The lotus posture directs the flow of *prāṇa* from *mūlādhāra* towards *sahasrāra cakra*. The pressure on the lower spine relaxes the nervous spine, and increases the blood flow to the abdominal area, stimulating the digestive process.

Do not sit in this position if you have sciatica, sacral injury, weak, injured or stiff knees as kneecaps and ligaments can be damaged. One should not force the body into padmāsana.

Often children under the age of seven sit naturally and easily in this lotus pose, as they sit mainly on the floor at school. From the age of seven, they spend more time sitting in chairs, thereby losing some flexibility.

Verses 4 to 7: Vīrāsana, Siṃhāsana and Siddhāsana

एकं पादमथैकस्मिन्विन्यस्योरुणि संस्थितः ।
इतरस्मिंस्तथा चोरुं वीरासनमुदीरितम् ।।४।। दक्षिणं सव्यगुल्फेन दक्षिणेन तथेतरम् ।
हस्तौ च जान्वोः संस्थाप्य स्वाङ्गुलीश्च प्रसार्य च ।।५।।
व्यात्तवक्त्रं निरीक्षेत नासाग्रं सुसमाहितः । सिंहासनं भवेदेतत्पूजितं योगिभिः सदा ।।६।। योनिं वामेन संपीद्य मेढ्रादुपरि दक्षिणम् ।
भ्रूमध्ये च मनोलक्ष्यं सिद्धासनमिदं भवेत् ।।७।।

ekaṃ pādamathaikasminvinyasyoruṇi saṃsthitaḥ itarasmiṃs-tathā coruṃ vīrāsanāmudīritam (4)
dakṣiṇaṃ savyagulphena dakṣiṇena tathetaram hastau ca jānvoḥ saṃsthāpya svāṅgulīśca prasārya ca (5)
vyāttavaktraṃ nirīkṣeta nāsāgraṃ susamāhitaḥ siṃhāsanaṃ bhavedetatpūjitaṃ yogibhiḥ sadā (6)
yoniṃ vāmena saṃpīḍya meḍhrādupari dakṣiṇam bhrū-madhye ca manolakṣyaṃ siddhāsanamidaṃ bhavet (7)

Vocabulary

vinyasi: placing; *ekam pādam*: one foot; *ekasmin ūruṇi*: on one thigh; *ca tathā*: and then; *itarasmin:* other; *ūrum:* thigh; *udīritam*: is called; *vīrāsanām*: vīrāsana, the hero pose; *saṃsthāpya*: placing; *dakṣiṇam*: right; *savya-gulphena*: with the left ankle; *hastau jānvoḥ:* hands on the knees; *ca svāṅgulīḥ prasārya:* and the fingers extended; *vaktram:* mouth; *vyātta:* opened wide; *nirīkṣeta susamāhitaḥ:* gazing intently at; *nāsāgram*: tip of the nose; *etat bhavet siṃhāsanam*: this is siṃhāsana, the lion pose; *sadā pūjitam yogibhiḥ*: forever honoured by the yogis; *saṃpīḍya*: pressing; *yoniṃ*: perineum; *vāmena*: with the left; *dakṣiṇam*: right one; *upari*: above; *meḍhrāt*: genitals; ca: and; *manolakṣyam*: fixing the mind; *bhrūmadhye*: on the eyebrow centre; *idam bhavet*: this is; *siddhāsanam*: siddhāsana, accomplished pose.

Translation

Placing one foot on one [opposite] thigh and then the other [foot] under its [opposite] thigh is called *vīrāsana*, the hero pose. Placing together the right ankle with the left one and the left at the right (i.e. crossing the ankles), the hands on the knees and the fingers extended, the mouth opened wide, gazing intently at the tip of the nose, this is *siṃhāsana*, the lion pose, forever honoured by the yogis. Pressing the perineum with the left [heel], the right one above the genitals [and] fixing the mind on the eyebrow centre, this is *siddhāsana*, accomplished pose.

Commentary

Vīrāsana

In this pose the left upper arm rests on the knee of the left leg, so that the chin can rest in the palm of the left hand. The eyes are lightly closed. The meditator in this posture seems to be contemplating on some worldly or spiritual matter. That is why the posture is also known as the thinker's or philosopher's pose. It is said to be named after *Mahāvīra* (Great Hero) which is another name for *Hanumān*, the monkey god in the *Ramāyana*, who embodied the heroic qualities of courage, strong character and selflessness. Vīrāsana is beneficial for the kidneys, liver, reproductive and abdominal organs. It helps mind and body to relax. Fix your attention on ājña cakra at the eyebrow centre, developing the power of concentration and clarity of mind.

Siṃhāsana

Siṃhāsana is a completely balanced posture as there is no strong pressure on any part of the body. If one keeps the eyes closed, gazing at the eyebrow centre, a meditative or relaxed state is produced. It can alleviate problems of the throat.

In siṃhāsana, the lion sits silently, waiting. This is the meditative attitude, which the yogi develops in order to enter deep states of consciousness. So, in this sense, siṃhāsana is also a major meditation āsana. Siṃhāsana is a powerful posture, just as its namesake, the lion, is a powerful creature.

Siddhāsana

The word '*siddha*' means 'accomplished' or 'perfected'. It refers to one, who is accomplished in yoga through the mastery of this pose. Siddhāsana and padmāsana are the two most important meditative poses. The other meditation poses are modifications, some of which may be practised more easily and others that are even more difficult. The body is firmly locked in siddhāsana and the feet are less likely to become numb.While padmāsana aims at achieving total balance of the prāṇas for the awakening of suṣumnā, siddhāsana activates the lower centres and redirects the reproductive energy upward to the brain to be used for higher meditation.

Siddhāsana stops the blood pressure from falling too low, and awakens ājña cakra, the psychic centre at the mid-brain, due to the connection between mūlādhāra and ājña. When ājña cakra is awakened, the higher dimension of consciousness is experienced. For these reasons, sitting in siddhāsana for prolonged periods is considered to bring about the meditative state in itself.

Siddhāsana can only be practised by men. Siddha Yoni Āsana is the female equivalent, where the lower heel is pressed into the opening of the vagina and the upper heel rests against the clitoris, and the toes of both feet are placed between the thighs and calf muscles.

Verses 8 to 12: Bhadrāsana, Muktāsana and Māyūrāsana

गुल्फौ तु वृषणस्याधः सीवन्याः पार्श्वयोः क्षिपेत् । पादपापार्श्वे तु पाणिभ्यां दृढं बद्धा सुनिश्चलम् । भद्रासनं भवेदेतत्सर्वव्याधिविषापहम् ।।८।।

संपीड्य सीविनीं सूक्ष्मां गुल्फेनैव तु सव्यतः । सव्यं दक्षिणगुल्फेन मुक्तासनमुदीरितम् ।।९।।

अवष्टभ्य धरां सम्यक्तलाभ्यां तु करद्वयोः । हस्तयोः कूर्परै चापि स्थापयेन्नाभिपार्श्वयोः ।।१०।।

समुन्नतशिरः पादो दण्डवद्व्योम्नि संस्थितः । मयूरासनमेतत्तु सर्वपापप्रणाशनम् ।।११।।

शरीरान्तर्गताः सर्वे रोगा विनश्यन्ति । विषाणि जीर्णानि ।।१२।।

gulphau tu vṛṣaṇasyādhaḥ sīvanyāḥ pārśvayoḥ kṣipet
pādapārśve tu pāṇibhyāṃ dṛḍhaṃ baddhā suniścalam
bhadrāsanaṃ bhavedetatsarvavyādhiviṣāpaham (8)
saṃpīḍya sīvinīṃ sūkṣmāṃ gulphenaiva tu savyataḥ savyaṃ
dakṣiṇagulphena muktāsanamudīritam (9)
avaṣṭabhya dharāṃ samyak talābhyāṃ tu karadvayoḥ
hastayoḥ kūrparai cāpi sthāpayennābhipārśvayoḥ (10)
samunnataśiraḥ pādo daṇḍavadvyomni saṃsthitaḥ
māyūrāsanametattu sarvapāpapraṇāśanam (11)
śarīrāntargatāḥ sarve rogā vinaśyanti viṣāṇi jīrṇāni (12)

Vocabulary

tu: now; *kṣipet*: putting; *gulphau*: ankles; *vṛṣaṇasya-adhaḥ*: under the testes; *pārśvayoḥ*: beside; *sīvanyāḥ*: perineum; *pāda-pārśve*: knees out to the side; *baddhā*: held; *dṛḍham*: firmly; *suniścalam*: stable; *pāṇibhyām*: with the hands; *etat bhavet*: this is; *bhadrāsana*, the gracious pose; *sarva-vyādhi-viṣāpaham*: antidote to all disease; *saṃpīḍya:* pressing; *savyataḥ*: right side; *sūkṣmām sīvinīm*: soft perineum; *gulphena*: with the heel; tu: then; *savyam*: left; *dakṣiṇa-*

gulphena: with the right heel; *udīritam*: is called; *muktāsana*: muktāsana, the liberated pose; *dharām*: holding; *avaṣṭabhya*: tightly; *talābhyām*: soles; *samyak*: together; *karadvayoḥ*: with the two palms; *ca*: and; *sthāpayet*: placing; *kūrparai*: elbows; *nābhi-pārśvayoḥ*: against the sides of the navel; *hastayoḥ*: both hands; *śiraḥ*: head; *samunnata*: raised; *pādaḥ*: legs; *daṇḍavat*: straight; *vyomni*: in the air; *tu etat*: then this; *māyūrāsana*: māyūrāsana, the peacock pose; *praṇāśanam*: remover of; *sarva-pāpa*: all obstructions; *sarve rogāḥ*: all diseases; *antar-gatāḥ*: have entered; *śarīra*: body; *vinaśyanti*: are destroyed; *viṣāṇi jīrṇāni*: poisons are digested.

Translation

Now putting the ankles under the testes beside the perineum, knees out to the sides, held firmly [and] stable with the hands, this is *bhadrāsana*, the gracious pose, the antidote to all disease. Pressing the right side [of] the soft perineum with the [left] heel, then the left [side] with the right heel is called *muktāsana*, the liberated pose. Holding tightly the soles [of the feet] together with the two palms [of the hands], and placing the elbows against the sides of the navel, both hands [on the ground], head raised, legs straight in the air, then this [is] *māyūrāsana*, the peacock pose, remover of all obstructions. [Then] all diseases [which] have entered the body are destroyed; the poisons are digested.

Commentary

Bhadrāsana

The word '*bhadra*' means 'gentle', 'gracious' or 'blessed'. This āsana automatically induces *mūla bandha*, the perineal lock, and is used for the awakening of mūlādhāra cakra, the root psychic centre. The practitioner should keep the awareness on mūlādhāra cakra and the natural breath or the nose tip. For this reason, it is also called *mūlabandhāsana* in some of the classical texts. It is an important posture for the conservation of sexual energy, and helps to tone the reproductive and eliminatory organs. Therefore, it keeps the body free from toxic buildup in the lower regions and helps to avert disease. Bhadrāsana is an excellent meditation pose for the advanced practitioner, whose knees, ankles and feet are very flexible.

Muktāsana

Muktāsana, the liberated pose, is another name for siddhāsana. The left heel is under the anus, the right heel above it. It can be practised by both sexes.

Māyurāsana

Māyurāsana, the peacock pose, is mentioned in this upaniṣad and in many classical texts on yoga, due to its powerful influence on the *maṇipura cakra* and the digestive system. The other postures mentioned in this section are all sitting postures. The purpose of including this major āsana here may have been for health reasons. The Indian subcontinent is hot and humid for many months of the year. Continuous heat and humidity affect the metabolism, causing toxins and bacteria to proliferate. The verse describes the practice, and then states that it will remove all obstructions. Digestive and metabolic ailments are considered to be the mother of all disease. For the yogi they are a great impediment, because the core energy becomes weak and unbalanced, making it very difficult to continue or progress in sādhana.

Māyurāsana massages the abdominal organs and stimulates the intestinal peristalsis. It removes toxins and develops mental and physical balance. Therefore the practitioner should keep the awareness on both maintaining balance and maṇipura cakra. 'Just as a peacock can kill and digest snakes without being affected by the poison, this āsana enables the practitioner to digest and metabolise the residual toxins and poisons in the body.'[13]

Do not attempt this posture if you have high blood pressure, any heart ailment, hernia, peptic or duodenal ulcer, if you have any sign of illness or physical weakness, or if you are pregnant.

Verses 13 to 15: Mastery of āsana

येन केनासनेन सुखधारणं भवत्यशक्तस्तत्समाचरेत् ।।१३।।

येनासनं विजितं जगत्त्रयं तेन विजितं भवति ।।१४।।

यमनियमासनाभ्यासयुक्तः पुरुषः प्राणायामं चरेत् ।येन नाड्यः शुद्धा भवन्ति ।।१५।।

yena kenāsanena sukhadhāraṇaṃ bhavatyaśaktastatsam-ācaret (13)
yenāsanaṃ vijitaṃ jagattrayaṃ tena vijitaṃ bhavati (14)
yamaniyamāsanābhyāsayuktaḥ puruṣaḥ prāṇāyāmaṃ caretyena nāḍyaḥ śuddhā bhavanti (15)

Vocabulary

yena bhavati: whoever is; *aśaktaḥ*: unable; *tat:* this; *samācaret:* should practise thoroughly; *kena-āsanena*: whichever āsana; *sukha-dhāraṇam*: hold comfortably; *tena*: thus; bhavati vijitam āsana: one has mastery over āsana; *vijitam jagat-trayam*: mastery over the three worlds; *puruṣaḥ*: person; *yuktaḥ*: established in; *yama-niyama-āsana-abhyāsa*: yama, niyama [and] āsana practice; *prāṇāyāmaṃ caret*: should perform prāṇāyāma; *yena*: thus; *nāḍyaḥ*: *nāḍīs*; *bhavanti*: become; *śuddhā*: purified.

Translation

Whoever is unable [to do] this [posture] should practise thoroughly whichever postures [one can] hold comfortably. Thus one [who] has mastery over āsana [has] mastery over the three worlds. The person established in yama, niyama [and] āsana practice should perform *prāṇāyāma*. Thus the nāḍīs become purified.

Commentary

According to this verse, the mastery of āsana gives one victory over the three worlds. Here, the three worlds can also be analogous with the body, energy and mind. Mastery of āsana gives flexibility, sensitivity and control over the physical body. It activates and rebalances the prāṇas, energies sustaining the body, and purifies, steadies and focuses the mind. Āsana should always be practised at least two hours after eating and before prāṇāyāma. Regular practice of prāṇāyāma eliminates toxins from the *nāḍīs*, enabling the vital energy to flow freely.

Fourth Section

Verse 1: Śāṇḍilya Inquires

अथ हैनमथर्वाणं शाण्डिल्यः पप्रच्छ केनोपायेन नाड्यः शुद्धाः स्यूः । नाड्यः कतिसंख्याकाः । तासामुत्पक्तिः कीदृशी । तासु कति वायवस्तिष्ठन्ति । तेषां कानि स्थानानि । तत्कर्माणि कानि । देहे यानि यानि विज्ञातव्यानि तत्सर्वं मे ब्रूहीति ॥१॥

atha hainamatharvāṇaṃ śāṇḍilyaḥ papraccha kenopāyena nāḍyaḥ śuddhāḥ syūḥ; nāḍyaḥ katisaṃkhyākāḥ; tāsāmutpaktiḥ kīdṛśī; tāsu kati vāyavastiṣṭhanti; teṣāṃ kāni sthānāni; tatkarmāṇi kāni; dehe yāni yāni vijñātavyāni tatsarvaṃ me brūhīti. (1)

Vocabulary
atha: now; *śāṇḍilyaḥ papraccha*: Śāṇḍilya asked; *inam atharvāṇam*: Lord Atharvan; *kena-upāyena*: by what means; *nāḍyaḥ: nāḍīs; syūḥ śuddhāḥ*: might be purified; *kati nāḍyaḥ*: how many nāḍīs; *saṃkhyākāḥ*: are there in number; *kīdṛśī*: how; *tāsām utpaktiḥ*: do they arise; *kati vāyavaḥ*: which vital airs; *tiṣṭhanti*: are located; *tāsu*: in them; *kāni*: which; *teṣāṃ sthānāni*: are their seats; *kāni tat-karmāṇi*: what are their actions; *me brūhīti*: please tell me; *tat-sarvam*: all that; *yāni vijñātavyāni*: which is to be known; *dehe*: in the body.

Translation
Now Śāṇḍilya asked Lord Atharvan: "By what means might the nāḍīs be purified? How many nāḍīs are there in number? How do they arise? Which vital airs are located in them? Which are their seats? What are their actions? Please tell me all that which is to be known in the body."

Commentary
Having been instructed in yama, niyama, āsana and the

influence of āsana on body, energy and mind by Atharvan, Śāṇḍilya now wants to understand everything there is to be known about the nāḍīs or energy currents, and vāyus (prāṇas) or vital airs in the pranic or subtle body.

Verses 2 to 5a: The Pranic Body

स होवाचाथर्वाः अथेदं शरीरं षण्णवत्यङ्गुलात्मकं भवति ।
शरीरात्प्राणो द्वादशाङ्गुलाधिको भवति ।।२।।
शरीरस्थं प्राणमग्निना सह योगाभ्यासेन समन्यूनं वा यः
करोति स योगिपुङ्गवो भवति ।।३।।
देहमध्ये शिखिस्थानं त्रिकोणं तप्तजाम्बूनदप्रभं मनुष्याणाम ।
चतुष्पदां चतुरश्रम् । विहङ्गानां वृत्ताकारम् ।
तन्मध्ये शुभा तन्वी पावकी शिखा तिष्ठति ।।४।।
गुदाद्द्व्यङ्गुलादूर्ध्वं मेढ्राद्द्व्यङ्गुलादधो देहमध्यं
मनुष्याणांभवति ।चतुष्पदां हृन्मध्यम् ।
विहगानां तुन्दमध्यम् ।५।

sa hovācātharvāḥ athedaṃ śarīraṃ ṣaṇṇavatyaṅgulātmakaṃ bhavatiśarīrātprāṇo dvādaśāṅgulādhiko bhavati (2)
śarīrasthaṃ prāṇamagninā saha yogābhyāsena samam-anyūnaṃ vā yaḥ karoti sa yogipuṅgavo bhavati (3)
dehamadhye śikhisthānaṃ trikoṇaṃ taptajāmbūnadaprabhaṃ manuṣyāṇāmcatuṣpadāṃ caturaśram; vihaṅgānāṃ vṛttākāramtanmadhye śubhā tanvī pāvakī śikhā tiṣṭhati (4)
gudāddvyaṅgulādūrdhvaṃ meḍhrāddvyaṅgulādadho deha-madhyaṃ manuṣyāṇāṃ bhavaticatuṣpadāṃ hṛnmadhyam; vihagānāṃ tundamadhyam (5a)

Vocabulary

atha: now; *atharvāḥ*: Atharvan; *āvāca:* replied; *idam śarīram*: this body; *ātmakam bhavati*: consists of; *ṣaṇṇavati-aṅgula*: ninety-six digits; *prāṇaḥ*: *prāṇa*; *adhikaḥ bhavati*: extends; *dvādaśa-aṅgula*: twelve digits; *śarīrāt*: beyond the body; *yaḥ*: whoever; *saha yogābhyāsena*: with regular yoga practice; *karoti*: makes; *prāṇam śarīrastham*: prāṇa in the body; *samamanyūnaṃ vā*: equal to or not less; *agninā*: than the fire; *sa bhavati*: he becomes; *yogi-puṅgavaḥ*: best of yogis; *manuṣ*

-yāṇām: in humans; *śikhi-sthānam*: region of fire; *trikoṇam*: triangular; *prabham*: radiant; *tapta-jāmbūnada*: molten gold; *deha-madhye*: middle of the body; *catuṣpadām*: in four-footed animals; *caturaśram*: quadrangular; *vihaṅgānām*: in birds; *vṛttākāram*: round; *tat-madhye*: in its centre; *tiṣṭhati*: is situated; *śubhā*: auspicious; *tanvī*: subtle; *pāvakī*: purifying; *śikhā*: flame; *dvi-aṅgulāt*: two digits; *ūrdhvam*: above; *gudāt*: anus; *adhaḥ*: below; *meḍhrāt*: sexual organ; *bhavati*: is; *deha-madhyam*: centre of the body; *manuṣyāṇām*: in humans; *catuṣpadām:* in four-footed animals; *hṛt-madhyam*: centre of the heart; *vihagānām*: in birds; *tunda-madhyam*: centre of the abdomen.

Translation

Now Atharvan replied: "This body consists of ninety-six digits [in length]. Prāṇa extends twelve digits beyond the body. Who-ever with regular yoga practice makes the prāṇa in the body equal to or not less than the fire [in it], he becomes the best of yogis. In humans, the region of fire, [which is] triangular [and as] radiant [as] molten gold, [is] in the middle of the body. In four-footed animals, [it is] quadrangular. In birds [it is] round. In its centre is situated the auspicious, subtle, purifying flame. Two digits above the anus [and] two digits below the sexual organ is the centre of the body in humans. In four-footed animals, [it is] the centre of the heart. In birds, [it is] the centre of the abdomen.

Commentary

The pranic body, also known as the subtle body, gives energy, life and movement to the physical body with its many organs and systems. It is described as ninety-six *aṅgulas*, digits or finger widths, which may amount to about seven to eight feet (210 to 240cm). Although the pranic body is contained within the physical, it often extends beyond it. The verse says that the prāṇa in the body should not be less than the fire in the triangle in the centre of the body. If it is less, it is like the smouldering remains of a fire, and the person lacks vitality, energy and motivation. In yoga, all the practices work on the subtle, or pranic, body in various ways to rebalance and awaken it. At the centre of this field is the *śikhisthāna*, the region of fire. In yoga, we also refer to this region as the *agni maṇḍala*, and it too plays an important role in the awakening of the subtle energies. It is described here as radiant as molten gold, just like the gold on the banks of the River Jambūnada, where the wet mud, dried by the air and sun, is said to produce large quantities of gold.

Verses 5b to 7: Maṇipura Cakra

देहमध्यं नवाङ्गुलं चतुरङ्गुलमुत्सेधायतमण्डाकृति ॥५॥

तन्मध्ये नाभिः ।

तत्र द्वादशारयुतं चक्रम् ।तच्च मध्ये पुण्यपापप्रचोदितो जीवो

भ्रमति ॥६॥

तन्तुपञ्जरमध्यस्थलूतिका यथा भ्रमति तथा चासौ तत्र

प्राणाश्चरति ।देहेऽस्मिञ्जीवः प्राणारूढो भवेत् ॥७॥

dehamadhyaṃ navāṅgulaṃ
caturaṅgulamutsedhāyatamaṇḍākṛti (5b)
tanmadhye nābhiḥ; tatra dvādaśārayutam cakramtacca
madhye puṇyapāpapracodito jīvo bhramati (6)
tantupañjaramadhyasthalūtikā yathā bhramati tathā cāsau
tatra prāṇaścaratidehe 'smiñjīvaḥ prāṇārūḍho bhavet (7)

Vocabulary

nava-aṅgulam: nine digits; *deha-madhyam*: centre of the body; *catuḥ-aṅgulam*: four digits; *utsedha-āyatam*: width and length; *aṇḍākṛti*: oval; *tat-madhye*: in its middle; *nābhiḥ*: navel; *tatra*: there; *cakram*: cakra; *utam*: with; *dvādaśa-ara*: twelve spokes; *ca*: and; *tat madhye*: in its midst; *jīvaḥ*: *jīva*, individual soul; *bhramati*: wanders; *pracoditaḥ*: impelled by; *puṇya-pāpa*: good and bad; *yathā . . tathā*: just as . . so; *lūtikā*: spider; *bhramati*: wanders; *madhyastha*: among; *tantu*: threads; *pañjara*: web; *asau prāṇaḥ*: that prāṇa; *carati tatra*: roams about there; *asmin dehe*: in this body; *jīvaḥ*: jīva; *bhavet*: is; *prāṇa-ārūḍhaḥ*: carried by prāṇa.

Translation

Nine digits [from] the centre of the body [and] four digits [in] width and length [is] an oval. In its middle [is] the navel. There [is] a cakra with twelve spokes, and in its midst the *jīva* wanders, impelled by its good and bad [actions]. Just as a spider wanders among the threads of a web, so that prāṇa roams about there. In this body, the jīva is carried by prāṇa.

Commentary

The oval here refers to the *kanda*, the root where the three main *nāḍīs*, or energy channels, *īḍā, piṅgalā* and *suṣumnā*, unite and separate. The cakra referred to is *maṇipura*, described as having twelve spokes, although usually it is considered to have ten. The main prāṇa of maṇipura is *samāna*, which moves from left to right and right to left, providing the energy for digestion. Two other prāṇas meet at the navel: *prāṇa*, which moves up and down between navel and throat, and *apāna*, which moves up and down between perineum and navel.

The verse says the *jīva* wanders about 'impelled by its good and bad [actions]', meaning that here the individual self is subject to the karmas of present and past lives. The jīva is trapped in this web of prāṇas, until the *kuṇḍalinī* awakens, and the jīva travels up to the higher cakras, where it identifies with the *ātman*, the universal Self.

Verse 8: Kuṇḍalinī

नाभेस्तिर्यगाध ऊर्ध्वं कुण्डलिनीस्थानम ।अष्टप्रकृतिरूपाऽष्टधा
कुण्डलीकृता कुण्डलिनी शक्तिर्भवति ।यथावद्वायुसंचारं
जलान्नादीनि परितः स्कन्धपार्श्वषु निरुध्यैनं मुखेनैव समावेष्ट्य
ब्रह्मरन्ध्रं योगकाले चापानेनाग्निना च स्फुरति ।हृदयाकाशो
महोज्ज्वला ज्ञानरूपा भवति ।।८।।

nābhestiryagādha ūrdhvaṃ kuṇḍalinīsthānamaṣṭaprakṛtirūpā 'ṣṭadhā kuṇḍalīkṛtā kuṇḍalinī śaktirbhavatiyathāvadvāyusaṃcāraṃ jalānnādīni paritaḥ skandhapārśvaṣu nirudhyainaṃmukhenaiva samāveṣṭya brahmarandhraṃ yogakāle cāpānenāgninā ca sphuratihṛdayākāśo mahojjvalā jñānarūpā bhavati (8)

Vocabulary

tiryaga-adhaḥ: lying below; *nābheḥ*: navel; *ūrdhvam*: above; *kuṇḍalinī-sthānam*: seat of the kuṇḍalinī; *kuṇḍalinī śaktiḥ*: *kuṇḍalinī śakti*; *bhavati*: has; *rūpā*: form; *aṣṭa-prakṛtiḥ*: eight prakṛtis (elements of nature); *kṛtā*: making; *aṣṭadhā kuṇḍalīḥ*: eightfold coils; *vāyu-saṃcāram*: movement of vital air; *yathāvat*: duly; *nirudhya*: controls; *jala-anna-(adīni)*: (possession of) water and food; *paritaḥ*: all around; *skandha-pārśvaṣu*: beside the *skandha*; *samāveṣṭya*: she covers; *mukhena*: with her mouth; *brahmarandhram*: *brahmarandhra*; *ca*: and; *sphurati*: breaks forth; *yoga-kāle*: at the time of yoga; *apānena-agninā*: by the fire of apāna; *mahot-jvalā*: great blaze; *jñāna-rūpā*: form of wisdom; *bhavati*: appears; *hṛdaya-ākāśaḥ*: in the heart space.

Translation

Lying below the navel [and] above [it is] the seat of the kuṇḍalinī. *Kuṇḍalinī śakti* has the form [of] eight *prakṛtis* (elements of nature), making eightfold coils. The movement of the vital air duly controls the food and water all around beside the *skandha*. She covers with her mouth [the way to] the *brahmarandhra*, and breaks forth at the time of yoga by the fire of apāna. A great blaze in the form of wisdom appears in the heart space.

Commentary

Kuṇḍalinī is the power of Consciousness (*cit-śakti*). Its literal meaning is 'she who is coiled'. Kuṇḍalinī śakti therefore is known as the serpent power, containing the potential divine or infinite energy of the cosmos, pure consciousness. The kuṇḍalinī energy residing at the kanda is in a more dynamic state, ready to awaken and ascend. When she is awakened at maṇipura cakra, she will ascend to the higher cakras and not fall down again to mūlādhāra or *svādhiṣṭhāna*.

The kuṇḍalinī has the form of the eight elements of nature, which she deposits at the cakras on her descent through the suṣumnā. First she deposits the three elements of mind: *buddhi* (intellect), *citta* (memory) and *ahaṃkāra* (individual self), at *ājña cakra* at the top of the spinal column. Next she descends to *viśuddhi cakra*, behind the throat, and deposits the element of space. Then she descends to *anāhata cakra*, behind the heart, and deposits the element of air. Next she descends to *maṇipura cakra*, behind the navel, and deposits the element of fire. She continues on her journey down to *svādhiṣṭhāna cakra*, behind the pubis, and deposits the energy of water, and finally she descends to *mūlādhāra cakra*, above the perineum, and deposits the energy of earth.

These five elements: earth, water, fire, air and space, along with the three elements of mind: buddhi, citta and ahaṃkāra, make eight elements of nature, which all human beings are comprised of. These eight elements represent the evolution of the kuṇḍalinī energy from divine to material, which is the cause of creation. Having assumed the earthly form through the combination and permutation of these elements, one must constantly consume food and water, and breathe air. The continuous intake of these earthly elements blocks the *brahmarandhra*, the opening of the *brahma nāḍī* at the fontanelle, holding the spirit in the body, in the same way that the kuṇḍalinī blocks the opening of suṣumnā at the lower centres with her own mouth at the kanda.

The 'movement of vital air' refers to samāna, which moves from side to side, stimulating digestion. When yoga practices are performed, prāṇa, the upward vital air, and apāna, the downward vital air, come together at the navel centre, *maṇipura kṣetram*, creating a powerful hot energy, awakening maṇipura cakra, and shooting up to anāhata cakra, where the aspiring yogi lives in universal wisdom.

Verses 9 to 11: Fourteen Nāḍīs

मध्यस्थकुण्डलिनीमाश्रित्य मुख्या नाड्यश्चतुर्दश भवन्ति ।
इडा पिङ्गला सुषुम्ना सरस्वती वारुणी पूषा हस्तिजिह्वा
यशस्विनी विश्वोदरी कुहूः शङ्खिनी पयस्विनी अलम्बुसा
गान्धारीति नाड्यश्चतुर्दश भवन्ति ।।९।।
तत्र सुषुम्ना विश्वधारिणी मोक्षमार्गेति चाचक्षते ।
गुदस्य पृष्ठभागे वीणादण्डाश्रिता मूर्धपर्यन्तं विज्ञेया व्यक्ता
सूक्ष्मा वैष्णवी भवति ।।१०।।
सुषुम्नायाः सव्यभागे इडा तिष्ठति । दक्षिणभागे पिङ्गला ।
इडायां चन्द्रश्चरति । पिङ्गलायां रविः । तमोरूपश्चन्द्रः ।
रजोरूपो रविः । विषभागो रविः ।अमृतभागश्चन्द्रमाः ।
तावेव सर्वकालं धत्तः ।
सुषुम्ना कालभोक्तृ भवति ।सुषुम्नापृष्ठपार्श्वयोः सरस्वतीकुहू
भवतः ।
यशस्विनीकुहूमध्ये वारुणी प्रतिष्ठिता भवति । पूषासरस्वतीमध्ये
पयस्विनी भवति ।कन्दमध्येऽलम्बुसा भवति । सुषुम्ना पूर्वपूर्वभागे
मेढ्रान्तं कुहूर्भवति ।कुण्डलिन्या अधश्चोर्ध्वं वरुणी सर्वगामिनी
भवति । यशस्विनी सौम्या च पादाङ्गुष्ठान्तमिष्यते ।पिङ्गला
चोर्ध्वगा याम्यनासान्तं भवति । पिङ्गलायाः पृष्ठतो याम्यनेत्रान्तं
पूषा भवति ।याम्यकर्णान्तं यशस्विनी भवति । जिह्वाया ऊर्ध्वान्तं
सरस्वती भवति ।आसव्यकर्णान्तमूर्ध्वगा शङ्खिनी भवति ।
इडापृष्ठभागात्सव्यनेत्रान्तगा गान्धारी भवति
।पायुमूलादधोर्ध्वगाऽलम्बुसा भवात । एतासु चतुर्दशसु नाडीष्वन्या
नाड्यः संभवन्ति ।तास्वन्यास्तास्वन्या भवन्तीति विज्ञेयाः ।

यथाऽश्वत्थादिपत्रं सिराभिर्व्याप्तमेवं शरिरं नाडीभिर्व्याप्तम ॥११॥*madhyasthakuṇḍalinīmāśritya mukhyā nāḍyaścaturdaśa bhavantiiḍā piṅgalā suṣumnā sarasvatī vāruṇī pūṣā hastijihvā yaśasvinī viśvodarī kuhūḥśaṅkhinī payasvinī alambusā gāndhārīti nāḍyaścaturdaśa bhavanti (9)tatra suṣumnā viśvadhāriṇī mokṣamārgeti cācakṣategudasya pṛṣṭhabhāge vīṇādaṇḍāśritā mūrdhaparyantaṃ vijñeyā vyaktā sūkṣmā vaiṣṇavī bhavati (10)suṣumnāyāḥ savyabhāge iḍā tiṣṭhati; dakṣiṇabhāge piṅgalā; iḍāyāṃ candraścarati;piṅgalāyāṃ raviḥ; tamorūpaścandraḥ; rajorūpo raviḥ; viṣabhāgo raviḥ;amṛtabhāgaścandramāḥ; tāveva sarvakālaṃ dhattaḥ; suṣumnākālabhoktṛ bhavati;suṣumnāpṛṣṭhapārśvayoḥ sarasvatīkuhū bhavataḥ; yaśasvinīkuhūmadhye vāruṇī pratiṣṭhitā bhavati; pūṣāsarasvatīmadhye payasvinī bhavati;gāndhārīsarasvatīmadhye yaśasvinī bhavati; kandamadhye 'lambusā bhavati;suṣumnāpūrvabhāge meḍhrāntaṃ kuhūrbhavati;kuṇḍalinyā adhaścordhvaṃ varuṇī sarvagāminī bhavati;yaśasvinī saumyā ca pādāṅguṣṭhāntamiṣyate;piṅgalā cordhvagā yāmyanāsāntaṃ bhavati;yāmyakarṇāntaṃ yaśasvinī bhavati; jihvāyā ūrdhvāntaṃ sarasvatī bhavati;āsavyakarṇāntamūrdhvagā śaṅkhinī bhavati;iḍāpṛṣṭhabhagātsavyanetrāntagā gāndhārī bhavati;pāyumūlādadhordhvagā 'lambusā bhavati;etāsu caturdaśasu nāḍīṣvanyā nāḍyaḥ saṃbhavanti;tāsvanyāstāsvanyā bhavantīti vijñeyāḥ;yathā 'śvatthādipattraṃ sirābhirvyāptamevaṃ śarīraṃ nāḍībhirvyāptam (11)*

Vocabulary

āśritya: having recourse to; *madhyastha-kuṇḍalinī*: kuṇḍalinī located in the centre; *bhavanti*: are; *caturdaśa*: fourteen; *mukhyā nāḍyaḥ*: main nāḍīs; *nāḍyaḥ-caturdaśa*: fourteen nāḍīs; *iti*: thus; *tatra*: among them; *ācakṣate*: is declared; *viśva-dhāriṇī*: sustainer of the universe; *ca iti*: and thus; *mokṣa-mārga*: way to liberation; *āśritā*: dwelling in; *vīṇā-*

daṇḍa: spinal column; *pṛṣṭhabhāge*: from the back; *gudasya:* of the anus; *mūrdha-paryantam*: right up to the crown of the head; *bhavati vijñeyā*: she is regarded as; *vyaktā sūkṣmā:* manifest, subtle; *vaiṣṇavī*: power of Viṣṇu; *savyabhāge*: on the left; *suṣumnāyāḥ:* of suṣumnā; *tiṣṭhati iḍā:* is located iḍā; *dakṣiṇabhāge piṅgalā*: on the right piṅgalā; *candraḥ carati iḍāyām*: moon moves in iḍā; *raviḥ piṅgalāyām*: sun in piṅgalā; *candraḥ*: moon; *tamaḥ rūpaḥ*: nature of tamas; *raviḥ*: sun; *rajaḥ rupaḥ*: nature of rajas; *viṣa-bhāgaḥ*: share of poison; *amṛta*: nectar; *tau*: they both; *dhattaḥ*: determine; *sarva-kālam*: all time; *bhavati*: is; *kāla bhoktṛ*: consumer of time; *sarasvatī-kuhū*: sarasvatī and kuhū; *bhavataḥ*: are; *pṛṣṭha-pārśvayoḥ*: at the back and to the side of; *vāruṇī pratiṣṭhitā bhavati:* vāruṇī is situated; *yaśasvinī-kuhū-madhye:* between yaśasvinī and kuhū; *payasvinī bhavati*: payasvinī is; *pūṣā-sarasvatī-madhye*: between pūṣā and sarasvatī; *yaśasvinī bhavati:* yaśasvinī is; *gāndhārī-sarasvatī-madhye:* between gāndhārī and sarasvatī; *alambusā bhavati:* alambusā is; *kanda-madhye*: in the centre of the navel; *kuhūḥ-bhavati:* kuhū is; *suṣumnā-pūrvabhāge*: in front of suṣumnā; *meḍhrāntam*: up to the genital organ; *varuṇī sarvagāminī bhavati*: vāruṇī goes everywhere; *adhaḥ-ca-ūrdhvam kuṇḍalinyā*: below and above kuṇḍalinī; *ca saumyā yaśasvinī*: and auspicious yaśasvinī; *iṣyate*: leads; *pāda-aṅguṣṭha-antam*: to the tip of the big toes; *ca piṅgalā*: and piṅgalā; *bhavati ūrdhvagā*: goes upwards to; *yāmya-nāsa-antam*: right nostril; *pūṣā bhavati*: pūṣā is; *piṅgalāyāḥ pṛṣṭhataḥ*: behind piṅgalā; *yāmya-netra-antam*: up to the right eye; *yaśasvinī bhavati*: yaśasvinī goes; *yāmya-karṇa-antam*: up to the right ear; *sarasvatī bhavati*: sarasvatī goes; *ūrdhva-antam*: to the upper side; *jihvāyāḥ*: of the tongue; *śaṅkhinī bhavati ūrdhvagā*: śaṅkhinī goes upwards; *āsavya-karṇa-antam*: to the left ear; *gāndhārī bhavati gā*: gāndhārī goes; *iḍā-pṛṣṭha-bhagāt*: from behind iḍā; *savya-netra-anta*: to the left eye; *alambusā bhavati gā*: alambusā goes; *adha-ūrdhva*: downwards and upwards; *pāyu-mūlāt*: from the base of the anus; *etāsu caturdaśasu nāḍīṣu*: from these fourteen nāḍīs; *anyāḥ nāḍyaḥ*: other nāḍīs; *saṃbhavanti*: arise; *tāsu anyāḥ bhavanti*: from these others arise; *tāsu anyāḥ*: from these others; *iti vijñeyāḥ*: thus they should be known; *yathā*: just as; *pattram*: leaf; *aśvattha-ādi*: holy fig tree and others; *vyāptam*: is pervaded; *sirābhiḥ*: with veins; *evam*: so; *śarīram*: body; *nāḍībhiḥ-vyāptam*: is pervaded with nāḍīs.

Translation

Having recourse to kuṇḍalinī located in the centre, are fourteen main nāḍīs. The fourteen nāḍīs are thus: *iḍā piṅgalā suṣumnā sarasvatī vāruṇī pūṣā hastijihvā yaśasvinī viśvodarī kuhūḥ śaṅkhinī payasvinī alambusā gāndhārī*. Among them, suṣumnā is declared the sustainer of the universe, and thus the way to liberation. Dwelling in the spinal column from the back of the anus right up to the crown of the head, she is regarded as the manifest, subtle power of Viṣṇu.

On the left of suṣumnā is located iḍā, on the right [is] piṅgalā. The moon moves in iḍā, the sun in piṅgalā. The moon [has] the nature of *tamas*, the sun of *rajas*. The sun [has] the share of poison, the moon nectar. They both determine all time. Suṣumnā is the consumer of time.

Sarasvatī and kuhū are at the back and to the side of suṣumnā [respectively]. Vāruṇī is situated between yaśasvinī and kuhū. Payasvinī is between pūṣā and sarasvatī. Yaśasvinī is between gāndhārī and sarasvatī. Alambusā is in the centre of the navel. Kuhū is in front of suṣumnā up to the genital organ. Vāruṇī goes everywhere, below and above kuṇḍalinī, and auspicious yaśasvinī leads to the tip of the big toes, and piṅgalā goes upwards to the right nostril.

Pūṣā is behind piṅgalā [and goes] up to the right eye. Yaśasvinī goes up to the right ear. Sarasvatī goes to the upper side of the tongue. Śaṅkhinī goes upwards to the left ear. Gāndhārī goes from behind iḍā to the left eye. Alambusā goes downwards and upwards from the base of the anus.

From these fourteen nāḍīs, other nāḍīs arise. From these others arise, and from these others; thus they should be known. Just as the leaf [of] the holy fig tree and others is pervaded with veins, so the body is pervaded with nāḍīs.

Commentary

Of the seventy-two thousand nāḍīs in the body, there are fourteen main nāḍīs, listed above, which originate from the kanda, the bulb-shaped origin of the nāḍīs. Different texts describe the location of the kanda either just above mūlādhāra cakra, or just above the perineum and terminating at maṇipura or at maṇipura cakra.14 The verse says 'suṣumnā is declared the sustainer of the universe', because the *śakt*i, the divine energy, flows through it from mūlādhāra cakra at the base of the spine to sahasrāra at the crown of the head, where the cosmic energy first enters the body. Just as Viṣṇu supports the universe, suṣumnā supports the physical body as it moves up the spine. It is the only nāḍī which ascends to the *brahmarandra* (brahmic fissure) at the crown of the head, and transcends the duality of iḍā (moon) and piṅgalā (sun), left and right.

The sun, being active and bright, is rajasic. The moon, being receptive and dark, is tamasic. When the energy flows in suṣumnā, there is *sattva*, balance and luminosity. The sun can be poisonous because it burns. A crescent moon is the symbol of *bindu*, the point at the top back of the head, the centre of creation. When bindu is awakened, nectar flows down to *viśuddhi cakra*, and then permeates the body's system. 'They both (sun and moon) indicate Time or Kāla, and Suṣumnā devours Kāla. For on that path, entry is made into timelessness.'15

Kuhū rises to the upper part of suṣumnā, which glows like the full moon. Kuhū goes up and down the back of the throat, behind the nostrils. Iḍā terminates at the left nostril and piṅgalā at the right. Suṣumnā represents the balanced flow of both nostrils together. Sarasvatī goes to the tongue. The location of Hastijihvā has been omitted; usually it is described as going to the toes of the left foot. Viṣvodarā is at the centre of the kanda.

The description of the major nāḍīs is found in several upaniṣads and classical texts, such as the *Śiva Swarodaya*. The yogis and rishis of old had seen these channels during their meditation, and later described what they had seen to their devotees and disciples. In the early times such instruction had to be remembered, as there were very few capable scribes. Hence, we find similarities as well as differences in regard to the names and placements of these subtle channels.

In the *Śiva Swarodaya*, for example, kuhū is located in the reproductive organs, so we can assume that it rises through the body to the upper part of suṣumnā. Again, yaśasvinī is said to flow up to the right ear in this text, while the *Śiva Swarodaya* describes it flowing up to the left ear. Pūṣā is said to terminate at the right eye in this text, while in Śiva Swarodaya it is the right ear. Śaṅkhinī goes to the anal region, according to *Śiva Swarodaya*, and to the left ear, according to this text. Both texts mention that gāndhārā goes to the left eye.

Verses 12 to 14: The Ten Vāyus

प्राणापानसमानोदानव्याना नागकूर्मकृकरदेवदत्तधनञ्जय एते दश वायवः सर्वासु नाडीषु चरन्ति

।।१२।।आस्यनासिकाणठनाभिपादाङ्गुष्ठद्वयकुण्डल्यदश्चोर्ध्वभागेषु प्राणाः संचरति ।श्रोत्राक्षिकटिगुल्फघ्राणगलस्फिग्देशेषु व्यानः संचरति

।गुदमेढ्रोरुजानूदरवृषणकटिजङ्घानाभिगुदाग्न्यगारेष्वपानः संचरति । सर्वसंधिस्थ उदानः ।पादहस्तयोरपि सर्वगात्रेषु सर्वव्यापी समानः ।भुक्तान्नरसादिकं गात्रेऽग्निना सह

व्यापयन्द्विसप्ततिसहस्रेषु नाडीमार्गेषु चरन्समानवातग्निना सह साङ्गोपाङ्गकलेवरं व्याप्नोति ।नागादिवायवः पञ्च

त्वगस्थ्यादिसंभवाः ।तुन्दस्थं जलमन्नं च रसादिषु समीरितं तुन्दमध्यगतः प्राणस्तानि पृथक्कुर्यात् ।अग्नेरुपरि जलं स्थाप्य जलोपर्यन्नादीनि संस्थाप्य स्वयमपानं संप्राप्य तेनैव सह मारुतः प्रयाति देहमध्यगतं ज्वलनम् ।वायुना पालितो वह्निरपानेन शनैर्देहमध्ये ज्वलाति ।ज्वलनो ज्वालाभिः प्राणेन कोष्ठमध्यगतं जलमत्युष्णमकरोत् ।जलोपरि समर्पितव्यञ्जनसंयुक्तमन्नं वह्निसंयुक्तवारिणा तप्नमकरोत् ।तेन

स्वेदमूत्रजलरक्तवीर्यरूपरसपुरीषादिकं प्राणः पृथक्कुर्यात्

।समानवायुना सह सर्वासु नाडीषु रसं व्यापयञ्छ्वासरुपेण देहे वायुश्चरति ।नवभिर्व्योमरन्ध्रैः शरीरस्य वायवः कुर्वन्ति विण्मूत्रादिविसर्जनम् ।निश्वासोच्छ्वासकासश्च प्राणकर्मोच्यते । विण्मूत्रादिविसर्जनमपानवायुकर्म ।हानोपादानचेष्टादि व्यानकर्म । देहस्योन्नयनादिकमुदानकर्म ।शरीरपोषणादिकं समानकर्म ।

उद्गारादि नागकर्म । निमीलनादि कूर्मकर्म ।क्षुत्करणं कृकरकर्म । तन्द्रा देवदत्तकर्म । श्लेष्मादि धनञ्जयकर्म ।।१३।।एवं नाडीस्थानं वायुस्थानं तत्कर्म च सम्यग्ज्ञात्वा नाडीसंशोधनं कुर्यात् ।।१४।।

prāṇāpānasamānodānavyāna nāgakūrmakṛkaradevadattadhanañjaya ete daśa vāyavaḥ sarvāsu nāḍīṣu caranti (12) āsyanāsikākaṇṭhanābhipādāṅguṣṭhadvayakuṇḍalyadaścordh vabhāgeṣu prāṇāḥ saṃcaratiśrotrākṣikaṭigulphaghrāṇagalasphigdeśeṣu vyānaḥ saṃcaratigudameḍhrorujānūdaravṛṣaṇakaṭijaṅghānābhigud āgnyagāreṣvapānaḥ saṃcaratisarvasaṃdhistha udānaḥ pādahastayorapi; sarvagātreṣu sarvavyāpī samānaḥbhuktānnarasādikaṃ gātre 'gninā saha vyāpayandvisaptatisahasreṣu nāḍīmārgeṣu caransamānavāyuragninā saha sāṅgopāṅgakalevaraṃ vyāpnotināgādivāyavaḥ pañca tvagasthyādisaṃbhavāḥtundasthaṃ jalamannaṃ ca rasādiṣu samīritaṃ tundamadhyagataḥ prāṇastāni pṛthakkuryātagnerupari jalaṃ sthāpya jaloparyannādīni saṃsthāpya svayamapānaṃ saṃprāpya tenaiva saha mārutaḥ prayāti dehamadhyagataṃ jvalanamvāyunā pālito vahnirapānena śanairdehamadhye jvalatijvalano jvālābhiḥ prāṇena koṣṭhamadhyagataṃ jalamatyuṣṇamakarotjalopari samarpitavyañjanasaṃyuktamannaṃ vahnisaṃyuktavāriṇā tapnamakarottena svedamūtrajalaraktavīryarūparasapurīṣādikaṃ prāṇaḥ pṛthakkuryāt samānavāyunā saha sarvāsu nāḍīṣu rasaṃ vyāpayañchvāsarupeṇa dehe vāyuścaratinavabhirvyomarandhraiḥ śarīrasya vāyavaḥ kurvanti viṇmūtrādivisarjanamniśvāsocchvāsakāsaśca prāṇakarmocyate; viṇmūtrādivisarjanamapānavāyukarmahānopādānaceṣṭādi vyānakarma; dehasyonnayanādikamudāna samānakarmaśarīrapoṣaṇādikaṃ samānakarma; udgārādi nāgakarma; nimīlanādi kūrmakarmakṣutkaraṇaṃ kṛkarakarma; tandrā devadattakarma; śleṣmādi

dhanañjayakarma (13)
evaṃ nāḍīsthānaṃ vāyusthānaṃ tatkarma ca samyagjñātvā nāḍīsaṃśodhanaṃ kuryāt (14)

Vocabulary

ete daśa vāyavaḥ: these ten vital airs; *caranti*: move; *sarvāsu nāḍīṣu*: in all the nāḍīs; *prāṇāḥ saṃcarati*: prāṇa moves through; *āsya*: face; *nāsikā*: nostrils; *kaṇṭha*: throat; *nābhi*: navel; *dvaya*: two; *pāda-aṅguṣṭha*: big toes; *kuṇḍalī-adaḥ-ca-ūrdhva-bhāgeṣu*: in the lower and upper parts of the kuṇḍalī; *vyānaḥ saṃcarati*: vyāna moves; *deśeṣu*: in the areas; *śrotra*: ears; *akṣi*: eyes; *kaṭi*: loins; *gulpha*: ankles; *ghrāṇa*: nose; *gala*: throat; *sphig*: buttocks; *apānaḥ saṃcarati*: apāna moves in; *guda*: anus; *meḍhra*: genitals; *ūru*: thighs; *jānu*: knees; *udara*: stomach; *vṛṣaṇa*: testicles; *kaṭi*: hips; *jaṅghā*: calves; *nābhi*: navel; *guda-agni-agāreṣu*: anus in the abode of fire; *udānaḥ sthaḥ*: udāna is in; *sarva-saṃdhi*: all the joints; *api*: as well as; *pāda-hastayoḥ*: feet and hands; *samānaḥ vyāpī sarva*: samāna spreads everywhere; *sarva-gātreṣu*: through all the limbs; *vyāpayan*: causing to pervade; *-ādikam*: first; *anna-rasa*: food and drink; *bhukta*: consumed; *saha agninā*: together with the fire; *caran*: moving through; *dvisaptatisahasreṣu nāḍīmārgeṣu*: seventy two thousand nāḍīs; *vāyuḥ samāna*: vital air [of] samāna; *saha agninā*: with its fire; *vyāpnoti*: permeates; *sāṅga*: confluence; *upāṅga*: divisions; *kalevaram*: body.

vāyavaḥ pañca: five vāyus; *nāga-ādi:* Nāga and others; *saṃbhavāḥ*: enter; *tvag-asthi-ādi*: skin and bones etc.; *prāṇa-stāni*: prāṇa there; *gataḥ*: having gone to; *tunda-madhya*: centre of the navel; *pṛthakkuryāt*: separates; *jalam-annam*: water and food; *tunda-stham*: situated around the navel; *samīritam*: stirring; *rasādiṣu*: in the fluids etc; *sthāpya*: having placed; *jalam*: water; *agneḥ-upari*: above the fire; *saṃsthāpya*: having put together; *anna-ādīni*: food etc; *jala-upari*: upon the water; *saṃprāpya*: arriving at; *svayam-apānam*: apāna itself; *mārutaḥ*: vital air; *prayāti*: goes forth;

tena saha: with it; *deha-madhya-gatam*: right to the centre of the body; *pālitaḥ*: feeding; *jvalanam*: fire; *vāyunā*: with energy; *śanaiḥ jvalati*: it burns more and more brightly; *deha-madhye*: in the centre of the body; *jvalanaḥ*: fire; *jvālābhiḥ*: with its flames; *akaro*t: makes; *jalam*: water; *gatam*: has gone to; *prāṇena*: through prāṇa; *koṣṭha-madhya*: centre of the bowels; *ati-uṣṇa*: very hot; *vahni-saṃyukta-vāriṇā*: fire together with the water; *tapnam-akarot*: heats; *annam-saṃyuktam-vyañjana*: food and condiments; *samarpita*: placed; *jala-upari*: above the water; *tena*: then; *prāṇaḥ pṛthakkuryāt*: prāṇa separates; *sveda*: sweat; *mūtra*: urine; *jala*: water; *rakta*: blood; *vīrya*: semen; *purīṣa-ādikam*: faeces and others; *rūpa-rasa*: form of fluid.

vyāpayan: causing to spread; *rasam*: fluid; *saha*: together with; *samāna-vāyunā*: samāna vāyu; *sarvāsu nāḍīṣu*: in all the nāḍīs; *vāyuḥ carati*: vāyu moves; *dehe*: in the body; *śvāsa-rupeṇa*: in the form of breath; *vāyavaḥ*: vāyus; *visarjanam kurvanti*: discharge; *viṇmūtra-ādi*: faeces and urine etc; *navabhiḥ randhraiḥ*: through the nine openings; *śarīrasya*: of the body; *vyoma*: air; *ucyate*: it is said; *prāṇa-karma*: action of prāṇa; *kāsaḥ*: coughing; *śvāsa*: inhalation; *ca*: and; *niśvāsot*: exhalation; *apāna-vāyu-karma*: action of apāna vāyu; *visarjanam*: discharging; *viṇmūtra-ādi*: faeces and urine etc; through the nine openings; *śarīrasya*: of the body; *vyoma*: air; *ucyate*: it is said; *prāṇa-karma*: action of prāṇa; *kāsaḥ*: coughing; *śvāsa*: inhalation; *ca*: and; *niśvāsot*: exhalation; *apāna-vāyu-karma*: action of apāna vāyu; *visarjanam*: discharging; *viṇmūtra-ādi*: faeces and urine etc; *vyāna-karma*: action of vyāna; *hāna-upādāna-ceṣṭa-ādi*: giving, taking and moving etc; *udāna-karma*: action of udāna; *unnayana-ādi*: straightening etc; *dehasya*: of the body; *samāna-karma*: action of samāna; *poṣaṇa-ādikam*: nourishing etc; *śarīra*: body; *nāga-karma*: action of nāga; *udgāra-ādi*: vomiting etc; *kūrma-karma*: action of kūrma; *nimīlan-ādi*: closing eyelids etc; *kṛkara-karma*: action of kṛkara; *kṣut-karaṇam*: cause of hunger; *devadatta-karma*:

action of devadatta; *tandrā*: lassitude; *dhanañjaya-karma*: action of dhanañjaya; *śleṣma-ādi*: phlegm etc.

evam: thus; *samyagjñātvā*: having a complete knowledge of; *nāḍī-sthānam*: seat of the nāḍīs; *vāyu-sthānam*: seat of the vāyus; *ca tat-karma*: and their actions; *kuryāt*: one should undertake; *nāḍī-saṃśodhanam*: purification of the nāḍīs.

Translation

Prāṇa, apāna, samāna, udāna, vyāna, nāga, kūrma, kṛkara, devadatta, dhanañjaya: these ten vital airs move in all the nāḍīs. Prāṇa moves through the face, nostrils, throat, navel, two big toes [and] in the lower and upper parts of the kuṇḍalī. Vyāna moves in the areas [of] the ears, eyes, loins, ankles, nose, throat and buttocks. Apāna moves in the anus, genitals, thighs, knees, stomach, testicles, hips, calves, navel, [and] the anus in the abode of fire. Udāna is in all the joints as well as the feet and hands. Samāna spreads everywhere through all the limbs. Causing first the food and drink consumed to pervade the body together with the fire, [and] moving through the seventy two thousand nāḍīs, the vital air [of] samāna with its fire permeates the confluence [of] the divisions [of] the body.The five vāyus, nāga and others, enter the skin and bones etc.

The prāṇa there, having gone to the centre of the navel, separates the water and food situated around the navel, stirring [them] in the fluids etc. Having placed the water above the fire [and] put together the food etc upon the water, arriving at the apāna itself, the vital air goes forth with it right to the centre of the body, feeding the fire with energy [so that] it burns more and more brightly in the centre of the body. The fire, with its flames, makes the water, [which] has gone through prāṇa to the centre of the bowels, very hot. The fire, together with the water, heats the food and condiments placed above the water. Then prāṇa separates the sweat, urine, water, blood, semen, faeces and others [in] the form of fluid.

The prāṇa, together with samāna vāyu, causing the fluid to spread in all the nāḍīs, moves in the body in the form of breath. The vāyus discharge the faeces and urine etc through the nine openings of the body [into] the air [outside]. It is said the action of prāṇa [is] coughing, inhalation and exhalation. The action of apāna vāyu [is] discharging faeces and urine. The action of vyāna [is] giving, taking and moving. The action of udāna [is] the straightening of the body. The action of samāna [is] nourishing the body. The action of nāga [is] vomiting. The action of kūrma [is] closing [and opening] the eyelids. The action of kṛkara [is] the causing of hunger. The action of devadatta [is] lassitude. The action of dhanañjaya [is] phlegm.

Thus, having a complete knowledge of the seat of the nāḍīs [and] of the vāyus and their actions, one should undertake the purification of the nāḍīs.

Commentary

These verses name the five major and five minor prāṇas. The locations given here may differ to those given in other classical texts. The five major prāṇas are: prāṇa, apāna, vyāna, samāna, and udāna. These five prāṇas continuously sustain the physical body with vitality and life. Of these five, prāṇa is considered to be the most important. It flows upward from the navel to the heart and in the nostrils. It supports the lungs and heart. Vyāna flows in the region of the shoulders, neck and head, sustaining the sensory organs, such as ears, eyes, nose, tongue, as well as the nervous system and the brain. Apāna flows downward from the navel to the anus, hips, thighs and knees. It sustains the reproductive and excretory organs. Udāna flows in the hands and feet. Samāna flows throughout the whole body. The five minor prāṇas, beginning with nāga, are said to be located in the skin and bones.

Again, the location of the prāṇas is different, according to the *Śiva Swarodaya*, which says that prāṇa is at the heart, samāna at the navel region, udāna at the throat, and vyāna pervades the whole body.

Of the five major energies, prāṇa is the energy responsible for sighing, coughing and exhalation. Apāna is responsible for evacuation of faeces, urine, gas and wind, and the foetus at the time of birth. Samāna vitalises the entire body. Udāna flows upward and mobilises the hands and feet. Vyāna flows in the region of the shoulders, neck and head, and vitalises the senses and brain.

The verse then describes how prāṇa and apāna stimulate the digestive process around maṇipura cakra in the small instestine, the main organ of digestion.

Of the five minor prāṇas, *nāga* is responsible for belching, vomiting and hiccuping. *Dhanaṃjaya* gives lustre to the skin. *Kūrma* causes blinking and shutting of the eyes. *Kṛkara* causes hunger and *devadatta* is the cause of sleep.

Fifth Section

Verse 1: Preparation for Yoga Practice

यमनियमयुत: पुरुषः सर्वसङ्गविवर्जितः कृतविद्यः
सत्यधर्मरतो जितक्रोधो गुरुशुश्रूषानिरतः
पितृमातृविधेयःस्वाश्रमोक्तसदाचारविद्वच्छिक्षितः
फलमूलोदकान्वितं तपोवनं प्राप्य रम्यदेशे
ब्रह्मघोषसमन्वितेस्वधर्मनिरतब्रह्मवित्समावृते
फलमूलपुष्पवारिभिः सुषंपूर्णे देवायतने नदीतीरे ग्रामे नगरे
वापिसुशोभनमठं नात्युच्चनीचायतमल्पद्वारं गोमयादिलिप्तं
सर्वरक्षासमन्वितं कृत्वा तत्र वेदान्तश्रवणंकुर्वन्योगं
समारभेत् ।।१।।

yamaniyamayutaḥ puruṣaḥ sarvasaṅgavivarjitaḥ kṛtavidyaḥ satyadharmaratojitakrodho guruśuśrūśāniratah pitṛmātṛ-visheyaḥ svāśramoktasadācāravidvacchikṣitaḥphalamūloda kānvitaṃ tapovanaṃ prāpya ramyadeśe brahmaghoṣa-samanvite svadharmaniratabrahmavitsamāvṛte phalamūlapuṣpavāribhiḥ susaṃpūrṇe devāyatanenadītīre grāme nagare vāpi suśobhanamaṭhaṃ nātyuccanīcāyatamalpadvāraṃgomayādiliptaṃ sarvarakṣāsamanvitaṃ kṛtvā tatra vedāntaśravaṇaṃ kurvanyogaṃ samārabhet (1)

Vocabulary

puruṣaḥ: person; *yama-niyama-yutaḥ*: practises the yamas and niyamas; *vivarjitaḥ*: avoids; *sarva-saṅga*: all company; *kṛta-vidyaḥ*: has completed [his] studies; *rataḥ*: delights in; *satya-dharma*: truth and righteousness; *jita-krodhaḥ*: has over -come anger; *rataḥ*: rejoices in; *guru-śuśrūśāni*: serving the guru; *visheyaḥ*: obedient to; *pitṛ-mātṛ*: father and mother; *śikṣitaḥ*: has been educated in; *vidvat*: wise; *sadācāra*:

virtuous conduct; *ukta*: instructed in; *sva-āśrama*:his stage of life; *prāpya*: arrives at; *tapovanam*: sacred grove; *anvitam*: replete with; *phala-mūla-udaka*: fruit, roots and water; *ramyadeśe*: in a pleasing spot; *samanvite*: resounding with; *brahmaghoṣa*: sacred chants; *samāvṛte*: protected by; *brahmavit*: knowers of Brahma; *nirata*: intent on; *sva-dharma*: their own dharma; *kṛtvā*: builds; *suśobhana-maṭham*: beautiful monastery; *vā-api*: either . . or; *devāyatane*: in a temple; *susaṃpūrṇe*: with plenty of; *phala-mūla-puṣpa-vāribhiḥ*: fruits, roots, flowers and streams; *nadītīre*: on a river bank; *grāme*: in a village; *nagare*: in a town; *sarva-rakṣā-samanvitam*: possessing every protection; *yatam-alpa-dvāram*: closed small door; *nāti-ucca-nīcā*: neither high or low; *liptam*: is smeared with; *ādi*: first; *gomaya*: cow-dung; *tatra*: there; *vedāntaśravaṇam*: listening to Vedānta; *samārabhet*: he should begin; *kurvan-yogam*: to practise yoga.

Translation

The person [who] practises the yamas and niyamas, avoids all company, has completed his studies, delights in truth and righteousness, has overcome anger, rejoices in serving his guru, obedient to [his] father and mother, has been educated in wise [and] virtuous conduct [and] instructed in his stage of life, [then] arrives at a sacred grove replete with fruit, roots and water in a pleasing spot resounding with sacred chants [and] protected by knowers of Brahma intent on their own dharma, [then] builds a beautiful monastery either in a temple with plenty of fruits, roots, flowers and streams, or on a river bank or in a village or town, possessing every protection [and which has] a closed small door, [is] neither [too] high nor low, [and is] smeared first with cow-dung. There, listening to Vedānta, he should begin to practise yoga.

Commentary

This verse gives a long list of prerequisites for anyone who is committed to the path and goal of yoga. That person should practise the yamas and niyamas sincerely and diligently to clear the mind, avoid outside influences, finish his schooling, does not have a mind disturbed by anger, serves his spiritual master with love and appreciation. He knows how to behave with wisdom and compassion, and lives according to the demands of his stage of life. Then he should find a beautiful place in nature to meditate, which has been purified by the mantras of realised or very evolved persons. This should have all his basic needs, fresh food and water. He should make himself a meditation hut, suitable for one person, with a door, and smeared with cow dung for insulation. Then, having listened to and absorbed the wisdom of Vedānta, he can now begin to practise yoga.

Verses 2 to 3: Meditating on Agnimaṇḍala

आदौ विनायकं संपूज्य स्वेष्टदेवतां नत्वा पूर्वोक्तासने स्थित्वा प्राङ्मुख उदङ्मुखो वापि मृद्वासनेषुजितासनगतो विद्वान्समग्रीवशिरोनासाग्रदृग्भ्रूमध्ये शशभृद्विम्बं पश्यन्नेत्राभ्याममृतं पिबेत् ।द्वादशमात्रया इडया वायुमापूर्योदरे स्थितंज्वालावलीयुतंरेफबिन्दुयुक्तमग्निमण्डल-युतंध्यायेद्रेचयेत्पिङ्गलया ।
पुनः पिङ्गलयाऽपूर्व कुम्भित्वा रेचयेदिडया ।।२।।
त्रिचतुस्त्रिचतुःसप्तत्रितुर्मासपर्यन्तं त्रिसंधिषु तदन्तरालेषु च षट कृत्व आचरेन्नाडीशुद्धिर्भवति ।ततः शरीरे लघुदीप्तिवह्निवृद्धिनादाभिव्यक्तिर्भवति ।।३।।

ādau vināyakaṃ saṃpūjya sveṣṭadevatāṃ natvā pūrvoktās-ane sthitvāprāṅmukha udaṅmukho vāpi mṛdvāsaneṣu jitāsanagatovidvānsamagrīvaśironāsāgradṛgbhrūmadhye śaśabhṛdvimbaṃpaśyannetrābhyāmamṛtaṃ pibet;dvādaśa-mātrayā iḍayā vāyumāpūryodare sthitaṃ jvālāvalīyutaṃrephabinduyuktamagnimaṇḍalayutaṃ dhyāyedrecayetpiṅgalayā;punaḥ piṅgalayā 'pūrva kumbhitvā recayediḍayā (2)
tricatustricatuḥsaptatricaturmāsaparyantaṃ trisaṃdiṣu tadantarāleṣu ca ṣaṭ kṛtvā ācarennāḍīśuddhirbhavati;tataḥ śarīre laghudīptivahnivṛddhinādābhivyaktirbhavati (3)

Vocabulary

ādau: firstly; *saṃpūjya*: having paid homage to; *vināyakam*: Vināyaka; *natvā*: having bowed to; *sva-iṣṭa-devatām*: his Iṣṭa Devatā; *sthitvā*: remaining; *āsane*: in a posture; *pūrva-ukta*: described before; *vā . . api*: either . . or; *prāṅmukhaḥ*: facing east; *udaṅmukhaḥ*: facing north; *jita-āsana*: posture perfected; *mṛdu-āsaneṣu*: on soft seats; *vidvān*: wise person; *grīva-śira*: neck and head; *sama*: aligned; *dṛk*: gazing at;

nāsāgra: nosetip; *paśyan*: observing; *bimbam*: sphere; *bhṛd*: supporting; *śaśa*: hare; *bhrūmadhye*: at the eyebrow centre; *pibet*: drinks; *amṛtam*: nectar; *netrābhyām*: through his eyes; *iḍayā vāyumāpūrya*: inhaling the air through iḍā; *dvādaśa-mātrayā*: for twelve mātrās; *dhyāyet*: he should meditate on; *agnimaṇḍala*: ring of fire; *sthitam udare*: situated in the abdomen; *jvālāvalīyutam*: encircled with flames; *repha-bindu-yuktam*: as well as on the point of the letter *'raṃ'*; *recayet-piṅgalayā*: he should exhale through piṅgalā; *punaḥ*: again; *piṅgalayā āpūrvaḥ*: inhaling through piṅgalā; *kumbhitvā*: retaining; *recayet-iḍayā*: he should exhale through iḍā.

saptatricatuḥ-māsa-paryantam: for twenty-one up to twenty eight months; *kṛtvā*: having practised; *ṣaṭ*: six; *tri-saṃdiṣu*: at the three sandhyās (junctions); *ca tad-antarāleṣu*: and in the intervals; *ācaret*: he should practise; *nāḍī-śuddhiḥ*: purification of the nāḍīs; *tataḥ*: then; *śarīre*: when the body; *bhavati*: becomes; *laghu-dīpti*: light and bright; *vahni-vṛddhi*: inner fire increases; *nāda-abhivyaktiḥ*: inner sound is expressed.

Translation

Firstly, having paid homage to Vināyaka [and] bowed to his Iṣṭa-Devata, [then] remaining in a posture described before, facing either east or north, the posture perfected on soft seats, the wise person, neck and head aligned, gazing at the nose tip, observing the sphere supporting the hare at the eyebrow centre, drinks the nectar through his eyes. Inhaling the air through iḍā for twelve mātrās, he should meditate on the ring of for twelve mātrās, he should meditate on the ring of fire situated in the abdomen as encircled with flames, as well as on the point of the letter 'raṃ', [and then] exhale through piṅgalā. Again, inhaling through piṅgalā [and] retaining [the breath], he should exhale through iḍā.

For twenty-one up to twenty-eight months, having practised

six [times] at the three sandhyās and in the intervals, he should practise purification of the nāḍīs. Then, when the body becomes light and bright, the inner fire increases [and] the inner sound is expressed.

Commentary

Vināyaka, whose literal meaning is Remover, is another name for Gaṇeśa, the elephant-headed deity who removes obstacles. Sun, which represent life, and on which we depend for life, rises in the east. North also means upwards in Sanskrit, so in facing north, one is looking up towards the higher consciousness. The person aspiring to yoga should be sitting comfortably, so as to remain still in meditation, the head, neck and spine should be in alignment allowing the prāṇa to flow freely. There are many words for 'moon' in Sanskrit, theson aspiring to yoga should be sitting comfortably, so as to remain still in meditation, the head, neck and spine should be in alignment allowing the prāṇa to flow freely. There are many words for 'moon' in Sanskrit, the most common being *candra*. Here the sage has chosen the poetic *śaśabhṛdvimbam*, whose literal meaning is 'the sphere supporting the hare'. The sphere is the body of the moon and the hare refers to the mountains and valleys of the moon, which from afar form the shape of a hare. The verse then says the yogin should practise nāḍī śodhana, meditating on the ring of fire, agnimaṇḍala, at maṇipura cakra, and its bīja mantra *ram*. When he has done this practice three times a day at dawn, midday and evening for up to two years and four months, the nāḍīs are purified, the vitality increases, and the nāda, the inner sound, can be heard.

Sixth Section

Verses 1 and 2: Prāṇāyāma

प्राणापानसमायोगः प्राणायामो भवाति ।रेचकपूरककुम्भकभेदेन स त्रिविधः ।ते वर्णात्मकाः । तस्मात्प्रणव एव प्राणायामः ।।१-२।।

prāṇāpānasamāyogaḥ prāṇāyāmo bhavati;recakapūrakakumbhakabhedena sa trividhaḥ; te varṇātmakāḥ; tasmātpraṇava eva prāṇāyāmaḥ (1-2)

Vocabulary

prāṇāyāmaḥ bhavati: prāṇāyāma is; *prāṇa-apāna-samāyogaḥ*: union of prāṇa and apāna; *bhedena*: with a division; *trividhaḥ*: three kinds; *recaka-pūraka-kumbhaka*: exhalation, inhalation and retention; *te ātmakāḥ*: they consist of; *varṇa*: group of letters; *tasmāt*: thus; *prāṇāyāmaḥ*: prāṇāyāma; *praṇavaḥ*: praṇava.

Translation

Prāṇāyāma is the union of prāṇa and apāna, with a division of three kinds: exhalation, inhalation and retention. They consist of a [particular] group of letters. Thus prāṇāyāma is praṇava.

Commentary

Prāṇāyāma consists of three parts: inhalation, retention and exhalation. These three components are said to resonate with three sounds: inhalation—'A', retention— 'U' and exhalation 'M'. These three sounds form the *praṇava, Aum*. Therefore, prāṇāyāma is formed by praṇava.

Verses 3 to 4: Gāyatrī Savitrī Sarasvatī

पद्माद्यासनस्थः पुमान्नासाग्रे
शशभृद्बिम्बज्योत्स्नाजालवतानिताकारमूर्तोरक्ताङ्गी हंसवाहिनी
दण्डहस्ता बाला गायत्री भवति ।उकारमूर्तिः श्वेताङ्गी ताक्ष्र्यवाहिनी
युवती चक्रहस्ता सावित्री भवति ।मकारमूर्तिः कृष्णाङ्गी
वृषभवाहिनी वृद्धा त्रिशूलधारिणी सरस्वती भवति ।।३।।
अकारादित्रयाणां सर्वकारणमेकाक्षरं परंज्योतिः प्रणवं भवतीति
।।४।।

padmādyāsanasthaḥ pumānnāsāgre śaśabhṛdbimbajyotsnājālavatānitākāramūrtoraktāṅgī haṃsavāhinī daṇḍahastā bālā gāyatrī bhavati;ukāramūrtiḥ śvetāṅgī tārkṣyavāhinī yuvatī cakrahastā sāvitrī bhavati;makāramūrtiḥ kṛṣṇāṅgī vṛṣabhavāhinī vṛddhā triśūladhāriṇī sarasvatī bhavati (3)akārāditrayāṇāṃ sarvakāraṇamekākṣaraṃ paraṃjyotiḥ praṇavaṃ bhavatīti (4)

Vocabulary

staḥ: seated in; *padma-ādi-āsana*: lotus or other posture; *pumān*: person; *gāyatrī bālā raktāṅgī*: Gāyatrī, a girl of the colour of Indian madder; *ānitā*: surrounded by; *jālavat*: web; *jyotsnā*: rays; *bimba*: disk; *śaśabhṛt*: moon; *vāhinī*: borne by; *haṃsa*: swan; *daṇḍa*: mace; *hasta*: hand; *bhavati*: she is; *mūrta*: form; *akāra*: sound A; *sāvitrī*: Sāvitrī; *yuvatī*: young woman; *śvetāṅgī*: colour white; *cakra-hastā*: discus in hand; *vāhinī*: mounted on; *tārkṣya*: garuḍa; *bhavati*: is; *mūrtiḥ*: form; *ukāra*: sound U; *sarasvatī*: Sarasvatī; *vṛddhā*: old woman; *kṛṣṇāṅgī*: colour black; *dhāriṇī*: holding; *triśūla*: trident; *vāhinī*: mounted on; *vṛṣabha*: bull; *bhavati*: is; *mūrtiḥ*: form; *makāra*: sound M; *iti*: thus; *paraṃ-jyotiḥ*: supreme light; *praṇavam*: sound Om; *bhavati*: is; *eka-akṣaram*: one sound; *kāraṇa*: cause; *sarva*: all; *trayāṇām*: three; *akāra-ādi*: beginning with the sound A.

Translation

Seated in the lotus or other posture, a person [should visualise] on the nosetip Gāyatrī, a girl [of] the colour of Indian madder, surrounded by a web [of] rays from the disk [of] the moon [and] borne by a swan, a mace [in] her hand, she is the form [of] the sound A. Sāvitrī, a young woman [of] the colour white, a discus in [her] hand, mounted on a garuḍa, is the form of the sound U. Sarasvatī, an old woman [of] the colour black, holding a trident [and] mounted on a bull, is the form [of] the sound M. Thus the supreme light, the praṇava Om, is the one sound [which is] the cause of all three, beginning with the sound A.

Commentary

Just as Brahma, Viṣṇu and Śiva are the three male representations of creation, preservation and destruction, so Gāyatrī, Sāvitrī and Sarasvatī are the three female forms of the one Śakti. Gāyatrī has the quality of creativity, Sāvitrī, the daughter of the solar deity Savitṛ, the qualof the one Śakti. Gāyatrī has the quality of creativity, Sāvitrī, the daughter of the solar deity Savitṛ, the qualThe garuḍa, half human, half eagle, is a devotee of Viṣṇu. He is the vehicle (vahana) of Viṣṇu whose banner he is depicted on. Garuda represents birth and heaven, and is the enemy of all snakes.

Verse 5: Prāṇāyāma on AUM

ध्यायेत इडया बाह्याद्वायुमापूर्य षोडशमात्राभिरकारं
चिन्तयन्पूरितं वायुं चतुःषष्टिमात्राभिःकुम्भयित्वोकारं
ध्यायन्पूरितं पिङ्गलया द्वात्रिंशन्मात्रया मकारमूत्रिध्यानेनैवं
क्रमेण पुनः पुनः कुर्यात् ।।५।।

*dhyāyet iḍayā bāhyādvāyumāpūrya ṣoḍaśamātrābhirakāraṃ
cintayanpūritaṃvāyuṃ catuḥṣaṣṭimātrābhiḥ
kumbhayitvokāraṃ dhyāyanpūritaṃ
piṅgalayādvātriṃśanmātrayā makāramūtridhyānenaivaṃ
krameṇa punaḥ punaḥ kuryāt (5)*

Vocabulary

āpūrya: having inhaled; *bāhyāt-vāyum*: external air; *iḍayā*: through iḍā; *ṣoḍaśa-mātrābhiḥ*: for sixteen mātrās; *dhyāyet*:one should meditate on; *akāram*: sound A; *kumbhayitvā*:retaining; *pūritam vāyum*: inhaled air; *catuḥṣaṣṭi-mātrābhiḥ*:for sixty-four mātrās; *cintayam ukāram*: meditating on the sound U; *pūritam*: inhaled; *piṅgalayā*: through piṅgalā; *dvātriṃśat-mātrayā*: for thirty-two mātrās; *dhyānena*:medita-ting on; *makāra-mūtri*: form of the sound M; *kuryāt*: one should do; *punaḥ punaḥ*: again and again; *krameṇa*: in the order.

Translation

Having inhaled the external air through iḍā for sixteen mātrās, one should meditate on the sound A. Retaining the inhaled air for sixty-four mātrās [at the same time] meditating on the sound U, [one should then exhale] the inhaled [air] through piṅgalā for thirty-two mātrās, meditating on the form of the sound M. One should do [this] again and again in the [same] order.

Commentary

The yoga upaniṣads recommend that nāḍī śodhana

prāṇāyāma be combined with repetition of the praṇava, Aum, as well as the ratio of 16:64:32. This version of nāḍī śodhana should not be undertaken until one has mastered the basic practice, and slowly increased the ratio.

A mātrā is a unit of measurement to calculate the time spent in breathing practices. It is defined in *Yoga Cūdāmani Upaniṣad* as the time a single breath takes to fill the lungs. According to *Yoga Tattva Upaniṣad* it is the time taken to snap one's fingers after circling the knee with one's hand. The *Tattva Vaiṣāradī* says one must circle the knee three times. The *Mārkandeya Purāṇa* says it is the time taken to open and close one's eyes.[16]

Seventh Section

Verse 1: Nāḍī Śodhana Prāṇāyāma

अथासनदृढो योगी वशी मितहिताशनः सुषुम्नानाडीस्थमलशोषार्थं योगी बद्ध्वपद्मासनो वायुं चन्द्रेणापूर्ययथाशक्ति कुम्भयित्वा सूर्येण रेचित्वा पुनः सूर्येणापूर्य कुमभयित्वा चन्द्रेण विरेच्य यया त्यजेत्तया संपूर्य धारयेत् ।तदेते श्लोका भवन्तिप्राणं प्रागिडया पिबेन्नियमितं भूयोऽन्यया रेचयेत्पीत्वा पिङ्गलया समीरणमथो बद्ध्वात्यजेद्वामया ।सूर्याचन्द्रमसोरनेन विधिनाऽभ्यासं सदा तन्वतां शुद्धा नाडिगणा भवन्ति यमिनां मासान्नयादूर्ध्वतः ।।१।।

athāsanadṛḍho yogī vaśī mitahitāśanaḥ suṣumnānāḍīsthamalaśoṣārthaṃ yogībaddhvapadmāsano vāyuṃ candreṇāpūrya yathāśakti kumbhayitvā sūryeṇarecitvā punaḥ sūryeṇāpūrya kumbhayitvā candreṇa virecya yayā tyajettayā saṃpūrya dhārayet;tadete ślokā bhavantiprāṇaṃ prāgiḍayā pibenniyamitam bhūyo'nyayā recayetpītvā piṅgalayā samīraṇamatho baddhvā tyajedvāmayā;sūryācandramasoranena vidhinā'bhyāsaṃ sadā tanvatāṃ śuddhā nāḍigaṇābhavanti yamināṃ māsānnayādūrdhvataḥ (1)

Vocabulary

atha: now; *āsana-dṛḍhaḥ*: firm in the posture; *mitahitāśanaḥ vaśī*: established in perfect [self]-control; *yogī*: yogin; *baddhvapadmāsanaḥ*: fixed in padmāsana; *śoṣa-artham*: in order to remove; *mala*: impurities; *suṣumnā-nāḍī-stha*: from suṣumnā and the nāḍīs; *āpūrya*: inhaling; *vāyum*: air; *candreṇa*: through the left nostril; *kumbhayitvā*: should hold; *yathāśakti*: as long as he is able; *recitvā*: then exhale; *sūryeṇa*: through the right; *punaḥ*: again; *sūryeṇa-āpūrya*: inhaling through the right nos-tril; *kumbhayitvā*: holding; *virecya candreṇa*: exhaling through the left; *saṃpūrya*: inhaling; *tayā yayā*: that through which; *tyajet*: he exhales; *dhārayet*: he should hold;

ete ślokāḥ: these verses; *bhavanti*: are; *tad*: thus; *prāk*: first; *pibet*: one should draw the breath in; *iḍayā*: through iḍā; *niyamitam*: as prescri-bed; *bhūyaḥ*: then; *recayet*: exhale; *anyayā*: other; *atha*: then; *pītvā piṅgalayā*: inhaling through piṅgalā; *samīraṇam*: air; *baddhvā*: retaining; *tyajet vāmayā*: he exhales through the left; *yamināṃ*: those of self-control; *tan*: continually; *sadā*: forever; *abhyāsam*: practising; *anena vidhinā*: through this method; *sūryācandramasāḥ*: sun and moon; *nāḍigaṇāḥ*: all the nāḍīs; *śuddhāḥ*: are purified; *māsāt-nayāt-ūrdhvataḥ*: in one month or more.

Translation

Now, firm in the posture [and] established in perfect [self]-control, the yogin, fixed in padmāsana, should, in order to remove impurities from suṣumnā and the nāḍīs, inhale the air through the left nostril, hold [it] as long as one is able, then exhale through the right. Again, inhaling through the right nostril, holding it, exhaling through the left, then inhaling that through which he exhales, one should hold [it]. These verses are thus: First one should draw the breath in through iḍā as prescribed, then exhale through the other [nostril]. Then inhaling the air through piṅgalā, retaining [it], one exhales through the left. [For those who] have self-control, continually [and] forever practising through this method [of] sun and moon, all the nāḍīs are purified in one month or more.

Commentary

In this verse the left and right nostrils are referred to as iḍā and piṅgalā. Iḍā is the flow of lunar or mental energy, which passes through the left nostril. Piṅgalā is the flow of solar or vital energy, which passes through the right nostril. The purpose of balancing the breath is to balance these two flows of energy. Then the practice of kumbhaka, internal breath retention, activates suṣumnā, the spiritual flow of energy.

In the first half of the round, one inhales through the left nostril and exhales through the right. In the second half, one inhales through the right nostril and exhales through the left. This process equalises the flow of breath in both the left and right nostrils, which in turn regulates the iḍā and piṅgalā nāḍīs, the parasympathetic and sympathetic nervous system and the right and left hemispheres of the brain.

Retention of the breath, as described here, is an important aspect of this practice, as it activates the suṣumnā nāḍī and the central nervous system, unifying the two hemispheres of the brain. The effects of this practice on the nervous system, the pranic system and the brain, make it an important requisite for meditation and all higher sādhanas.

Verses 2 to 6: Kumbhaka

प्रातर्मध्यन्दिने सायमर्धरात्रे तु कुम्भकान्शनैरशीतिपर्यन्तं चतुर्वारं समभ्यसेत् ।।२।।

कनीयसि भवेत्स्वेदः कम्पो भवति मध्यमे ।उत्तिष्ठत्युत्तमे प्राणरोधे पद्मासनं भवेत् ।।३।।

जलेन श्रमजातेन गात्रमर्दनमाचरेत् ।दृढता लगुता चापि तस्य गात्रस्य जायते ।।४।।

अभ्यासकाले प्रथमं शस्तं क्षीराज्यभोजनम् ।ततोऽभ्यासे स्थिरीभूते न तावन्नियमग्रहः ।।५।।

यथा सिंहो गजो व्याघ्रो भवेद्वश्यः शनैःशनैः ।तथैव सेवितो वायुरन्यथा हन्ति साधकम् ।।६।।

prātarmadhyandine sāyamardharātre tu kumbhakānśanairaśītiparyantaṃ caturvāraṃ samabhyaset (2)
kanīyasi bhavetsvedaḥ kampo bhavati madhyameuttiṣṭhatyuttame prāṇarodhe padmāsanaṃ bhavet (3)
jalena śramajātena gātramardanamācaretdṛḍhatā lagutā cāpi tasya gātrasya jāyate (4)
abhyāsakāle prathamaṃ śastaṃ kṣīrājyabhojanamtato'bhyāse sthirībhūte na tāvanniyamagrahaḥ (5)
yathā siṃho gajo vyāghro bhavedvaśyaḥ śanaiḥśanaiḥtathaiva sevito vāyuranyathā hanti sādhakam (6)

Vocabulary

samabhyaset: one should practise; *kumbhakān*: retention of the breath; *śanaiḥ*: slowly; *aśiti-paryantam*: up to eighty times; *prātaḥ*: early morning; *madhyandine*: midday; *sāyam*: evening; *ardharātre*: midnight; *caturvāram*: four weeks;

bhavet prāṇa-rodhe: when there is suppression of the breath; *kanīyasi*: in the beginning; *bhavati*: there is; *svedaḥ*: perspiration; *madhyame*: in the middle; *kampaḥ*: trembling; *uttame*: finally; *uttiṣṭhati*: levitation; *mardanam-ācaret*: one should massage; *gātra*: body; *jalena śrama*: perspiration; *jātena*: is produced; *ca āpi*: and then; *tasya gātrasya*: this body; *jāyate*: becomes; *dṛḍhatā lagutā*: firm and light; *prathamam*: early; *abhyāsa-kāle*: in the time of practice; *śastam*: excellent; *bhojanam*: food; *kṣīra-ājya*: milk and ghee; *sthirībhūte*: if one has become firm; *na tāvat*: not yet; *abhyāse*: in the practice; *grahaḥ*: one should adhere to; *niyama*: rule; *yathā*: just as; *siṃhaḥ*: lion; *gajaḥ*: elephant; *vyāghraḥ*: tiger; *bhavet*: can be; *śanaiḥśanaiḥ*: gradually; *vaśyaḥ*: tamed; *tathaiva*: likewise; *vāyuḥ*: breath; *sevitaḥ*: can be managed; *anyathā*: otherwise; *hanti*: it kills; *sādhakam*: aspirant.

Translation

One should practise retention of the breath slowly up to eighty times early morning, midday, evening [and] midnight for four weeks. When there is, [seated in] padmāsana, suppression of the breath, in the beginning there is perspiration, in the middle [stage] there is trembling [and] finally levitation. One should massage the body when perspiration is produced, and then this body becomes firm and light. Early in the time of practice, an excellent food is milk and ghee. If one has not yet become firm in the practice, one should adhere to this rule. Just as the lion, elephant [and] tiger can be gradually tamed, likewise the breath can be managed, otherwise it kills the aspirant.

Commentary

The verse says to practise *kumbhaka* (breath retention) at the four junctions or intervals (known as *sandhya*) of dawn, midday, evening and midnight, as these are the times when the transition is made from one part of the day to the next. The three sandhyas (dawn, midday and dusk) are the traditional prayer times of Brahmanas.

The word *kumbhaka* comes from the root *kumbha*, meaning a 'vessel' or 'pot'. In order to retain the breath inside, the diaphragm expands, so that the belly forms a pot, where the air is stored for a duration of time.

Kumbhaka, the retention of breath or prāṇa, is the basis of prāṇāyāma. Prāṇa is the vital energy or life force, constantly moving in all beings, and which also moves in and out with the breath. Ordinarily, the prāṇa of an individual moves throughout the body, and also flows outside, whenever the senses connect with people, places and things. Every interaction is an exchange of prāṇa. The practice of kumbhaka developed, because the yogis of old wished to conserve their prāṇa in order to awaken the consciousness.

The practices of prāṇāyāma rebalance the prāṇās and nervous system, preparing the body and mind for higher yoga practices. The verse states the outer effects of prāṇāyāma. At first result there is perspiration, because the practice causes the body to become heated. This perspiration is different to ordinary perspiration, and should not be washed off directly, but rather wiped off with a soft, clean cloth.

In the next stage of prāṇāyāma, trembling arises due to activation of the prāṇās and nāḍīs. In the third stage, when the practice is mastered, the prāṇās expand throughout the body and there is the experience of lightness. In this stage the body may levitate easily. When these three stages are practised repeatedly, the highest stage is attained.

Fresh milk and ghee are recommended, because they maintain the mucus lining of the digestive tract and alimentary canal and neutralise excessive heat and acidity in the stomach.

Verses 7 to 13: Effects of Nāḍī Śodhana Prāṇāyāma

युक्तंयुक्तं त्यजेद्वायुं युक्तंयुक्तं च पूरयेत् ।युक्तंयुक्तं च बन्धीयादेवं सिद्धिमवाप्नुयात् ।।७।।

यथेष्टधारणाद्वायोरनलस्य प्रदीपनम् ।नादाभिव्यक्तिरारोग्यं जायते नाडीशोधनात् ।।८।।

विधिवत्प्राणसंयामैर्नाडीचक्रे विशोधिते ।सुषुम्नावदनं भित्त्वा सुखाद्विशति मारुतः ।।९।।

मारुते मध्यसंचारे मनःस्थैर्यं प्रजायते ।यो मनः सुस्थिरो भावः सैवावस्था मनोन्मनी ।।१०।।

पूरकान्ते तु कर्तव्यो बन्धो जालन्धराभिधः ।कुम्भकान्ते रेचकादौ कर्तव्यस्तूड्डियाणकः ।।११।।

अधस्तात्कुञ्चनेनाशु कण्ठसंकोचने कृते ।मध्ये पश्चिमतानेन स्यात्प्राणो ब्रह्मनाडिगः ।।१२।।

अपानमूर्ध्वमुत्थाप्य प्राणं कण्ठादधो नयन् ।योगी जराविनिर्मुक्तः षोडशो वयसा भवेत् ।।१३।।

yuktaṃyuktaṃ tyajedvāyuṃ yuktaṃyuktaṃ ca pūrayetyuktaṃyuktaṃ ca bandhīyādevaṃ siddhimavāpnuyāt (7)
katheṣṭadhāraṇādvāyoranalasya pradīpanamnādābhivyaktirārogyaṃ jāyate nāḍīśodhanāt (8)
vidhivatprāṇasaṃyāmairnāḍīcakre viśodhitesuṣumnāvadanaṃ bhittvā sukhādviśati mārutaḥ (9)
mārute madhyasaṃcāre manaḥsthsiryaṃ prajāyateyo manaḥ susthiro bhāvaḥ saivāvasthā manonmanī (10)
pūrakānte tu kartavyo bandho jālandharābhidhaḥkumbhakānte recakādau kartavyastūḍḍiyāṇakaḥ (11)
adhastātkuñcanenāśu kaṇṭhasaṃkocane kṛtemadhye paścimatānena syātprāṇo brahmanāḍigaḥ (12)

apānamūrdhvamutthāpya prāṇaṃ kaṇṭādadho nayanyogī jarāvinirmuktaḥ ṣoḍaśo vayasā bhavet (13)

Vocabulary

pūrayet: one should inhale; *vāyum*: air; *yuktaṃyuktam*: proper-ly; *tyajet*: one should exhale; *ca*: and; *yuktaṃyuktam bandhī-yāt*: with proper retention; *evam*: thus; *avāpnuyāt*: one will attain; *siddhim*: success; *yathā*: just; *dhāraṇāt*: by holding; *vāyoḥ*: of the two breaths; *iṣṭa*: in the approved way; *nāḍī-śodhanāt*: by purification of the nāḍīs; *pradīpanam*: fanning; *analasya*: of the fire; *nādā-abhivyaktiḥ*: clarity of inner sounds *ārogyam*: good health; *jāyate*: are produced; *nāḍī-cakre*: when the nāḍīs and cakras; *viśodhite*: have been purified; *vidhivat-prāṇasaṃy-āmaiḥ*: through appropriate suspension of the breath;*vadanam mārutaḥ*: breath; *bhittvā suṣumnā*: having broken into suṣumnā; *viśati*: spreads; *sukhāt*: joyfully; *mārute*: when the air; *madhya-saṃcāre*: moves up the middle; *manaḥ*: mind; *prajāyate*: becomes; *sthairyam*: steady; *yaḥ manaḥ*: the mind; *bhāvaḥ*: having become; *susthiraḥ*: stable; *eva*: now; *āvasthā*: in a state; *manonmani*: mindlessness; *bandhaḥ jālandhara-abhidhaḥ*: contraction named *jālandhara*; *kartavyaḥ*: is to be done; *pūrakānte*: after inhaling; *tu*: then; *kumbhakānte recakādau*: after retaining and exhaling; *uḍḍiyāṇakaḥ karta-vyaḥ*: *uḍḍiyāṇa bandha* is to be done; *kaṇṭha-saṃkocane kṛte*: when the throat is contracted; *adhastāt-kuñcanena-āśu*: and immediately closed below; *prāṇaḥ brahma-nāḍi-gaḥ*: prāṇa moves up *brahma nāḍī*; *madhye paścimatānena*: in the middle of the back; *apānam-ūrdhvam-utthāpya*: having caused apāna to rise upwards; *prāṇaṃ kaṇṭhāt-adhaḥ nayan*: drawing the prāṇa down from the throat; *yogī jarā-vinirmuktaḥ*: yogin, freed from old age; *bhavet ṣoḍaśo vayasā*: becomes like a sixteen year old youth.

Translation

One should inhale the air properly, exhale properly and with proper retention. Thus one will attain success. Just by the holding of the two breaths in the approved way [and] by purification of the nāḍīs, the fanning of the fire, clarity of inner sounds [and] good health are produced. When the nāḍīs and cakras have been purified through appropriate suspension of the breath, the breath, having broken into suṣumnā, spreads joyfully [up it]. When the air moves up the middle, the mind becomes steady. The mind, having become stable, [is] now in a state [of] mindlessness. The contraction named jālandhara is to be done after inhaling. Then, after retaining and exhaling, *uḍḍiyāna bandha* is to be done. When the throat is contracted and immediately closed below, the prāṇa moves up *brahma nāḍī* in the middle of the back. Having caused apāna to rise upwards, drawing the prāṇa down from the throat, the yogin, freed from old age, becomes like a sixteen year old youth.

Commentary

These verses emphasise that, for the practice to be beneficial, full inhalation, retention (without straining) and complete exhalation are necessary. This process equalises the flow of breath in both the left and right nostrils, which in turn regulates the iḍā and piṅgalā nāḍīs, the parasympathetic and sympathetic nervous systems and the right and left hemispheres of the brain.

Then the deep influx of prāṇa invigorates the body with more oxygen, eliminating toxins from the blood. Retention of the breath, as described here, is an important aspect of this practice, as it activates the suṣumnā nāḍī and the central nervous system, unifying the two hemispheres of the brain.The effects of the practice of nāḍī śodhana prāṇāyāma on the mind are clarity, stillness and increased concentration. *Nāda*, the most subtle inner sound, may be heard. The effects on the nervous system, the pranic system and the brain, make it an important requisite for meditation and all higher sādhanas, as the mind is now in a state of *manonmani* (mindlessness), where there are no activities in the mind, which has gone beyond the conscious, subconscious and unconscious states.

Jālandhara bandha is performed by bending the head forward after inhalation, so that the chin touches the chest. In this pose, the awareness is focused on the point where the chin meets the chest. Bending the head forward in this manner contracts the region of viśuddhi cakra, which is located behind the throat pit. Exhalation takes place after the head is raised. By pressing on iḍā and piṅgalā nāḍīs, the bandha diverts the prāṇa to pass through suṣumnā. It clears the nasal passages and regulates the flow of blood and prāṇa to the heart, head and endocrine (thyroid and para-thyroid) glands in the neck.

The word 'jālandhara' is comprised of the words *jāla* meaning 'net', and *dhara* 'flow'. According to the philosophy of Tantra, the *amṛta*, or nectar of life, flows down through the body from *bindu*, which is located at the top back of the head. The regular practice of jālandhara bandha activates viśuddhi cakra, and enables it to become a processing centre for the flow of amṛta.

Uḍḍīyāna bandha is known as the abdominal lock. It is performed by drawing the abdomen inward and then upward, exercising the diaphragm and abdominal organs, thereby causing an upsurge of energy. It lightly massages and tones the heart muscles, and by toning the abdominal organs, increases the gastric fire and eliminates toxins in the digestive tract.

The word *uḍḍīyāna* means 'to rise up', 'to fly up'. Uḍḍīyāna bandha is the psychic lock, which causes the prāṇa, or the amṛta, that is collected and stored at maṇipura cakra, to fly upward through the suṣumnā nāḍī to the brain and the higher centres of consciousness. *Brahma* is the subtlest and innermost nāḍī of the three nāḍīs in suṣumnā, through which the kuṇḍalinī ascends.

Verses 13.1 to 13.4: Destruction of Disease (1)

सुखासनस्थो दक्षनाड्या बहि:स्थं पवनं समाकृष्याकेशमानखाग्रं कुम्भयित्वा सव्यनाड्या रेचयेत् ।तेन कपालशोधनं वातनाडीगतसर्वरोगसर्वविनाशनं भवति ।।१३-१।।
हृदयादिकण्ठपर्यन्तं सस्वनं नासाभ्यां शनै: पवनमाकृष्य यथाशक्ति कुम्भयित्वा इडया विरेच्य गच्छंस्तिष्ठनकुर्यात ।तेन श्लेष्महरं जठराग्निवर्धनं भवति ।।१३-२।।
वक्त्रेण सीत्कारपूर्वकं वायुं गृहीत्वा यथाशक्ति कुम्भयित्वा नासाभ्यां रेचयेत् ।तेन क्षुत्तृष्णालस्यनिद्रा न जायन्ते ।।१३-३।।
जिह्वया वायुं गृहीत्वा यथाशक्ति कुम्भयित्वा नासाभ्यां रेचयेत् ।तेन गुल्मप्लीहज्वरपित्तक्षुधादीनि नश्यन्ति ।।१३-४।।

sukhāsanastho dakṣanāḍyā bahiḥsthaṃ pavanaṃ samākṛṣyākeśamānakhāgraṃkumbhayitvā savyanāḍyā recayettena kapālaśodhanaṃ vātanāḍīgatasarvarogasarvavināśanaṃ bhavati (13.1)
hṛdayādikaṇṭhaparyantaṃ sasvanaṃ nāsābhyāṃ śanaiḥ pavanamākṛṣya yathāśaktikumbhayitvā iḍayā virecya gacchaṃstiṣṭhankuryāt tena śleṣmaharaṃ jaṭharāgnivardhanaṃ bhavati (13.2)
vaktreṇa sītkārapūrvakaṃ vāyuṃ gṛhītvā yathāśakti kumbhayitvā nāsābhyāṃ recayettena kṣuttṛṣṇālasyanidrā na jāyante (13.3)
jihvayā vāyuṃ gṛhītvā yathāśakti kumbhayitvā nāsābhyāṃ recayettena gulmaplīhajvarapittakṣudhādīni naśyanti (13.4)

Vocabulary

sukha-āsana-sthaḥ: seated in a comfortable posture; *samākṛṣyā*: drawing; *pavanam*: air; *bahiḥ-stham*: from outside; *dakṣa-nāḍyā*: through the right nāḍī; *kumbhayitva*: retaining; *agram*: top; *keśam*: hair; *ānakha*: toe-nails; *recayet*: one should exhale; *savya-nāḍyā*: through the left nāḍī; *tena*:

through this; *kapāla-śodhanam*: brain is purified; *sarva roga*: every disease; *vāta-nāḍī-gata*: gone into the vāta nāḍī; *bhavati vināśanam*: is destroyed; *ākṛṣya*: having drawn in; *śanaiḥ*: slowly; *pavanam*: vital air; *sasvaram*: noisily; *nāsābhyām*: through both nostrils; *hṛdayā-ādi*: from the heart; *kaṇṭha-paryantam*: up to the throat; *kumbhayitvā*: retained; *yathāśakti*: as long as one is able; *iḍayā virecya*: exhaled through iḍā; *gacchaṃs-tiṣṭhan-kuryāt*: one should go and rest; *tena*: thus; *bhavati haram*: re-moves; *śleṣma*: phlegm; *jaṭhara*: hunger; *agni-vardhanam*: stimulating digestion; *pūrvakam*: first; *gṛhītvā*: having taken in; *vāyum*: air; *sītkāra*: with a hissing sound; *vaktreṇa*: through the mouth; *kumbhayitvā yathāśakti*: retained as long as one is able; *recayet*: one should exhale; *nāsābhyām*: through both nostrils; *tena*: hence; *kṣut*: hunger; *tṛṣṇa*: thirst; *ālasya*: idleness; *nidrā*: sleep; *na jāyante*: do not arise; *gṛhītvā*: having taken in; *vāyum*: air; *jihvayā*: through the tongue; *kumbhayitvā yathāśakti*: retained as long as one is able; *nāsābhyām recayet*: one should exhale through both nostrils; *tena*: thereby; *gulma-plīha*: diseases of the spleen; *jvara*: fever; *pitta*: bile; *kṣudha-ādīni*: hunger etc; *naśyanti*: are destroyed.

Translation

Seated in a comfortable posture, drawing the air from outside through the right nāḍī [and] retaining [it from] the top [of] the hair [to] the toe-nails, one should exhale through the left nāḍī. Through this, the brain is purified [and] every disease [which] has gone into the *vāta nāḍī* is destroyed. Having slowly drawn in the vital air noisily through the nostrils from the heart up to the throat, retained it as long as one is able, exhaled through iḍā, one should go and rest. Thus this removes phlegm [and] hunger, stimulating digestion.

Having first taken in the air with a hissing sound through the mouth, [and] retained it as long as one is able, one should exhale through both nostrils. Hence, hunger, thirst, idleness

[and] sleep do not arise. Having taken in the air through the tongue, [and] having retained it as long as one is able, one should exhale through both nostrils. Thereby diseases of the spleen, fever, bile and hunger are destroyed.

Commentary

Prāṇāyāma is a means to extend the internal fields of prāṇa, and in this way many diseases can be resolved. Many diseases are due to excess or deficiency of prāṇa. The best times to practise prāṇāyāma are before sunrise, at dawn, at noon, and at dusk. If this is not possible or practical, it can also be performed at any other time.

The first practice described here is *sūrya bheda prāṇāyāma,* where one inhales through piṅgalā (right) nāḍī and exhales through iḍā (left) nāḍī. This is a very powerful practice, which should only be done under the guidance of a qualified teacher. It produces heat in the body, and corrects imbalances of the wind element (*vāta doṣa*). The vāta nāḍī runs along the back of the neck and head into the brain, managing the formation and elimination of gas.

Next, the cooling methods of prāṇāyāma, performed by inhaling through the mouth, are described. The first is *sītkarī prāṇāyāma*. The hissing sound is produced by inhaling through the teeth. By continuously drawing the breath in through the open mouth, over the tongue, the yogi is freed from heat and fatigue, and attains good health. The second is *śītalī prāṇāyāma*, where one draws the breath in through the tongue, which is curled around to form a tube. At the end of inhalation, the breath should be held at the root of the tongue. In this way one should drink the nectar steadily, obtaining total happiness. *Lalana cakra*, a minor centre, which holds the nectar, is located at the root of the tongue. When this practice is mastered, the nectar becomes profuse and the experience of bliss is ongoing.

Verses 13.5 to 13.6: Sahita and Kevala Kumbhaka

अथ कुम्भकः । स द्विविधः सहितः केवलश्चेति ।
रेचकपूरकयुक्तः सहितः । तद्विवर्जितः केवलः ।
केवलसिद्धिपर्यन्तं सहितमभ्यसेत् ।केवलकुम्भके सिद्धे
त्रिषु लोकेषु न तस्य दुर्लभं भवति ।
केवलकुम्भकात्कुण्डलिनीबोधो जयते ।।१३-५।
।ततः कृशवपुः प्रसन्नवदनो निर्मललोचनोऽभिव्यक्तनादो
निर्मुक्तरोगजालो जितबिन्दुः पट्वग्निर्भवति ।।१३-६।।
atha kumbhakaḥ; sa dvividhaḥ sahitaḥ kevalaśceti;recakapūrakayuktaḥ sahitaḥ; tadvivarjitaḥ kevalaḥ;kevalasiddhiparyantaṃ sahitamabhyaset;kevala-kumbhake siddhe triṣu lokeṣu na tasya durlabhaṃ bhavati;kevalakumbhakātkuṇḍalinībodho jayate (13.5)
tataḥ kṛśavapuḥ prasannavadano nirmalalocano 'bhivyakta -nādo nirmuktarogajālo jitabinduḥ paṭvagnirbhavati (13.6)

Vocabulary

atha: now; *kumbhakaḥ*: kumbhaka; *iti*: is; *dvividhaḥ*: of two kinds; *sahitaḥ ca kevalaḥ*: sahita and kevala; *sahitaḥ yuktaḥ*: sahita is connected with; *pūraka recaka*: inhalation and exhal -ation; *tad-vivarjitaḥ*: that excludes; *kevala-siddhi-paryantam*: until perfection in kevala; *sahitam-abhyaset*: one should prac-tise sahita; *kevala-kumbhake siddhe*: if [there is] perfection in kevala kumbhaka; *bhavati*: there is; *na tasya*: nothing; *durla-bham*: difficult to attain; *triṣu lokeṣu*: in the three worlds; *kevala-kumbhakāt*: through kevala kumbhaka; *jayate kuṇḍa-linī-bodhaḥ*: comes knowledge of kuṇḍalinī; *tataḥ*: then; *kṛśa -vapuḥ*: lean in body; *prasanna-vadanaḥ*: serene of counte-nance; *nirmala-locanaḥ*: bright-eyed; *abhivyakta-nādaḥ*: inner sounds distinct; *nirmukta*: freed from; *roga-jālaḥ*: from the web of disease; *jita-binduḥ*: seed subdued; *agniḥ bhavati*: fire becomes; *paṭu*: intense.

Translation

Now *kumbhaka* is of two kinds, *sahita* and *kevala*. Sahita is connected with inhalation and exhalation. That [which] excludes [these is] kevala. Until [there is] perfection in kevala, one should practise sahita. If [there is] perfection in *kevala kumbhaka*, there is nothing difficult to attain in the three worlds. Through kevala kumbhaka comes knowledge of kuṇḍalinī. Then, [when the yogin is] lean in body, serene of countenance, bright-eyed, the inner sounds distinct, freed from the web of disease [and his] seed subdued, the fire becomes intense.

Commentary

There are two types of *kumbhaka: sahita*, retention practised by intentionally holding the breath, and *kevala*, spontaneous breath retention. *Sahita* or deliberate retention is also of two types: *antar kumbhaka*, where the breath is held inside, after inhalation, and *bahir kumbhaka*, where the breath is held outside, after exhalation.

The practice of *sahita kumbhaka* leads to *kevala kumbhaka*, where breath suspension takes place by itself, during deep meditation. During this state the pressure in the lungs becomes the same as the atmospheric pressure, allowing the respiratory process to cease and the lungs to rest. When the breath ceases, the mind becomes totally still, and the veil that separates the mind from the higher consciousness is raised. Therefore, the most important aspect of prāṇāyāma is kumbhaka, and in the ancient texts prāṇāyāma is also known as kumbhaka.

In order to master kumbhaka, the yogin must gradually gain control over the breathing process. For this reason, great emphasis has been placed on the inhalation and exhalation during prāṇāyāma practice. Control of the breath leads to control of prāṇa, and control of prāṇa leads to control of the mind. By regulating the flow of breath, one can calm the mind in preparation for higher meditation. Hence, the above verse states that the yogin, who practises sahita prāṇāyāma, will have the power of kevala, the power to transcend the mind and experience the pure consciousness.

Sahita kumbhaka involves the breathing process and extension of the breath, whereas kevala kumbhaka, which arises spontaneously, does not. A number of prāṇāyāma practices are therefore included in sahita, such as *sūrya bheda*, *ujjāyī*, *śītalī*, and *bhastrikā*. Each of these practices involves a particular type of inhalation and exhalation, for the regulation of the prāṇas and the mind. However, all four utilise the same method of retention, so these comprise sahita kumbhaka.

In the previous verses the method of nāḍī śodhana prāṇāyāma was described. This method focuses on the ratio of breath through the alternate nostrils with the addition of kumbhaka, breath retention, at the end of each inhalation. Nāḍī śodhana was the main prāṇāyāma practised earlier, and it remains so even today, because of its balancing effects on the prāṇas, nervous system, and mind. The perfection of nāḍī śodhana is kevala kumbhaka, spontaneous breath retention, in which there is complete cessation of the breath for a period of time.

Cessation of the breath is an important stage of yoga, because it allows the deeper states of consciousness to be accessed effortlessly. When the breath stops, the mind becomes absolutely still. In this state of total stillness, the yogin is able to penetrate the subconscious and unconscious states. The active mind is the barrier to achieving in-depth meditation. When the mind is stilled as a result of kevala kumbhaka, meditation dawns effortlessly.

The verse further states that for the yogin, who is able to access the three states of consciousness through kevala kumbhaka, spontaneous breath retention, nothing remains unattainable in the three worlds. The three states of consciousness: conscious, subconscious and unconscious, which can be accessed during spontaneous breath retention, are related to the three planes of existence: earthly, intermediary or purgatory, and heavenly. Through kevala kumbhaka the yogin can experience the bliss of *kuṇḍalinī*, the spiritual energy.

Verses 14 to 16: Vaiṣṇavī and Khecarī Mudrā

अन्तर्लक्ष्यं बहिर्दृष्टर्निमेषोन्मेषवर्जिता ।एषा सा वैष्णवी मुद्रा सर्वतन्त्रेषु गोपिता ।।१४।।

अन्तर्लक्ष्यविलीनचित्तपवनो योगी सदा वर्तते दृष्ट्या निश्चलतारया बहिरधः पश्यन्नपश्यन्नपि ।मुद्रेयं खलु खेचरी भवति सा लक्ष्यैकताना शिवा शून्याशून्यविवर्जितं स्फुरति सा तत्त्वं सदं वैष्णवी ।।१५।।

अर्धोन्मीलितलोचनः स्थिरमना नासाग्रदत्तेक्षणश्चन्द्रार्कावपि लीनतामुपनयन्निष्पन्दभावोत्तरम् ।ज्योतीरूपमशेषहृयरहितं देदीप्यमानं परं तत्त्वं तत्परमस्ति वस्तुविषयं शाण्डल्य विद्धीह तत् ।।१६।।

antarlakṣyaṃ bahirdṛṣṭarnimeṣonmeṣavarjitāeṣā sā vaiṣṇavī mudrā sarvatantreṣu gopitā (14)
antarlakṣyavilīnacittapavano yogī sadā vartate dṛṣṭyā niścalatārayā bahiradhaḥ paśyannapaśyannapi;mudreyaṃ khalu khecarī bhavati sā lakṣyaikatānā śivāśūnyāśūnya-vivarjitaṃ sphurati sā tattvaṃ sadaṃ vaiṣṇavī (15)
ardhonmīlitalocanaḥ sthiramanā nāsāgradattekṣaṇaś-candrār-kāvapi līnatāmupanayanniṣpandabhāvottaram; jyotīrūpamaśeṣabāhyarahitaṃ dedīpyamānaṃ paraṃ tattvaṃtatparamasti vastuviṣayaṃ śāṇḍilya viddhīha tat (16)

Vocabulary

antar-lakṣyam: inner object; *bahiḥ-dṛṣṭaḥ*: while looking outside; *varjitā*: without; *nimeṣa-unmeṣa*: closing or opening the eyelids; *eṣā*: this is; *gopitā*: concealed; *sarva-tantreṣu*: in all the tantras; *citta-pavana*: mind and breath; *antarlakṣya-vilīna*: immersed in the inner object; *yogī*: yogin; *paśyan-api-napaśyan*: seeing yet not seeing; *bahiḥ-adhaḥ*: outside and below; *sadā*: continually; *vartate*: remains intent on; *dṛṣṭyā*: looking; *niścala-tārayā*: with motionless pupils; *khalu*: now;

iyam: this; *khecarī*: khecarī mudrā; *sā bhavati*: it has; *ekatānā*: one sense object; *lakṣya*: goal; *śivā*: auspicious; *tattvam sadam*: true seat; *vaiṣṇavī*: of Viṣṇu; *śūnya-aśūnya-vivarjitam*: neither void nor non-void; *sphurati*: shines brightly; *locanaḥ*: eyes; *ardha-unmīlita*: half-closed; *sthira-manā*: firm mind; *īkṣaṇaḥ*: eyes; *nāsāgra-datta*: fixed on the nosetip; *līnatām-upanayan*: becoming absorbed in; *candra-arkau*: moon and sun; *uttaram*: then; *niṣpanda-bhāva*: in an immoveable state; *asti*: is; *jyotī-rūpam*: form of light; *rahitam*: free from; *aśeṣabāhya*: all externals; *dedīpyamānam*: radiant; *param tattvam*: Supreme Truth; *param vastuviṣayam*: Absolute Reality; *viddhīha tat śāṇḍilya*: know this, o Śāṇḍilya!

Translation

[Concentration on] an inner object while looking outside without closing or opening the eyelids, this is *vaiṣṇavī mudrā,* concealed in all the tantras. Mind and breath immersed in the inner object, the yogin, seeing, yet not seeing, [what is] outside and below, remains continually intent on looking with motionless pupils.

Now this is khecarī mudrā. It has one sense object [as its] goal, [which is] auspicious. The true seat of Viṣṇu, [which is] neither void nor non-void, shines brightly. With eyes half-closed [and] a firm mind, eyes fixed on the nose-tip, becoming absorbed in the sun and moon, then in an immoveable state, [the yogin] is of the form of light free from all externals, [and is] radiant, the Supreme Truth, the Absolute Reality. Know this, o Śāṇḍilya!

Commentary

Vaiṣṇavī mudrā is also known as *śāṃbhavī mudrā*, where the yogin is aware only of an inner object of concentration while keeping the eyes open. It was one of the secret methods of tantra to access deeper states of awareness, and was taught only to those initated by the guru.

Khecarī mudrā, the tongue lock, is one of the most highly regarded yoga practices. It is discussed at length in many of the upaniṣads, as well as in the classical haṭha yoga texts. There are two versions of this practice: the *rāja yoga* method and the *haṭha yoga* method. The rāja yoga method simply involves folding the tongue back, so that the under surface presses against the roof of the mouth, and the tip reaches into the region at the back of the throat. The word *khecarī* comes from two roots: *khe*, meaning 'sky' and *carya*, meaning 'one who roams'. The yogi, who perfects khecarī, is considered to be liberated while living. He is able to roam freely in the space of consciousness, unaffected by the limitations and associations of the mind and the world. In this sense, khecarī is synonymous with mokṣa, because it bestows liberation on its practitioners.

The yogin seeks to attain Viṣṇu, the supreme consciousness, through the practices of yoga and meditation. In this sense, Viṣṇu, the supreme being, is the universal light, which is seen by those, who travel the path of self-realisation or enlightenment. This light is what guides the seeker on his chosen path towards the true essence of himself and of all existence.

Verses 17 to 23: Dissolution of Mind

तारं ज्योतिषि संयोज्य किंचिदुन्नमयन्भ्रुवै ।पूर्वाभ्यासस्य मार्गोऽयमुन्मनीकारकः क्षणात् ।।१७।।

तस्मात्खेचरीमुद्रामभ्यसेत् । तत उन्मनी भवति ।ततो योगनिद्रा भवति ।

लब्धयोगनिद्रस्य योगिनः कालो नास्ति ।।१७-१।।

शक्तिमध्ये मनः कृत्वा शक्तिं मानसमध्यगाम् ।

मनसा मन आलोक्य शाणडिल्य त्वं सुखी भव ।।१८।।

खमध्ये कुरु चात्मानमात्ममध्ये च खं कुरु ।सर्वं च खमयं कृत्वा न किंचिदपि चिन्तय ।।१९।।

बाह्यचिन्ता न कर्तव्या तथैवान्तरचिन्तका ।सर्वचिन्तां परित्यज्य चिन्मात्रपरमो भव ।।२०।।

कर्पूरमनले यद्वत्सैन्धवं सलिले यथा ।तथा च लीयमानं सन्मनस्तत्त्वे विलीयते ।।२१।।

ज्ञेयं सर्वप्रतीतं च तज्ज्ञानं मन उच्यते ।ज्ञानं ज्ञेयं समं नष्टं नान्यः पन्था द्वितीयकः ।।२२।।

ज्ञेयवस्तुपरित्यागाद्विलयं याति मानसम् ।मानसे विलयं याते कैवल्यमवशिष्यते ।।२३।।

tāraṃ jyotiṣi saṃyojya kiṃcidunnamayanbhruva pūrvābhyāsasya mārgo'yamunmanīkārakaḥ kṣaṇāt (17)
tasmātkhecarīmudrāmabhyaset; tata unmanī bhavatitato yoganidrā bhavati;
labdhayoganidrasya yoginaḥ kālo nāsti (17.1)
śaktimadhye manaḥ kṛtvā śaktiṃ mānasamadhyagāmmanasā mana ālokya śāṇḍilya tvaṃ sukhī bhava (18)
khamadhye kuru cātmānamātmamadhye ca khaṃ kurusarvaṃ ca khamayaṃ kṛtvā na kiṃcidapi cintaya (19)

bāhyacintā na kartavyā tathaivāntaracintakāsarvacintāṃ parityajya cinmātraparamo bhava (20)
karpūramanale yadvatsaindhavaṃ salile yathātathā ca līyamānaṃ sanmanastattve vilīyate (21)
jñeyaṃ sarvapratītaṃ ca tajñānaṃ mana ucyatejñānaṃ jñeyaṃ samaṃ naṣṭaṃ nānyaḥ panthā dvitīyakaḥ (22)
jñeyavastuparityāgādvilayaṃ yāti mānasammānase vilayaṃ yāte kaivalyamavaśiṣyate (23)

Vocabulary

saṃyojya: having merged; *tāram*: sound; *jyotiṣi*: in the light; *unnamayan*: raising; *bhru*: brows; *kiṃcit*: a little; *ayam*: this;
mārgaḥ: way; *pūrva-abhyāsasya*: of former practice; *kṣaṇāt*: immediately; *kārakaḥ unmanī*: brings forth *unmanī*, beyond mind; *tasmāt*: thus; *abhyaset*: one should practise; *tataḥ*: then; *bhavati*: there is; *yoga-nidrā*: deep relaxation; *yoginaḥ*: yogins; *labdha-yoganidrasya*: who have attained deep relaxation; *kālaḥ*: time; *na-asti*: does not exist; *kṛtvā*: having put; *manaḥ*: mind; *śakti-madhye*: in the midst of *śakti*; *śaktim gām*: śakti going; *mānasa-madhya*: into the midst of the mind; *ālokya*: observing; *manaḥ*: mind; *manasā*: with the mind; *śāṇḍilya tvam bhava*: o Śāṇḍilya, may you be; *sukhī*: happy; *kuru ātmānam*: place the *ātman*; *kha-madhye*: within the ether; *ca kham*: and the ether; *ātma-madhye*: within the ātman; *ca kṛtvā*: and having made; *sarvam khamayam*: everything ether; *na cintaya*: do not think of; *kiṃcit-api*: anything else; *bāhya-cintāḥ*: external thoughts; *na kartavyāḥ*: are not to be had; *tathaiva*: likewise; *antara-cintakāḥ*: internal thoughts; *parityajya*: having renounced; *sarva-cintām*: all thoughts; *bhava*: become; *paramaḥ mātra cin*: highest measure of thought; *yadvat*: just as; *yathā*: for instance; *karpūram*: camphor; *līyamānam*: becomes absorbed; *anale*: in fire; *ca saindhavam*: and salt; *salile*: in water; *tathā manaḥ*: so the mind; *vilīyate*: is absorbed; *sattattve*: in its true nature; *ucyate manaḥ*: is called mind; *ta-jñānam*: is knowing that;

sarva: all; *pratītam*: past; *ca jñeyam*: and is to be known; *jñānam jñeyam*: knowledge of past and future; *samam naṣṭam*: equally lost; *na anyaḥ*: no other; *dvitī-yakaḥ panthā*: second path; *parityāgāt*: by abandoning; *jñeya*: future knowledge; *vastu*: objects; *mānasam*: mind; *yāti vilayam*: goes into dissolution; *mānase yāte*: when the mind goes into; *vilayam*: dissolution; *avaśiṣyate*: there remains only; *kaivalyam*: *kaivalya.*

Translation
Having merged the sound in the light, raising the brows a little, this [is] the way of former practice [and] immediately brings forth unmanī. Thus one should practise khecarī mudrā. Then there is unmanī. Then there is yoga nidrā. [For] yogins who have attained deep relaxation, time does not exist. Having put the mind in the midst of śakti, śakti going into the midst of the mind, observing the mind with the mind, o Śāṇḍilya, may you be happy! Place the ātman within the ether, and the ether within the ātman, and having made everything ether, do not think of anything else. External thoughts are not to be had, likewise internal thoughts. Having renounced all thoughts, become the highest measure of thought. Just as for instance camphor becomes absorbed in fire and salt in water, so the mind is absorbed in its true nature. [That which] is called mind is knowing all that is past and [all that] is to be known. [When] knowledge of past and future [is] equally lost, [there is] no other second path. By abandoning future knowledge [of] objects, the mind goes into dissolution. When the mind goes into dissolution, there remains only kaivalya.

Commentary
As long as there is sound, there is the mind, because it is the mind that perceives the sound. When there is no more inner sound, there is the state beyond the mind, which is pure light and *unmanī*, beyond mind and thought. To achieve this state, one can practise khecarī mudrā and yoga nidrā, the practice of

deep relaxation, where the body sleeps and the mind remains awake, yet aware, calm and free from distraction. Śakti is the subtle power that creates the mind. Lord Atharvan tells Śāṇḍilya he will be happy when the mind is dissolved back into śakti, and when the ether element, which contains the mind, and the ātman, the true Self, are merged. Then the yogin reaches *kaivalya*, final liberation, the supreme state of consciousness beyond duality.

Verses 24 to 27: Yoga and Jñāna

द्वै क्रमौ चित्तनाशस्य योगो ज्ञानं मुनिश्वर ।

योगस्तद्वत्तिरोधो हि ज्ञानं सम्यगवेक्षणम् ।।२४।।

तस्मिन्निरोधते नूनमुशान्तं मनो भवेत् ।मनः

स्पन्दोपशान्त्यायं संसारः प्रविलीयते ।।२५।।

सूर्यालोकपरिस्पन्दशान्तौ व्यवहृतिर्यथा

।शास्त्रसज्जनसंपर्कवैराग्यासयोगतः ।।२६।।

अनास्थायां कृतास्थायां पूर्वं संसारवृत्तिषु

।यथाभिवाच्छितध्यानाच्चिरमेकतयोहितात् ।।२७।।

dvai kramau cittanāśasya yogo jñānaṃ
munīśvarayogastadvattirodho hi jñānaṃ samyag-
avekṣaṇam (24)
tasminnirodhate nūnamupaśāntaṃ mano bhavetmanaḥ
spandopaśāntyāyaṃ saṃsāraḥ pravilīyate (25)
sūryālokaparispandaśāntau
vyavhṛtiryathāśāstrasajjanasaṃparkavairāgyāsayogataḥ (26)
anāsthāyāṃ kṛtāsthāyāṃ pūrvaṃ
saṃsāravṛttiṣuyathābhivācchitadhyānācciramekatayohitāt (27)

Vocabulary

dvai kramau: two ways; *citta-nāśasya*: of destruction of *citta*; *yogaḥ jñānam*: yoga and jñāna; *munīśvara*: o excellent Sage; *tadvat*: thus; *yogaḥ tirodhaḥ*: yoga controls; *hi jñānam*: and jñāna; *samyak-avekṣaṇam*: correct understanding; *nūnam*: so; *tasmin-nirodhate*: when … is thus prevented; *manaḥ bhavet*: mind becomes; *upaśāntam*: calm; *spanda-upaśāntyāyam*: through the interruption of activity; *saṃsāraḥ manaḥ*: illusory mind; *pravilīyate*: becomes dissolved; *yathā*: as; *vyavhṛtiḥ*: action; *parispanda*: maintaining; *sūrya-āloka śāntau*: when the light of the sun has ceased; *yogataḥ*: by means of; *abhyā-sa*: yoga practice; *sat-jana-saṃparka*: keeping virtuous company; *śāstra*: sacred teachings; *vairagya*: detachment; *anāsth-*

āyām: indifference; *vṛttiṣu*: to the mental influences; *saṃsāra*: illusory world; *pūrvam*: previously; *kṛta-āsthāyām*: contemplated; *yathā*: then; *ekataya*: one by one; *dhyānāt*: through meditation; *ciram*: for a long time; *abhivācchita*: desires; *uhitāt*: are borne away.

Translation

The two ways of destruction of *citta* [are] *yoga* and *jñāna*, excellent Sage. Thus yoga controls [it], and jñāna [gives] correct understanding. So when [thinking] is thus prevented, the mind becomes calm. Through the interruption of activity, the illusory mind becomes dissolved. As when the action of maintaining the light of the sun has ceased, so by means of yoga practice, keeping virtuous company, sacred teachings, detachment [from sensory pleasures], [and] indifference to the mental influences of the illusory world, previously contemplated, then one by one, through meditation for a long time, the desires are borne away.

Commentary

Jñāna is the wisdom and highest knowledge arising from the inner experience of deep meditation. The word 'yoga' comes from the verb *yuj*, which means to join, yoke, unite. Yoga includes systems, practices and philosophies which lead the yogin to jñāna.

Just as jñāna in the absence of yoga will not be a sure path to attain liberation; similarly, the practice of yoga in the absence of jñāna will not lead to liberation.In order to progress on any given path the objective or goal must be known. Jñāna is the knowledge of paramātmā, the supreme consciousness. In the absence of this knowledge, the practice of yoga will have no ultimate goal or outcome. A *jñāni* is able to discriminate between the mind and the consciousness, the permanent and the impermanent, the inner truth and the outer experience.In the light of the sun, all darkness disappears. Similarly, in the light of knowledge, all ignorance, suffering and desires are removed. The cycle of saṃsāra (birth, death and rebirth) can no longer bind the person, who is illumined with self-knowledge. This person lives in the world, but not of it, and therefore does not undergo the suffering of life in the same way as someone, who identifies with the world and is ignorant of the Self.

Verses 28 to 36: Control of Prāṇa

एकतत्त्वदृढाभ्यासात्प्राणस्पन्दो निरुध्यते

।पूरकाद्यनिलायामाद्दृढाभ्यासादखेदजात् ।।२८।।

एकान्तध्यानयोगाच्च मनःस्पन्दो निरुध्यते ।

ओङ्कारोच्चारणप्रान्तशब्दतत्त्वानुभावनात् ।

सुषुप्ते संविदा ज्ञाते प्राणस्पन्दो निरुध्यते ।।२९।।

तालुमूलगतां यत्नाज्जिह्वयाक्रम्य घण्टिकाम् ।

ऊर्ध्वरन्ध्रं गते प्राणे प्राणस्पन्दो निरुध्यते ।।३०।।

प्राणे गलितसंवित्तौ तालूर्ध्वं द्वादशान्तगे ।

अभ्यासादूर्ध्वरन्ध्रेण प्राणस्पन्दो निरुध्यते ।।३१।।

द्वादशाङ्गुलपर्यन्ते नासाग्रे विमलेऽम्बरे ।

संविद्दृशि प्रशाम्यन्त्यां प्राणस्पन्दो निरुध्यते ।।३२।।

भ्रूमध्ये तारकालोकशान्तावन्तमुपागते ।

चितनैकतने बद्ध्वे प्राणस्पन्दो निरुध्यते ।।३३।।

ओमित्येव यदुद्भूतं ज्ञानं ज्ञेयात्मकं शिवम् ।

असंस्पृष्टविकल्पांशं प्राणस्पन्दो निरुध्यते ।।३४।।

चिरकालं हृदेकान्तव्योमसंवेदनान्मुने ।

अवासनमनोध्यानात्प्राणस्पन्दो निरुध्यते ।।३५।।

एभिः क्रमैस्तथान्यैश्च नानासंकल्पकल्पितैः ।

नानादेशिकवक्त्रस्थैः प्राणस्पन्दो निरुध्यते ।।३६।।

ekatattvadṛḍhābhyāsātprāṇaspando nirudhyatepūrakādyanilāyāmāddṛḍhābhyāsādakhedajāt (28)
ekāntadhyānayogācca manaḥspando nirudhyateoṅkāroccāraṇaprāntaśabdatattvānubhāvanāt-suṣupte saṃvidā jñāte prāṇaspando nirudhyate (29)
tālumūlagatāṃ yatnājjihvayākramya ghaṇṭikāmūrdhvaran-

dhraṃ gate prāṇe prāṇaspando nirudhyate (30)
prāṇe galitasaṃvittau tālūrdhvaṃ dvādaśāntageabhyāsādūrdhvarandhreṇa prāṇaspando nirudhyate (31)
dvādaśāṅgulaparyante nāsāgre vimale'mbaresaṃviddṛśi praśāmyantyāṃ prāṇaspando nirudhyate (32)
bhrūmadhye tārakālokaśāntāvantamupāgatecitanaikatane baddhve prāṇaspando nirudhyate (33)
omityeva yadudbhrūtaṃ jñānaṃ jñeyātmakaṃ śivamasaṃspṛṣṭavikalpāṃśaṃ prāṇaspando nirudhyate (34)
cirakālaṃ hṛdekāntavyomasaṃvedanānmune avāsanamanodhyānāt prāṇaspando nirudhyate (35)
ebhiḥ kramaistathānyaiśca nānāsaṃkalpakalpitaiḥnānādeśikavaktrasthaiḥ prāṇaspando nirudhyate (36)

Vocabulary

prāṇa-spandaḥ: movement of prāṇa; *nirudhyate*: is controlled; *dṛḍha-abhyāsāt*: by consistent yoga practice on; *eka-tattva*: one essential nature; *anila-āyāmāt*: by holding the breath; *pūraka-ādi*: first inhaling; *dṛḍha-abhyāsāt*: by consistent practice; *akheda-jāt*: does not cause fatigue; *ca dhyānayogāt*: and by deep meditation; *ekānta*: solitary; *manaḥ spandaḥ*: activity of the mind; *nirudhyate*: is restrained; *anubhāvanāt*: through direct experience; *śabda-tattva*: true essential nature of the sound; *prānta*: extremity; *oṅkāra-uccāraṇa*: enunciation of Aum; *saṃvidā jñāte*: when consciousness is known; *suṣupte*: in deep sleep; *prāṇa-spando nirudhyate*: vibration of prāṇa is controlled; *tālu-mūla-gatām*: passage at the root of the palate; *ghaṇṭikām*: small bell; *kramya*: is closed; *jihvayā*: by the tongue; *yatnāt*: with effort; *prāṇe gate*: prāṇa enters; *ūrdhva-randhram*: upper aperture; *galita-saṃvittau*: when consciousness is merged; *prāṇe*: with prāṇa; *abhyāsāt*: through yoga practice; *ūrdhva-randhreṇa*: through the upper aperture; *dvādaśānta*: *dvādaśānta* (*sahasrāra cakra*); *tālu-ūrdhvam*: above the palate; *saṃvid-dṛśi*: when the eye of consciousness; *praśāmyantyām*: becoming calm; *vimale ambare*: in the clear ether; *dvādaśa-āṅgula-paryante*: up to twelve digits; *nāsāgre*: from the nosetip; *prāṇa-spandaḥ nirudhyate*: vibrations of prāṇa cease; *citaḥ-na-ekatane*: when many thoughts; *upāgate*: arise; *baddhve*: bound up; *śāntau-antam*: they are finally extinguished; *tāraka-āloka*: in the world of *tāraka*; *bhrū-madhye*: at the eyebrow centre; *jñānam*: knowledge; *jñeya-ātmakam*: form of that which is to be known; *śivam*: auspicious; *asaṃspṛṣṭa*: untouched; *vikalpa-aṃśam*: oscillations through-out; *udbhrū*: brows raised; *om-iti-eva*: is just Aum; *tam*: then; *prāṇa-spandaḥ nirudhyate*: vibrations of prāṇa have ceased; *saṃvedanāt*: by being conscious of; *cirakālam*: for a long time; *vyoma*: space; *hṛd-ekānta*: within the heart; *mune*: o Sage; *dhyānāt*: by meditating on; *manaḥ*: mind; *avā-sana*: free from impressions; *tathā*: thus; *ebhiḥ kramaiḥ*: by these methods; *ca nānā anyaiḥ*: and by many others; *saṃkalpa kalpitaiḥ*: come to mind; *vaktra-sthaiḥ*: by the connection with the appearance of; *nānā-deśika*: many guides.

Translation

The movement of prāṇa is controlled by consistent yoga practice on the one essential nature. By holding the breath, first inhaling, by firm practice [which] does not cause fatigue, and by solitary deep meditation, the activity of the mind is restrained.

Through direct experience of the true essential nature of the sound [at] the extremity [of] the enunciation of Aum [and] when consciousness is known in deep sleep, the movement of prāṇa is controlled.

[When] the passage at the root of the palate, [like] a small bell, is closed by the tongue with effort, [and] the prāṅa enters the upper aperture, the movement of prāṇa is controlled.

When consciousness is merged with prāṇa, [and] when through yoga practice, [prāṇa goes] through the upper aperture into the *dvādaśānta* above the palate, the movement of prāṇa is controlled. When the eye of consciousness, becoming calm, [can see] in the clear ether up to twelve digits from the nosetip, the movements of prāṇa cease.

When many thoughts arise, bound up [in the mind], they are finally extinguished in the world of *tāraka* at the eyebrow centre [and] the movements of prāṇa cease. When the knowledge in the form of that which is to be known [is] auspicious, untouched by the oscillations throughout [the mind] and, brows raised, is just Aum, then the movements of prāṇa have ceased. By being conscious for a long time of the space within the heart, o Sage [and] meditating on the mind free from impressions, the movements of prāṇa cease. Thus by these methods and many others [which] come to mind [and] by the connection with the appearance of many guides, the movements of prāṇa cease.

Commentary

These verses list many ways in which the movements, vibrations, fluctuations of prāṇa are controlled or stopped, and the signs that they have ceased: kumbhaka without straining while meditating in a secluded place on one's essential nature; by experiencing, while chanting the mantra Aum, *turīya*, the fourth state, which transcends the three states of consciousness of waking, dreaming and sleeping; in deep sleep, when there is disassociation of the senses from both external and internal environments; when practising khecarī mudrā, where the uvula is closed by the underside of the tongue, so that the prāṇa in the form of the breath moves up through *brahmarandra* to *dvādaśānta* (*sahasrāra cakra)* twelve digits above the palate.[17] when ājña cakra (eye of consciousness, third eye) becomes still, there is expansion of awareness and intuition; when meditating on the light, *tāraka*, at *ājña cakra*, thoughts are dissolved in the light; [18] when one knows pure consciousness as praṇava, AUM; when meditating on the heart space (*hṛdayākāśa dhāraṇā*) where dwell memories and emotions, and meditating on the space of the mind (*cidākāśa dhāraṇā*) in which dwell thoughts, being aware of the flame of light (pure consciousness) behind them.

Finally, the verses emphasise that practice must be consistent and focused on the inner Self. They say that there are many other ways of controlling the prāṇa, including association with advanced spiritual masters.

Verses 36kha-38: Awakening Kuṇḍalinī

आकुञ्चनेन कुण्डलिन्याः कवाटमुद्धात्य मोक्षद्वारं विभेदयेत्
।।३६ ख।।

येन मार्गेण गन्तव्यं तद्द्वारं मुखेनाच्छाद्य प्रसुप्ता ।

कुण्डलिनी कुटिलाकारा सर्पवद्वेष्टिता भवति ।।३६ ग।।

साशक्तिर्येन चालिता स्यत्स तु मुक्ते भवति ।

सा कुण्डलिनी कण्ठोर्ध्वभागे सुप्ता चेद्योगिनां मुक्तये भवति ।

बन्धनायाधो मूढानाम ।।३६ घ।।

इडादिमार्गद्वयं विहाय सुषुम्नामार्गेणागच्छेत्तद्विष्णोः परमं
पदम् ।।३६ ङ।।

मरुदभ्यसनं सर्वं मनोयुक्तं समभ्यसेत् ।

इतरत्र न कर्तव्या मनोवृत्तिर्मनीषिना ।।३७।।

दिवा न पूजयेद्विष्णुं रात्रौ नैव प्रपूजयेत् ।सततं पूजयेद्विष्णुं
दिवारात्रं न पूजयेत् ।।३८।।

ākuñcanena kuṇḍalinyāḥ kavāṭamuddhātya mokṣadvāraṃ vibhedayet (36 kha)
yena mārgeṇa gantavyaṃ taddvāraṃ mukhenācchādya prasuptā kuṇḍalinī kuṭilākārā sarpavadveṣṭitā bhavati (36ga)
sāśaktiryena cālitā syātsa tu mukte bhavatisā kuṇḍalinī kaṇṭhordhvabhāge suptā cedyoginām muktaye bhavati bandhanāyādho mūḍhānām (36 gha)
iḍādimārgadvayaṃ vihāya suṣumnāmārgeṇāgacchettad-viṣṇoḥ paramaṃ padam (36 ṅ)
marudabhyasanaṃ sarvaṃ manoyuktaṃ samabhyasetitar-atra na kartavyā manovṛttirmanīṣinā (37)
divā na pūjayedviṣṇuṃ rātrau naiva prapūjayetsatataṃ pūjayedviṣṇuṃ divārātraṃ na pūjayet (38)

Vocabulary

uddhātya: having opened up; *ākuñcanena*: by contraction; *kavāṭam*: doorway; *kuṇḍalinyāḥ*: to kuṇḍalinī; *vibhedayet*: one can break through; *dvāram*: door; *mokṣa*: liberation; *ācchādya*: having covered; *mukhena*: with her mouth; *tad dvāram*: that door; *yena*: through which; *gantavyam*: one enters; *veṣṭitā*: coiled up; *sarpavat*: like a snake; *kuṭilā-kārā*: spiral form; *prasuptā bhavati*: is sleeping; *sa yena*: the one who; *syāt cālitā*: causes to move; *sā śaktiḥ*: this *śakti*; *bhavati mukte*: is liberated; *ced sā kuṇḍalinī*: if the kuṇḍalinī; *suptāḥ*: sleeps; *kaṇṭha-ūrdh-va-bhāge*: in the upper part of the neck; *yogināṃ*: of the yogins; *muktaye bhavati*: they will be liberated; *adhaḥ*: lower; *bandhan-āya*: bondage; *mūḍhānām*: of the ignorant; *vihāya*: moving away from; *mārga-dvayam*: two paths; *iḍā-ādi*: *iḍā* etc; *āgacchet*: she will go up to; *suṣumnā-mārgeṇa*: through the path of *suṣumnā*; *tad paramam padam viṣṇoḥ*: that supreme seat of Viṣṇu; *sarvam samabhyaset*: one should always practise; *marut-abhyasanam*: controlling the breath; *manaḥ-yuktam*: with concentration on the mind; *manaḥ-vṛttiḥ*: activity of the mind; *na kartavyā*: is not to be placed; *itaratra*: elsewhere; *manīṣinā*: by the wise person; *viṣnum na pūjayet*: one should not worship Viṣṇu; *divā eva*: by day only; *na prapūjayet*: nor worship; *rātrau*: by night; *pūjayet viṣṇum satatam*: one should worship Viṣṇu continually; *na divārātram*: not by day and night.

Translation

Having opened up by contraction the doorway to kuṇḍalinī, one can break through the door [to] liberation. Having covered with her mouth that door through which one enters, the kuṇḍalinī, coiled up like a snake in spiral form, is sleeping.

The one who causes this *śakti* to move is liberated. If the kuṇḍalinī sleeps in the upper part of the neck of the yogins, they will be liberated. [If she sleeps] in the lower [part], [there is] bondage of the ignorant. Moving away from the two paths of īḍa [and piṅgalā], she will go up through the path of suṣumnā to that supreme seat of Viṣṇu.

One should always practise controlling the breath with concentration on the mind. The activity of the mind is not to be placed elsewhere by the wise person. One should not worship Viṣṇu by day only, nor worship [him] by night [only]. One should worship Viṣṇu continually, not [only] by day and night.

Commentary

The verse infers that it is possible for a yoga aspirant to arouse the *kuṇḍalinī śakt*i, the cosmic energy sleeping coiled up at mūlādhāra cakra, causing her to ascend suṣumnā nāḍī through the levels of consciousness represented by the seven cakras, which denote our evolution from self-centredness towards realisation of the higher Self.

If the kuṇḍalinī goes beyond the *viśuddhi cakra* in the throat pit, the yogin will be freed from worldly identity. If she does not reach viśuddhi cakra, he will have no knowledge of the higher Self. 'She (kuṇḍalinī) sleeps because She is at rest. Then man's consciousness is awake to the world, Her creation, in which She is immanent. When She awakes and Yoga is completed, man sleeps to the world and enjoys super-worldly experience.'[19]

The yogin must worship Viṣṇu constantly, day and night. Viṣṇu's name means 'pervader', which refers to his omnipresence. He has the quality or guṇa of *sattwa*, meaning harmony, purity and goodness. The path of *Bhakti Yoga* is a devotional one, inspired by Viṣṇu, who is worshipped through his human incarnations (avatāras) Rāma and Kṛṣṇa. 'The supreme step of Viṣṇu, his highest seat, is the triple world of bliss and light, *paramam padam*, which the wise ones see extended in heaven like a shining eye of vision; It is the highest seat of Viṣṇu, that is the goal of the Vedic journey.'[20]

Verses 39 to 42gha: Khecarī Mudrā (2)

सुषिरा ज्ञानजनकः पञ्चस्रोतः समन्वितःतिष्ठते खेचरी मुद्रा त्वं हि शाण्डिल्य तां भज ।।३९।।

सव्यदक्षिणनाडीस्थो मध्ये चरति मारुतः ।

तिष्ठते खेचरी मुद्रा तस्मिन्स्थाने नसंशयः ।।४०।।

इडापिङ्गलयोर्मध्य शून्यं चैवानिलं ग्रसेत् ।तिष्ठतति खेचरी मुद्रा तत्र सत्यं प्रतिष्थम् ।।४१।।

सोमसूर्यद्वयोर्मध्ये निरालम्बतले पुनः ।संस्थिता व्योमचक्रे सा मुद्रा नाम्ना च खेचरी ।।४२ क।।

छेदनचालनदोहैः कलां परां जिह्वां कृत्वा दृष्टिं भ्रूमध्ये स्थाप्य कपालकुहरे जिह्वा विपरीतगा यदा भवति तदा खेचरी मुद्रा जायते ।जिह्वा चित्तं च खे चरति तेनोर्ध्वजिह्वः पुमानमृतो भवति ।।४२ ख।।

वामपादमूलेन योनिं संपीड्य दिक्षनपादं प्रसार्य तंकराभ्यां धृत्वा नासाभ्यां वायुमापूर्य कण्ठबन्धं समारोप्योर्ध्वतो वायुं धारयेत् ।

तेन सर्वक्लेशहानिः ।ततः पीयूषमिव विषं जीर्यते ।

क्षयगुल्मगुदावर्तजीर्नत्वगादिदेषा नश्यन्ति ।

एष प्राणजयोपायः सर्वमृत्यूपघातकः ।।४२ घ।।

suṣirā jñānajanakaḥ pañcasrotaḥ samanvitaḥtiṣṭhate khecarī mudrā tvaṃ hi śāṇḍilya tāṃ bhaja (39)
savyadakṣiṇanāḍīstho madhye carati mārutaḥtiṣṭhate khecarī mudrā tasminsthāne na saṃśayaḥ (40)
iḍāpiṅgalayormadhye śūnyaṃ caivānilaṃ grasettiṣṭhati khecarī mudrā tatra satyaṃ pratiṣtham (41)
somasūryadvayormadhye nirālambatale punaḥsaṃsthitā vyomacakre sā mudrā nāmnā ca khecarī (42 ka)
chedanacālanadohaiḥ kalāṃ parāṃ jihvāṃ kṛtvā dṛṣṭiṃbhrū-

madhye sthāpya kapālakuhare jihvā viparītagāyadā bhavati tadā khecarī mudrā jāyatejihvā cittaṃ ca khe carati tenordhvajihvaḥ pumānamṛto bhavati (42 kha)
vāmapādamūlena yoniṃ saṃpīḍya dikṣanapādaṃ prasārya taṃ karābhyāṃ dhṛtvā nāsābhyāṃ vāyumāpūrya kaṇṭha bandhaṃ samāropyordhvato vāyuṃ dhārayettena sarvakleśahāniḥtataḥ pīyūṣamiva viṣaṃ jīryatekṣayagulmagudāvartajīrnatvagādideṣā naśyantieṣa prāṇajayopāyaḥ sarvamṛtyūpaghātakaḥ (42 ga)
vāmapādapārṣṇiyonisthāne niyojya dakṣiṇacaraṇaṃ-vāmorūpari saṃsthāpya vāyumāpūrya hṛdaye cubukaṃ nidhāya yonimākuñcya manomadhye yathāśaktidhārayitvā svātmānaṃ bhāvayettenāparokṣasiddhiḥ (42 gha)

Vocabulary

suṣirā: opening; *jñāna-janakaḥ*: generating wisdom; *samanvitaḥ*: possesses; *pañca-srotaḥ*: five canals; *tiṣṭhate*: abides; *tvam tām bhaja*: (you) practise it; *tasmin-sthāne khecarī mudrā*: when one rests in khecarī mudrā; *mārutaḥ*: vital air; *savya-dakṣiṇa-nāḍī-sthaḥ*: having been in the left and right nāḍīs; *carati*: flows; *tiṣṭhate*: remains; *madhye*: in the middle; *na saṃśayaḥ*: there is no doubt; *graset*: one should swallow; *anilam*: air; *śūnyam*: void; *iḍā-piṅgalayoḥ-madhye*: between iḍā and piṅgalā; *tatra*: there; *khecarī mudrā tiṣṭhati*: khecarī mudrā is located; *pratiṣtham satyam*: seat of truth; *punaḥ*: again; *sā mudrā*: that mudrā; *khecarī nāmnā*: *saṃsthitā*: is situated; *vyoma-cakre*: in *ākāśa* cakra; *nirālamba-tale*: in the unsupported part; *soma-sūryadvayoḥ-madhye*: between the sun and the moon; *kṛtvā jihvām*: having made the tongue; *parām kalām*: another digit; *chedana-cālana-dohaiḥ*: by an incision, shaking and milking; *sthāpya dṛṣṭim*: fixing the gaze; *bhrūmadhye*: at the eyebrow centre; *yadā*: when; *jihvā bhavati viparītagā*: tongue is reversed; *kapāla-kuhare*: into the hole in the skull; *tadā jāyate*: then [this] becomes; *cittam carati*: citta moves; *jihvā*: with the togue; *khe*: in the ākāśa; *tena*: then; *pumān*: person; *ūrdhva-jihvaḥ*: tongue raised up; *bhavati amṛtaḥ*: becomes immortal;

saṃpīḍya: pressing; *yonim*: peri-neum; *vāma-pādamūlena*: with the left heel; *prasārya*: stretching out; *dikṣana-pādam*: right leg; *dhṛtvā tām*: grasping it; *karābhyām*: with both hands; *vāyum-āpūrya*: inhaling the air; *nāsābhyām*: through the nostrils; *dhārayet*: one should hold; *kaṇṭha-bandham*: throat lock; *samāropya vāyum*: raising the air; *ūrdhvataḥ*: upwards; *tena*: thus; *sarvakleśa*: every affliction; *hāniḥ*: is destroyed; *tataḥ*: then; *viṣam*: poison; *jīryate*: is digested; *iva*: like; *pīyūṣam*: nectar; *doṣāḥ*: problems; *kṣaya*: consumption; *gulma*: spleen; *guda-āvarta*: turning up of the anus; *jīrna*: old age; *tvag-ādi*: skin etc; *naśyanti*: are removed; *eṣa upāyaḥ*: this is the way; *prāṇajaya*: to conquer prāṇa; *upaghātakaḥ*: overcoming; *sarvamṛtyu*: every death; *niyojya*: pressing; *vāma-pādapārṣṇi*: left heel; *yoni-sthāne*: in the area of the perineum; *saṃsthāpya*: placing; *dakṣiṇa-caraṇam*: right foot; *vāma-ūrūpari*: on the left thigh; *vāyum-āpūrya*: inhaling the vital air; *nidhāya*: resting; *cubukam*: chin; *hṛdaye*: on the chest; *yonim-ākuñcya*: contracting the perineum; *dhārayitvā*: holding; *sva-ātmānam*: one's own ātman; *manomadhye*: within the mind; *yathā-śakti*: as long as possible; *bhāvayet*: one can realise.

Translation

The opening generating wisdom possesses five canals. Here abides khecarī mudrā. Practise it, o Śāṇḍilya! When one rests in khecarī mudrā, the vital air, having been in the left and right nāḍīs, flows [and] remains in the middle [nāḍī]. [About this] there is no doubt. One should swallow the air in the void between iḍā and piṅgalā. There khecarī mudrā is located, the seat of truth. Again, that mudrā, khecarī by name, is situated in ākāśa cakra in the unsupported part between the sun and the moon.

Having made the tongue another digit [in length] by an incision, shaking and milking [it], fixing the gaze at the eyebrow centre [and] when the tongue is reversed into the hole of the skull, then [this] becomes khecarī mudrā. [When] citta moves with the tongue in the ākāśa, then the person [whose] tongue is raised up becomes immortal. Pressing the perineum with the left heel, stretching out the right leg, grasping it [the right foot] with both hands [and] inhaling the air through the nostrils, one should hold the throat lock, raising the air upwards.

Thus every affliction is destroyed. Then poison is digested like nectar. The problems of consumption, the spleen, turning up of the anus, old age and skin etc. are removed. This is the way to conquer prāṇa, overcoming every [type of] death. Pressing the left heel in the area of the perineum, placing the right foot on the left thigh, inhaling the vital air, resting the chin on the chest, contracting the perineum, [then] holding one's own ātman within the mind as long as possible, one can realise [it].

Commentary

During the practice of khecarī mudrā, the prāṇa flows up suṣumnā. As said in above verses, the word khecarī comes from two roots: *khe*, meaning 'sky' and *carya*, meaning 'one who roams'. The yogi, who perfects khecarī, is able to roam freely in the space of consciousness, ākāśa, at ājña cakra.

The verse describes the haṭha yoga method which involves gradual cutting of the frenum under the tongue, and is therefore irreversible. By systematic cutting, massaging and stretching, the tongue gradually be comes elongated and can reach into the nasal cavity. This position of the tongue activates ājña cakra and blocks the descent of the nectar and the consciousness into the lower centres. One should meditate on the true Self in the space of the mind while holding the mudrā. Each stage of the haṭha yoga method needs to be done slowly and methodically and only under the guidance of an experienced master. Through this practice all afflictions can be overcome.

Verses 43 to 51: Destruction of Disease (2)

बाह्यात्प्राणं समाकृष्य पूरयित्वोदरे स्थितम् ।नाभिमध्ये च नासाग्रे पादाङ्गुष्ठे च यत्नतः ।।४३।।

धारयेन्मनसा प्राणं सन्ध्याकालेषु वा सदा ।सर्वरोगविनिर्मुक्तो भवेद्योगी गतक्लमः ।।४४ क।।

नासाग्रे वायुविजयं भवाति । नाभिमध्ये सर्वरोगविनाशः ।पादाङ्गुष्ठधारणाच्छरीरलघुता भवति ।।४४ ख।।

रसनाद्वायुमाकृष्य यः पिबेत्सततं नरः ।श्रमदाहौ तु न स्यातां नश्यन्ति व्याधयस्तथा ।।४५।।

सन्ध्ययोर्ब्राह्मणः काले वायुमाकृष्य यः पिबेत् ।
त्रिमासात्तस्य कल्याणी जायते वाक् सरस्वती ।।४६।।

एवं षण्मासाभ्यासात्सर्वरोगङिवृत्तिः ।
जिह्वया वायुमानीय जिह्वामूले निरोधयेत् ।
यः पिबेदमृतं विद्वान्सकलं भद्रमश्नुते ।।४७।।

आत्मन्यात्मानमिड्या धारयित्वा भ्रुवोऽन्तरे ।
विभेद्य त्रिदशाहारं व्याधिस्थोऽपि विमुच्यते ।।४८।।

नाडीभ्यां वायुमारोप्य नाभौ तुन्दस्य पार्श्वयोः ।
घटिकैकां वहेद्यस्तु व्याधिभिः स विमुच्यते ।।४९।।

मासमेकं त्रिसन्ध्यं तु जिह्वयारोप्य मारुतम् ।
विभेद्य त्रिदशाहारं धारयेत्तुन्दमध्यमे ।।५०।।

ज्वराः सर्वऽपि नश्यन्ति विषाणि विविधानि च ।
मुहूर्तमपि यो नित्यं नासाग्रे मनसा सह ।
सर्वं तरति पाप्मानं तस्य जन्मशतार्जितम् ।।५१।।

bāhyātprāṇaṃ samākṛṣya pūrayitvodare sthitamnābhi-

madhye ca nāsāgre pādāṅguṣṭhe ca yatnataḥ (43)
dhārayenmanasā prāṇaṃ sandhyākāleṣu vā
sadāsarvarogavinirmukto bhavedyogī gataklamaḥ (44 ka)
nāsāgre vāyuvijayaṃ bhavati; nābhimadhye sarvaroga-vināśaḥ pādāṅguṣṭhadhāraṇāccharīralaghutā bhavati (44 kha)
rasanādvāyumākṛṣya yaḥ pibetsatataṃ naraḥśramadāhau
tu na syātāṃ naśyanti vyādhayastathā (45)
sandhyayorbrāhmaṇaḥ kāle vāyumākṛṣya yaḥ
pibettrimāsāttasya kalyāṇī jāyate vāk sarasvatī (46)
evaṃ ṣaṇmāsābhyāsatsarvaroganivṛttiḥjihvayā vāyumānīya
jihvāmūle nirodhayetyaḥ pibedamṛtaṃ vidvānsakalaṃ
bhadramaśrute (47)
ātmanyātmānamiḍyā dhārayitvā bhruvo'ntarevibhedya
tridaśāhāraṃ vyādhistho'pi vimucyate (48)
nāḍībhyāṃ vāyumāropya nābhau tundasya pārśvayoḥ-
ghaṭikaikāṃ vahedyastu vyādhibhiḥ sa vimucyate (49)
māsamekaṃ trisandhyaṃ tu jihvayāropya mārutamvibhedya
tridaśāhāraṃ dhārayettundamadhyame (50)
jvarāḥ sarva'pi naśyanti viṣāṇi vividhāni camuhūrtamapi yo
nityaṃ nāsāgre manasā sahasarvaṃ tarati pāpmānaṃ tasya
janmaśatārjitam (51)

Vocabulary

samākṛṣya: having inhaled; *bāhyāt*: from outside; *pūrayitvā*: having filled; *sthitam udare*: place in the stomach; *dhārayet*: one should hold; *manasā*: with the mind; *nābhi-madhye*: in the centre of the navel; *ca nāsāgre*: and at the nosetip; *ca yatnataḥ*: and with great effort; *pādāṅguṣṭhe*: at the toes; *sandhyā-kāleṣu*: at the times of sunrise and sunset; *vā sadā*: or at all times; *yogī bhavet*: yogin becomes; *gataklamaḥ*: refreshed; *vinirmuktaḥ*: freed from; *sarva roga*: all disease; *nāsāgre*: at the nosetip; *vāyu bhavati vijayam*: vital air is mastered; *nābhi-madhye*: at the centre of the navel; *sarva-roga-vināśaḥ*: all diseases are destroyed; *dhāraṇat*: by holding; *pādāṅguṣṭha*: at the toes; *śarīra*: body; *bhavati*: becomes; *laghutā*: light; *naraḥ yaḥ*: the person who; *satatam pibet*: always drinks; *vāyum ākṛṣya*: air inhaled; *rasanāt*:

through the tongue; *na syātām*: does not have; *śrama-dāhau*: fatigue and fever; *tathā yaḥ*: then he who; *ākṛṣya vāyum*: having inhaled the air; *pibet*: drinks; *vyādhayaḥ*: mouth open; *sandhya-yoḥ*: at dawn and dusk; *brāhmaṇaḥ kāle*: at the time of Brahma; *tri-māsāt*: within three months; *tasya vāk*: his speech; *jāyate*: is born from; *kalyāṇī sarasvatī*: auspicious Sarasvatī; *evam*: thus; *ṣaṇ-māsa-abhyāsat*: after six months' practice; *sarva-roga-ni-vṛttiḥ*: all disease has disappeared; *vāyum-ānīya*: having brought in the air; *jihvayā*: through the tongue; *nirodhayet*: he should retain; *jihvā-mūle*: at the root of the tongue; *vidvānyaḥ pibet*: wise one who drinks; *amṛtam*: nectar; *aśnute*: gains; *sakalam bhadram*: every benefit;

dhārayitvā: holding; *ātmānam ātmani*: ātman in the ātman; *bhruvaḥ antare*: at the eyebrow centre; *iḍayā*: through iḍā; *vibhedya*: having pierced; *tridaśāhāram*: thirty times; *api*: even; *vyādisthaḥ*: very sick person; *vimucyate*: is freed; *yaḥ*: he who; *vāyum-āropya*: having inhaled the air; *nāḍībhyām*: through the nāḍīs; *vahet*: holds; *ghaṭika-ekam*: for twenty-four minutes; *nābhau*: in the navel; *pārśvayoḥ*: on both sides; *tundasya*: of the belly; *tu saḥ vimucyate*: then he is freed; *vyādhibhiḥ*: from disease; *jihvayā-āropya*: inhaling through the tongue; *māsam-ekam*: for one month; *trisandhyam*: three *sandhyas;* sunrise, noon, sunset; *vibhedya*: pierced; *tri-daśāhāram*: thirty times; *dhārayet*: he should hold; *mārutam*: vital air; *tunda-madhyame*: in the middle of the navel; *ca vividhāni viṣāṇi*: and several poisons; *api*: as well as; *sarva jvarāḥ*: all fevers; *naśyanti*: are destroyed; *yaḥ tarati*: whoever holds; *nityam*: regularly; *saha manasā*: together with the mind; *nāsāgre*: at the nosetip; *api muhūrtam*: even for a short time; *sarvam pāpmānam*: every wrongdoing; *arjitam*: committed; *tasya*: by him; *śata janma*: during one hundred births.

Translation

Having inhaled the prāṇa from outside [and] filled the place in the stomach [with it], one should hold [it] with the mind in the centre of the navel and at the nosetip and with great effort at the toes at the times of sunrise and sunset or at all times. The yogin becomes refreshed and freed from all disease. [With the prāṇa] at the nosetip, the vital air is mastered; at the centre of the navel, all diseases are destroyed. By holding [it] at the toes, the body becomes light. The person, who always drinks the air inhaled through the tongue, does not have fatigue and fever. Then, he who, having inhaled the air, drinks [it], mouth open, at dawn, dusk and at the time of Brahma, within three months his speech is born from the auspicious Sarasvatī. Thus after six months' practice, all disease has disappeared. Having brought in the air through the tongue, he should retain [it] at the root of the tongue. The wise one who drinks [this] nectar gains every benefit.

Holding the ātman in the ātman at the eyebrow centre, [having inhaled] through iḍā, [and] pierced it thirty times, even a very sick person is freed [from disease]. He who, having inhaled the air through the nāḍīs, holds it for twenty-four minutes in the navel [and] both sides of the belly, then he is freed from disease. Inhaling through the tongue for one month at sunrise, noon and sunset [and] pierced thirty times, he should hold the vital air in the middle of the navel, and several poisons as well as all fevers are destroyed. Whoever holds [the vital air] regularly together with the mind at the nosetip even for a short time, [destroys] every wrongdoing committed by him during one hundred births.

Commentary

Prāṇāyāma is a way of expanding the internal fields of prāṇa, and in this way many diseases can be cured which are caused by excess or deficiency of prāṇa. The best times to practise prāṇāyāma are before sunrise, at dawn, at noon, and at dusk. One should inhale slowly and deeply through both nostrils, drawing the breath downward into the abdomen until it is full. Holding the breath inside, one should concentrate on either the nose tip, the navel or the big toe.

By focusing the awareness at the nose tip, while holding the breath inside, one can control the prāṇa. The nose tip forms a bridge, connecting the three major nāḍīs, iḍā, piṅgalā and suṣumnā. Therefore, by concentrating at this point, while holding the breath inside, the prāṇas can be controlled. By focusing at the navel, all diseases disappear. The navel is related with manipura cakra, where the pranic storehouse is located. When the awareness is focused at this centre, the prāṇas expand and disease disappears. When the awareness is focused at the big toe, the body becomes very light, and is capable of moving easily and quickly, because the energy is held in the proximity of the feet. By drawing the breath in through the open mouth over the tongue, holding it at maṇipura cakra, the yogin is freed from over-heating and internal toxins produced by poor diet and indigestion. His speech is purified by the goddess of speech Sarasvatī.

Whoever concentrates with the prāṇa at the nosetip, thereby stimulating mūlādhāra cakra, enters into *turīya*, the fourth state of consciousness beyond the three states of waking, dreaming and sleeping, and the karma (results) of wrongdoings from previous lives are destroyed.

Verse 52a: Knowledge of All Worlds

तारसंयमात्सकलविषयज्ञानं भवति ।
नासाग्रे चित्तसंयमादिन्द्रलोकज्ञानम् ।
तदधश्चित्तसंयमादग्निलोकज्ञानम् ।
चक्षुषि चित्तसंयमात्सर्वलोकज्ञानम् ।
श्रोत्र चित्तस्य संयमाद्यमलोकज्ञानम् ।
तत्पार्श्वे संयमान्निरृति लोकज्ञानम् ।
पृष्ठभागे संयमाद्वरुणलोकज्ञानम् ।
वामकर्णे संयमाद्वायुलोकज्ञानम् ।
कण्ठे संयमात्सोमलोकज्ञानम् ।
वामचक्षुषि संयमाच्छिवलोकज्ञानम् ।
मूर्ध्नि संयमाद्ब्रह्मलोकज्ञानम् ।
पादाधोभागे संयमादतललोकज्ञानम् ।
पादे संयमाद्वितललोकज्ञानम्लोकज्ञानम् ।
पादसन्धौ संयमान्नितललोकज्ञानम् ।
जङ्घे संयमातसुतललोकज्ञानम् ।
जानौ संयमान्महातललोकज्ञानम् ।
ऊरौ चित्तसंयमाद्रसातललोकज्ञानम् ।
कटलौ चित्तसंयमात्तलातललोकज्ञानम् ।
नाभौ चित्तसंयमाद्भूलोकज्ञानम् ।
कुक्षौ संयमाद्भुवर्लोकज्ञानम् ।
हृदि चित्तस्य संयमात्स्वर्लोकज्ञानम् ।
हृदयोर्ध्वभागे चितसंयमान्महर्लोकज्ञानम् ।
कण्ठे चित्तसंयमाज्जनोलोकज्ञानम् ।

भ्रूमध्ये चित्तसंयमात्तपोलोकज्ञानम् ।
मूर्ध्नि चित्तसंयमात्सत्यलोकज्ञानम् ।५२।
tārasaṃyamātsakalaviṣayajñānaṃ bhavatināsāgre cittasaṃyamādindralokajñānamtadadhaścittasaṃyamād-agniloka jñānamcakṣuṣi cittasaṃyamātsarvalokajñānamśrotra cittasya saṃyamādyamalokajñānamtatpārśve saṃyamānnirṛtilokajñānampṛṣṭhabhāge saṃyamādvaruṇalokajñānamvāmakarṇe saṃyamādvāyulokajñānamkaṇṭhe saṃyamātsomalokajñānamvāmacakṣuṣi saṃyamācchivalokajñānammūrdhri saṃyamādbrahmalokajñānampādādhobhāge saṃyamādatalalokajñānampāde saṃyamādvitalalokajñānampādasandhau saṃyamānnitalalokajñānamjaṅghe saṃyamātsutalalokajñānamjānau saṃyamānmahātalalokajñānamūrau cittasaṃyamādrasātalalokajñānamkaṭau cittasaṃyamāttalātalalokajñānamnābhau cittasaṃyamādbhrūlokajñānamkukṣau saṃyamādbhruvarlokajñānamhṛdi cittasya saṃyamātsvarlokajñānamhṛdayordhvabhāge cittasaṃyamānmaharlokajñānamkaṇṭhe cittasaṃyamājjanolokajñānambhrūmadhye cittasaṃyamāttapolokajñānammūrdhri cittasaṃyamātsatyalokajñānam (52a)

Vocabulary

tāra-saṃyamāt: through concentration on Tāra; *jñānam bhavati*: one gains knowledge of; *sakala-viṣaya*: all subjects; *citta-saṃyamāt*: by holding the mind; *nāsāgre*: at the nosetip; *indra-loka-jñānam*: knowledge of the Indra world; *tat-adhaḥ*: below that; *cakṣuṣi*: in the eye; *śrotra*: in the ear; *tat-pārśve*: at the back of it; *vāma-karṇe*: in the left ear; *kaṇṭhe*: in the throat; *vāma-cakṣuṣi*: in the left eye; *mūrdhri*: in the head;

pāda-adhaḥ-bhāge: in the soles of the feet; *pāde*: in the feet; *pādasandhau*: in the ankles; *jaṅghe*: in the calves; *jānau*: in the knees; *ūrau*: in the thighs; *kaṭau*: in the loins; *nābhau*: in the navel; *kukṣau*: in the belly; *hṛdi*: in the heart; *hṛdaya-ūrdhva-bhāge*: in the place above the heart; *kaṇṭhe*: in the throat; *bhrūmadhye*: in the eyebrow centre; *mūrdhri*: in the head.

Translation

Through concentration on Tāra, one gains knowledge of all subjects. By holding the mind at the nosetip, one gains knowledge of the Indra world. By holding the mind below that, one gains knowledge of the Agni world. By holding the mind in the eye, one gains knowledge of all worlds; in the ear, knowledge of the Yama world; beside it, knowledge of the Nirṛti world; at the back [of the ear], knowledge of the Varuṇa world; in the left ear, knowledge of the Vāyu world; in the throat, knowledge of the Soma world; in the left eye, knowledge of the Śiva world; in the head, knowledge of the Brahma world; in the soles of the feet, knowledge of the Atala world; in the feet, knowledge of the Vitala world; in the ankles, knowledge of the Nitala world; in the calves, knowledge of the Sutala world; in the knees, knowledge of the Mahātala world; in the thighs, knowledge of the Rasātala world; in the loins, knowledge of the Talātala world; in the navel, knowledge of Bhūrloka; in the belly, knowledge of Bhruvarloka; in the heart, knowledge of the Suvar world; in the place above the heart, knowledge of the Mahar world; in the throat, knowledge of the Jana world; in the eyebrow centre knowledge of the Tapa world; in the head, knowledge of the Satya world.

Commentary

By concentration on Tāra, the Self in the form of light, one can gain knowledge of and insight into all worlds, which are states of being or consciousness.

There are the worlds of the deities and elements. The Indra world is heaven or pure consciousness. The Agni world is that of fire and sacrifice. 'By holding the mind in the eye' refers to *jñāna-cakṣus*, the inner eye through which the transcendental Self can be seen. The Varuṇa world is water, in particular the ocean. The Vāyu world is the wind or air. Soma governs rejuvenation and immortality. Śiva is cosmic consciousness, causing transformation. Brahma is the Creator, whose world is the realm of Īśvara, the highest level of cosmic existence.

The Atharva Veda lists seven higher worlds (*vyāhṛti*) and seven lower worlds *(pātāla*).

These are the seven higher planes of existence or states of consciousness. The verse says that knowledge of the *bhūrloka*, or earth plane, is at the navel, although it is usuallysaid to be at the base of the spine at *mūlādhāra cakra*. It is the first level of experience. From here the awareness becomes more and more subtle as one moves up through the *lokas*. *Bhūvarloka*, the intermediary or spacial plane, is in the pelvic area at *svādhiṣ-ṭhāna cakra*. *Suvarloka* is said to be in the heart, althoughusually it is said to be at *maṇipura cakra*. *Mahāloka* is in the heart at *anāhata cakra*. *Janoloka* is at the throat at *viśuddhi cakra*. *Tapoloka* is at the eyebrow centre at *ājña cakra*. And *Satyaloka*, the plane of absolute truth, is in the head at *sahasrāra cakra.*

Yama is the world of death. Nirṛti is at the lowest depths of the earth. Atala, Vitala, Nitala, Sutala, Rasātala and Talātala all represent regions in the lower planes of existence (pātāla) below mūlādhāra cakra.

In this body . . . there are seers and sages; all the stars and planets as well.

The Sun and Moon, agents of creation and destruction, also move in it. Ether, Air, Fire, Water and Earth are there also.
Shiva Samhita 21

Verse 52b: Saṃyama

धर्माधर्मसंयमादतीतानागतज्ञानम् ।तत्तज्जन्तुध्वनौ
चित्तसंयमात्सर्वजन्तुरुतज्ञानम् ।संचितकर्मणि
चित्तसंयमात्पूर्वजातिज्ञानम् ।परचित्ते चित्तसंयमात्परचित्तज्ञानम्
।कायरूपे चित्तसंयमादन्यादृश्यरूपम् ।
बले चित्तसंयमाद्धनुमादिबलम् ।
सूर्ये चित्तसंयमाद्भुवनज्ञानम्।चन्द्रे चित्तसंयमात्ताराव्यूहज्ञानम् ।
ध्रुवे तद्गतिदर्शनम् । स्वार्थसंयमात्पुरुषज्ञानम् ।
नाभिचक्रे कायव्यूहज्ञानम् ।कण्ठकूपे क्षुत्पिपासानिवृत्तिः ।
कूर्मनाड्यां स्थैर्यम् । तारे सिद्धदर्शनम् ।
कायाकाशसंयमादाकाशगमनम् ।
तत्तत्स्थाने संयमात्तत्त्सिद्धयो भवति ।।५२ ।।

dharmādharmasaṃyamādatītānāgatajñānamtattajjantu-dhvanau cittasaṃyamātsarvajanturutajñānamsaṃcitakarmaṇi cittasaṃyamātpūrvajātijñanamparacitte cittasaṃyamātparacittajñānamkāyarūpe cittasaṃyamādanyādṛśyarūpambale cittasaṃyamāddhanumādibalamsūrye cittasaṃyamādbhuvanajñānamcandre cittasaṃyamāttārāvyūhajñānamdhruve tadgatidarśanamsvārthasaṃyamātpuruṣajñānamnābhicakre kāyavyūhajñānamkaṇṭhakūpe kṣutpipāsānivṛttiḥkūrma-nāḍyāṃ sthairyamtāre siddhadarśanamkāyākāśasaṃyamādākāśagamanamtattat-sthāne saṃyamāttattatsiddhayo bhavati (52b)

Vocabulary

saṃyamāt: through constraint on; *dharma-adharma*: what is right and wrong; *jñānam*: one knows; *atīta-anāgata*: past and future; *citta-saṃyamāt*: by constraining the mind; *dhvanau*: on the sound; *tat-tat-jantu*: this and that creature; *jñānam*: ne can know; *ruta*: cry; *sarva-jantu*: all creatures; *citta-saṃyamāt*: by constraining the mind; *saṃcita-karmaṇi*: on past karmas; *jñānam*: one has knowledge of; *pūrva-jāti*: previous births; *citta-saṃyamāt*: by constraining; *para-citte*: on the mind of another; *jñānam*: one can know; *para-citta*: thoughts of others; *citta-saṃyamāt*: by constraining; *kāya-rūpe*: on the form of the body; *rūpam*: form; *anyāḥ*: others; *dṛśya*: can be seen; *bale*: on strength; *balam*: strength; *hanumā-ādi*: Hanumān and others; *sūrye*: on the sun; *jñānam*: one can know; *bhuvana*: cosmos; *candre*: on the moon; *tārā-vyūha*: formation of the fixed stars; *dhruve*: on the pole star; *darśanam*: one has insight; *tat-gati*: its movement; *sva-artha*: one's own Self; *puruṣa-jñānam*: knowledge of pure consciousness; *nābhi-cakre*: at the cakra at the navel; *kāya-vyūha*: group of bodies; *kaṇṭha-kūpe*: at the well of the throat; *nivṛttiḥ*: freedom from; *kṣut-pipāsā*: hunger and thirst; *sthairyam*: steadiness; *tāre*: in the pupil of the eye; *darśanam*: sight; *siddha*: perfected ones; *kāya-ākāśa*: *ākāśa* in the body; *ākāśa-gamanam*: one moves in the ākāśa; *tat*: thus; *yaḥ*: whoever; *saṃyamāt*: with constraint; *tat sthāne*: in any place; *bhavati*: becomes; *siddha*: seer.

Translation

By constraint on what is right and wrong, one knows the past and future. By holding the mind on the sound of this and that creature, one can know the cry of all creatures. By constraint on the mind on past karmas, one has knowledge previous births. By constraint on the mind of another, one can know the thoughts of others. By constraint on the form of the body, the form [of] other [objects] can be seen. By constraint on strength, the strength of Hanumān and others [can be attained]. By constraint on the sun, one can know the cosmos. By constraint on the moon, one can know the formation of the fixed stars. [By constraint on] the pole star, one has insight into its movement. By constraint on one's own Self, [one gains] knowledge of pure consciousness; at the cakra at the navel, [one gains] knowledge [of oneself as] a group of bodies; at the well of the throat, freedom from hunger and thirst; in the *kūrma nāḍī* [in the well of the throat], steadiness [of concentration]; in the pupil of the eye, the sight [of] the perfected ones. By constraint on the ākāśa in the body, one moves in the ākāśa. Thus, whoever [can practise] constraint in any place, becomes a seer.

Commentary

Saṃyama is constraint, one-pointed deep concentration. *Trayamekatra saṃyama* is the process of merging the last three stages of the eightfold path, so that they become one. They are *dhāraṇā* (concentration, deepening of mental awareness), *dhyāna* (meditative state) and *samādhi* (union with pure consciousness), *traya* meaning 'three', *eka* 'one' and *tra* 'to-gether'. Through this process the yogin can perceive the inner cause of the object of concentration. This concept is the subject of *Vibhūti-Pāda*, Chapter 3 of Patañjali's *Yoga-Sūtra*.

The Śiva-Sūtra of Vasugupta also stresses the importance of saṃyama. Georg Feuerstein's translation of verse 3.44 says: 'Through constraint *(saṃyama)* [i.e. through ecstatic identification with] the innermost centre of the nose, how [can the ultimate Reality not be realised] in the left, the right,and the central [channels of the life force]?' His interpretation of the verse is that the 'innermost centre of the nose' is the core of the life force or consciousness, and by practising saṃyama on that point, the yogin can realise the ultimate Reality irrespective of which nāḍī the prāṇa isflowing through. 22

The verse gives examples of the results of saṃyama. Once one can distinguish between right and wrong, one can understand the past and predict the future. By constraint on the cry of a living being, one can perceive the cause of all sounds as they move in ākāśa. Similarly, by constraint on another's mind, body and qualities such as strength, one can perceive their cause. By constraint on a heavenly body such as the sun, moon and pole star, one can understand the cosmos, and the cause of its cosmic bodies, their stillness or movements. By concentrating on maṇipura, the centre of dynamism, sending prāṇa throughout the whole body, one can perceive oneself as part of *mahā prāṇa*, the great cosmic energy which contains and gives life to all bodies. Through constraint on *viśuddhi* in the throat, the nectar from *bindu* does not drop down to maṇipura, but remains there at viśuddhi, nourishing the body. When *kūrma nāḍī* is awakened, the yogin is no longer distracted by the need or desire for food and drink. Byconstraint on the third eye, ājña cakra, one can hear, see and receive guidance from realised beings. By constraint on ākāśa one's intuition is highly developed. Therefore by constraint the yogin becomes a seer and a sage.

Eighth Section

Verses 1 and 2: Pratyāhāraḥ

अथ प्रत्याहारः । स पञ्चविधः विषयेषु विचरतामिन्द्रियाणां
बलादाहरणं प्रत्याहारः ।
यद्यत्पश्यति तत्सर्वमात्मेति प्रत्याहारः ।
नित्यविहितकर्मफलत्यागः प्रत्याहारः ।
सर्वविषयपराङ्मुखत्वं प्रत्याहारः ।
अष्टादशसु मर्मस्थानेषु क्रमाद्धारणं प्रत्याहारः ।।१।।
पादाङ्गुष्ठगुल्फजङ्घाजानूरुपायुमेढ्रनाभिहृदयकण्ठ-
कूपतालुनासाक्षिभ्रूमध्यललाटमूर्ध्नि स्थानानि ।
तेषु क्रमादारोहावरोहक्रमेण प्रत्याहरेत् ।।२।।

atha pratyāhāraḥsa pañcavidhaḥ viṣayeṣu vicaratām-indriyāṇāṃ balādāharaṇaṃ pratyāhāraḥyadyatpaśyati tatsarvamātmeti pratyāhāraḥnityavihitakarmaphalatyāgaḥ pratyāhāraḥsarvaviṣayaparāṅmukhatvaṃ pratyāhāraḥ-aṣṭādaśasu marmasthāneṣu kramāddhāraṇaṃ pratyāhāraḥ (1)
pādāṅguṣṭhagulphajaṅghājānūrupāyumeḍhranābhihṛdaya-kaṇṭhakūpatālunāsākṣibhrūmadhyalalāṭamūrdhri sthānāniteṣu kramādārohāvarohakrameṇa pratyāharet (2)

Vocabulary

atha: now; *sa pañcavidhaḥ*: it [is] of five kinds; *āharaṇam*: withdrawal; *balāt*: from the power; *indriyāṇām*: of the sense organs; *vicara*: moving; *viṣayeṣu*: in the objects of the senses; *tyāgaḥ*: renouncing; *phala*: fruits; *karma*: actions; *vihita*: performed; *nitya*: daily; *mukhatvam*: turning away from; *sarva-viṣaya*: all sense objects; *parāk*: of the outer world; *dhāraṇam*: concentration; *aṣṭādaśasu marma-sthāneṣu*: on eighteen parts of the body; *kramāt*: in the [following] order; *pāda*: feet; *aṅ-guṣṭha*: big toes; *gulpha*: ankles; *jaṅghā*: calves; *jānu*: knees;

ūru: thighs; *pāyu*: anus; *meḍhra*: penis; *nābhi*: navel; *hṛdaya*: heart; *kaṇṭha-kūpa*: well of the throat; *tālu*: palate; *nāsā*: nose; *akṣi*: eyes; *bhrū-madhya*: eyebrow centre; *lalāṭa*: forehead; *mūrdhri*: head; *sthānāni*: locations; *pratyāharet*: one should withdraw; *teṣu*: from these; *kramāt*: gradually; *āroha-avaroha-krameṇa*: in ascending and descending order.

Translation

Now *pratyāhāra*: it [is] of five kinds. Pratyāhāra [is] the withdrawal [of the mind] from the power of the sense organs moving in the objects of the senses.Whatever ones sees is all ātman: this is pratyāhāra. Renouncing the fruits of actions performed daily [is] pratyāhāra. Turning away from all sense objects of the outer world [is] pratyāhāra. Concentration on eighteen parts of the body in the [following] order [is] pratyāhāra. The feet, big toes, ankles, calves, knees, thighs, anus, penis, navel, heart, well of the throat, palate, nose, eyes, eyebrow centre, forehead and head [are their] locations. One should withdraw from these gradually, in ascending and descending order.

Commentary

Here begins the description of the inner path of meditation. In the path of *aṣṭāṅga yoga*, the eightfold yoga, the first four limbs are known as *bahiraṅga*, or outer branches.The last four are called *antaraṅga*, the inner branches. *Pratyāhāra* is the fifth limb of aṣṭāṅga yoga, and the first limb on the inner path, which leads to the following levels of *dhāraṇā*, one-pointed concentration, *dhyāna*, spontaneous meditation, and finally *samādhi*, transcendental consciousness.

Pratyāhāra is often defined as 'withdrawal of the senses'. This verse expands that definition, by stating that it is withdrawal of the mind from the sense organs and from the senses, for example, not paying attention to the eyes and therefore not seeing. The mind cannot be still and clear, as long as there is sensory input. When pratyāhāra has been mastered, the ātman, the inner Self, is clearly visible in everything. Renouncing the fruits of one's actions is *karma yoga*, which, the verse says, is pratyāhāra, because a a *karma yogi*, knowing that there is a higher force operating, acts with meditative awareness, and not ego gratification.

The five sense organs, eyes, ears, tongue, skin, and nose, are naturally attracted to those objects which can be seen, heard, tasted, touched and smelled. Through the practice of yama, niyama, āsana and prāṇāyāma, the practitioner gradually learns to direct the awareness back towards his or her own behaviour, discipline, bodily postures and breath. In this way, one prepares for the stage of pratyāhāra. By withdrawal of the senses from the external world, the inner journey towards the true Self can unfold.

Yoga Nidra is the practice of inducing a state of deep relaxation, where the body sleeps while the mind remains awake and aware. The practice includes awareness of the body and rotation of the mind through the various parts of the body withdrawing the senses from the external world.

When the stage of pratyāhāra has been mastered through regular meditative practice, this inner awareness can also be experienced, even while carrying out one's daily activities in the world. Once the practitioner is fully established in the state of sensory withdrawal, then, whatever actions one does throughout one's life, all can be done with full awareness of Brahma, the causal dimension or mind.

Ninth Section

Verse 1: Dhāraṇā

अथ धाराणा ।

सा त्रिविधा आत्मनि मनोधारणं दहराकाशे

बाह्याकाशधारणंपृथिव्यप्तेजोवाय्वाकाशेषु पञ्चमूर्तिधारनं

चेति ॥१॥

atha dhāraṇāsā trividhā ātmani manodhāraṇaṃ daharākāśe bāhyākāśadhāraṇaṃ pṛthivyaptejovāyvākāśeṣu pañcamūrtidhāraṇaṃ ceti (1)

Vocabulary

atha: now; *sā trividhāḥ*: it [is] of three kinds; *iti*: thus; *manaḥ-dhāraṇam*: holding the mind; *ātmani*: in the ātman; *dhāraṇam*: contemplating; *bāhya-ākāśa*: external ākāśa; *dahara-ākāśe*: in the small ākāśa; *ca*: and; *dhāraṇam*: concentrating on; *pañca-mūrti*: five forms; *pṛthivi-ap-tejaḥ-vāyu-ākāśeṣu*: in the earth, water, fire, air [and] ether.

Translation

Now *dhāraṇā*: it [is] of three kinds: thus, holding the mind in the *ātman*, contemplating the external *ākāśa* in the small ākāśa, and concentrating on the five forms [of the elements]: earth, water, fire, air and ether.

Commentary

Holding the mind in the *ātman* is concentration on the inner Self, the praṇava AUM and eternal Light.Concentration on the elements is also a way to connect with the basic elemental energies within oneself and in all beings of creation. The five elements are: ether, air, fire, water, and earth.

Practice: Concentration on the five elements

Sit quietly in a steady meditative posture and close the eyes.

Relax the whole body systematically, from head to toe. Develop the feeling of stillness within. Become aware of the natural rhythm of the breath. Focus the awareness at the nose-tip, and feel each inhalation and exhalation flowing in and out through the nostrils.

Now, leave the awareness of the breath and become aware of the element of space or ether, which surrounds you in all directions. Space is all pervasive. Feel that your entire body is also pervaded by space. The quality of space is stillness. See space wherever you look; inside of you and outside of you, there is nothing but space. Everything in creation exists in this same space. Draw your awareness deep within and focus on the space contained at the centre, or core, of your being.

Allow this perception of space to fade, and become aware of the element of air. While space is all pervasive and still, air is a gaseous substance in constant movement. Air moves all through the space and fills it with kinetic energy, like the movement of the wind or prāṇa. We can feel the movement of air on our skin and in the flow of our breath. Air is the breath of life and it travels all through us, enlivening every cell, organ and part. Our whole body breathes in the air from the atmosphere, and expels the air, which has been utilised by the cellular structures, from moment to moment. Focus on the element of air.

The movement of air produces friction, and heat or fire is produced. Fire has two qualities, heat and light. Become aware of the fire burning in your belly. Fire is a dynamic force, which has form and is visible. The heat produced by fire is responsible for the digestive and metabolic processes. The light enables us to see and thus to differentiate myself from another. Become aware of the fire burning within you.

When the heat of fire cools, water is produced. Water has the quality of fluidity and movement. Our bodies are more than 75% water, and the water is in constant flow and movement. Fluids are continually flowing to and from every cell, organ and part. Focus on the element of water, below the navel, in the pelvic region.

When water ceases its movement, it becomes still and solidifies into earth. Become aware of the earth element, which is dense, heavy and unmoving. Feel the quality of earth within you and around you. Feel the weight of the body, the bones, the muscle, the skin, the hair, the teeth, the nails. The body is supported by earth, nourished by earth, walks upon earth. Focus on the earth element at the pelvic floor. Feel the connection between the pelvic floor and the earth beneath you. 23

Tenth Section

Verse 1: Dhyānam

अथ ध्यानम् ।

तद्द्विविधं सगुणं निर्गुणं चेति ।सगुणं मूर्तिध्यानम् ।

निर्गुणमात्मयाथात्म्यम् ॥१॥

atha dhyānamtaddvividhaṃ saguṇaṃ nirguṇaṃ cetisaguṇaṃ mūrtidhyānam; nirguṇamātmayāthātmyam (1)

Vocabulary

atha: now; *iti*: so; *tad-dvividham*: this [is] of two kinds; *mūrti -dhyānam*: meditation on a form; *yathā*: whereas; *ātma ātmī-yam*: one's own Self.

Translation

Now *dhyānam*: so this [is] of two kinds, *saguṇa* and *nirguṇa*. Saguṇa [is] meditation on a form, whereas nirguṇa [is medita-tion on] one's own Self.

Commentary

Dhyāna is the third limb of *antaraṅga* in rāja yoga. *Pratyā-hāra* and *dhāraṇā*, the first and second limbs, require regular and vigilant practice. In pratyāhāra, the awareness is focused within the conscious and subconscious mind on the immediate and latent mental impressions and patterns. In dhāraṇā, the awareness is focused on one object or ideal within the conscious and subconscious mind, but there are breaks. The mind wanders and the practitioner brings it back again and again to the object of focus. In dhyāna, the awareness flows smoothly and steadily towards the object or ideal in the deep levels of the subconscious mind, without a break. From the stage of dhyāna onward, meditation takes place spontaneously and effortlessly.

Saguṇa dhyāna is meditation with form. 'Form' here means the pure qualities which are beyond the mind. In the state of saguṇa an awareness of the pure qualities is developed, which are beyond the qualities of nature, the *guṇas*, of *tamas*, *rajas* and *sattwa*. These are observed and reflected on in the stages of pratyāhāra and dhāraṇā, where one becomes aware of how they affect our personality, character and behaviour in daily life. Saguṇa dhyāna is meditation on a form which is beyond tamas, rajas and sattwa. *Brahma* is that form, the light, present in the three guṇas. 'Brahma is divine harmony. In this state the absolute truth, which is the remedy for all delusions, relating with time, space and object, is known. The yogi who becomes established in dhyāna has the direct experience of the supreme Brahma, the Lord of creation, and is no longer affected by the illusory appearances and experiences of the external world.' 24

Nirguṇa dhyāna is meditation without guṇas or qualities. The guṇas merge and fuse into one light, the eternal flame of spirit, *caitanya jyoti*.

Eleventh Section

Verse 1: Samādhiḥ

अथ समाधिः ।

जीवात्मपरमात्मैक्यावस्था त्रिपुटारहितापरमानन्दस्वरूपा शुद्धचैतन्यात्मिका भवति ।।१।।

atha samādhiḥjīvātmaparamātmaikyāvasthā tripuṭārahitāparamānandasvarūpā śuddhacaitanyātmikā bhavati (1)

Vocabulary

atha: now; *aikya*: union; *jīvātma*: individual self; *param-ātma*: cosmic Self; *rahitā*: free from; *tripuṭā avasthā*: three-fold state; *bhavati*: it is; *param-ānanda-svarūpā*: nature of supreme bliss; *ātmikā*: based on; *śuddha-caitanya*: pure consciousness.

Translation

Now *samādhi* [is] the union of the individual self [with] the cosmic Self, free from the threefold state. It is [of] the nature of supreme bliss, based on pure consciousness.

Commentary

Samādhi is the transcendental state of consciousness, in which all barriers and limitations of the conscious, subconscious, and unconscious are removed, while the body remains. It is a state of mind where only pure consciousness or pure awareness remains. The well-known phrase *sat-cid-ānanda* (existence-con-sciousness-bliss), the three essential aspects of the Absolute (Brahman) according to Vedānta, means that after all the thoughts, emotions and experiences of the mind have been transcended, there remains the indescr-ibable unique bliss of pure consciousness.

Chapter Two

Verses 1 to 6: Knowledge of Brahman

अथ ह शाण्डिल्यो ह व वै ब्रह्मऋषिश्चतुर्षु वेदेषु
ब्रह्मविद्यामलभमानः किं नामेत्यथर्वणंभगवन्तमुपसन्नः
पप्रच्छाधीहि भगवन् ब्रह्मविद्यां येन श्रेयोऽवाप्स्यामिति ।।१।।
स होवाचाथर्वा शाण्डिल्य सत्यं विज्ञानमनन्तं ब्रह्मा ।।२।।
यस्मिन्निदमोतं च प्रोतं च ।यस्मिन्निदं सं च विचैति सर्वं
यस्मिन्विज्ञाते सर्वमिदं विज्ञातं भवति ।
तदपाणिपादमचक्षुःश्रोत्रमजिह्वमशरीरमग्राह्यमनिर्देश्यम् ।।३।।
यतो वाचो निवर्तन्ते अप्राप्य मनसा सह ।
यत्केवलं ज्ञानगम्यम् ।
प्रज्ञा च यस्मात्प्रसृता पुराणी ।यदेकमद्वितीयम् ।
आकाशवत्सर्वगतं सुसूक्ष्मं निरञ्जनं निष्क्रयं सन्मात्रं
चिदानन्दैकरसं शिवं प्रशान्तममृतं तत्परं च ब्रह्म ।तत्त्वमसि
तज्ज्ञानेन हि विजानीहि ।।४।।
य एको देव आत्मशक्तिप्रधानः सर्वज्ञः सर्वेश्वरः
सर्वभूतान्तरात्मासर्वभूताधिवासः सर्वभूतनिगूढो
भूतयोनिर्योगैकगम्यः ।
यश्च विश्वं सृजति विश्वं बिभर्ति विश्वं भुङ्क्ते स आत्मा ।
आत्मनि तं तं लोकं विजानिहि ।।५।।
मा शोचीरात्मविज्ञानी शोकस्यान्तं गमिष्यसि ।।६।।

atha ha śāṇḍilyo ha vai brahmarṣiścaturṣu vedeṣubrahmavidyāmalabhamānaḥ kiṃ nāmetyatharvaṇaṃbhagavantamupasannaḥ papracchādhīhi bhagavanbrahmavidyāṃ yena śreyo'vāpsyāmīti (1)

sa hovācātharvā śāṇḍilya satyaṃ vijñānamanantaṃ brahmā (2)
yasminnidamotaṃ ca protaṃ cayasminnidaṃ saṃ ca vicaiti sarvaṃ yasminvijñāte sarvamidaṃ vijñātaṃ bhavatitadapāṇipādamacakṣuḥśrotramajihvamaśarīram-agrāhyama-nirdeśyam (3)
yato vāco nivartante aprāpya manasā sahayatkevalaṃ jñānagamyam; prajñā ca yasmātprasṛtā purāṇīyadekamadvitīyamākāśavatsarvagataṃ susūkṣmaṃ nirañjanaṃ niṣkrayaṃ sanmātraṃ cidānandaikarasaṃ śivaṃ praśāntamamṛtaṃ tatparaṃ ca brahmatattvamasi tajjñānena hi vijānīhi (4)
ya eko deva ātmaśaktipradhānaḥ sarvajñaḥ sarveśvaraḥsarvabhūtāntarātmā sarvabhūtādhivāsaḥ sarvabhūtanigūḍhobhūtayoniryogaikagamyaḥyaśca viśvaṃ sṛjati viśvaṃ bibharti viśvaṃ bhuṅkte sa ātmāātmani taṃ taṃ lokaṃ vijānihi (5)
mā śocīrātmavijñānī śokasyāntaṃ gamiṣyasi (6)

Vocabulary

atha: now; *brahma-ṛṣiḥ śāṇḍilyaḥ*: Brahma-Ṛṣi Śāṇḍilya; *labha*: not obtaining; *brahma-vidyām*: knowledge of Brahman; *caturṣu vedeṣu*: in the four Vedas; *upasannaḥ*: respectfully; *papracchāt*: approached; *bhagavantam atharvaṇam*: Lord Atharvan; *īhi*: desire; *iti*: asked; *bhagavan*: o Lord; *yena*: by what means; *vāpsyāmi*: can I obtain; *brahma-vidyām*: knowledge of Brahman; *śreyaḥ*: supreme.

atharvā uvācā: Atharvan replied; *brahmā satyam*: Brahman [is] truth; *vijñānam-anantam*: wisdom and infinity; *yasmin*: in which; *idam*: all this; *otam*: woven; *ca protam*: and pervaded by; *ca yasmin*: and in which; *idam vicaiti*: all this is manifested; *ca yasmin sarvam*: and in which all; *vijñāte*: is known; *bhavati sarvam vijñātam*: is all understood; *tad*: it; *a-pāṇi-pādam*: without hands and feet; *a-cakṣuḥ-śrotram*: without eyes and ears; *ajihvam*: without tongue; *aśarīram*: without body; *agrāhyam-anirdeśyam*: unattainable and indescribable; *yataḥ*: since; *aprāpya*: cannot be reached; *vācaḥ*: speech; *saha manasā*: together with mind; *nivartante*: must turn back; *yat-kevalam*: this pure consciousness; *jñāna-gamyam*: is attainable through jñāna; *yasmāt*: from which; *purāṇī prajñā*: ancient wisdom; *prasṛtā*: came forth; *yad-ekam-advitīyam*: that which is one and non-dual; *sarva-gatam*: moves in every-thing; *ākāśavat*: within ākāśa; *susūkṣmam*: subtle; *nirañjanam*: without blemish; *niṣkrayam*: invaluable; *sanmātram*: true essence; *eka-rasam*: only delight; *cit-ānanda*: bliss of consciousness; *śivam*: auspicious; *praśāntam-amṛtam*: calm and immortal; *param*: supreme; *tat brahma*: that [is] Brahman; *tattvam asi*: that thou art; *tat vijāni*: that you realise; *jñānena*: through jñāna;

yaḥ ekaḥ devaḥ: he who [is] the one Divine Being; *pradhānaḥ*: cause; *ātma-śakti*: power of ātma; *sarvajñaḥ*: omniscient; *sarveśvaraḥ*: lord of all; *antara-ātmā*: inner Self; *sarva-bhūta*: all beings; *sarvabhūta-adhivāsaḥ*: who dwells in all beings; *sarvabhūta-nigūḍhaḥ*: hidden in all beings; *bhūta-yoniḥ*: source of [all] beings; *yoga-eka-gamyaḥ*: accessible only by yoga; *cayaḥ*: and who; *sṛjati*: creates; *viśvam*: universe; *bibharti*: maintains; *bhuṅkte*: consumes; *vijāni-hi*: know; *tam tam lokam*: all worlds; *ātmani*: in the ātman; *mā śocīra*: do not grieve; *ātma-vijñānī*: knower of the Self; *gamiṣyasi*: you will reach; *śokasya-antam*: end of sorrow.

Translation

Now the Brahma-Ṛṣi Śāṇḍilya, not obtaining the knowledge of Brahman in the four Vedas, respectfully approached the Lord Atharvan [and with this] desire asked: "O Lord, by what means can I obtain the knowledge of Brahman, [who is] supreme?"

Atharvan replied: "Śāṇḍilya, Brahman [is] truth, wisdom [and] infinity, in which all this is woven and pervaded by, and in which all this is manifested and in which all [that] is known is all understood. It [is] without hands and feet, without eyes and ears, without tongue, without body, [and is] unattainable and indescribable. Since [Brahman] cannot be reached, speech together with mind must turn back. This pure consciousness is attainable through *jñāna*, from which ancient wisdom came forth. That which is one and non-dual, moves in everything within ākāśa, [is] subtle, without blemish, invaluable, the true essence, [whose] only delight [is] the bliss of consciousness, auspicious; calm and immortal, supreme, that [is] Brahman. That thou art. That you realise through jñāna.

He who [is] the one Divine Being, the cause of the power of the ātman, the omniscient, the lord of all, the inner Self of all beings, who dwells in all beings, hidden in all beings, the source of [all] beings, accessible only by yoga, and who creates the universe, maintains the universe [and] consumes the universe - he is *Ātmā*. Know all worlds in the ātman. Do not grieve, knower of the Self. You will reach the end of sorrow."

Commentary

Śāṇḍilya has the title Brahma-Ṛṣi, meaning he is a sage who is a member of the priestly caste. He says that although he is well-versed in the four Vedas, he still does not have the experiential spiritual knowledge, *jñāna*, of Brahman. He asks the Lord Atharvan how can he obtain this knowledge.

Atharvan begins by defining Brahman, who is truth, wisdom and infinity, who is the pure ever-expanding totality of consciousness, everywhere and in everything. It does not have the physical attributes of body, hands, feet, eyes, ears and tongue, and therefore cannot be attained through the five senses and the mind. It can only be attained through the pathof jñāna, which leads to reunion with the inner knowledge of consciousness. It moves in everything within ākāśa, ether, the first and most subtle element of nature, which contains all the other elements, including the mind, and which has all the divine qualities.

Ātmā is *paramātmā*, the Supreme Self of the whole universe, of the individual as well as the cosmos. Atharvan says *tattvam asi* (that thou art), emphasising that the true nature of the individual soul is identical with the Supreme Spirit pervading the universe, and that once Śāṇḍilya realises this, he will attain the bliss of pure consciousness, beyond suffering.

Chapter Three

First Section

Verses 1 to 6: Creation of the Universe

अथ हैनं शाण्डिल्योऽथर्वणं पप्रच्छ यदेकमक्षरं निष्क्रियं शिवं सन्मात्रं परंब्रह्मतस्मात्कथमिदं विष्वं जायते कथं स्थीयते कथमस्मिल्लीयतेतन्मे संशयं छेत्तुमर्हसीति ।।१।।
स होवाचाथर्वा सत्यं शाण्डिल्य परब्रह्म निष्क्रियमक्षरमितिअथाप्यस्यारूपस्य ब्यह्मणस्त्रीणि रूपानि भवन्ति सकलं निष्कलं सकलनिष्कलं चेति ।।२-३।।
यत्सत्यं विज्ञानमानन्दं निष्क्रियं निरञ्जनं सर्वगतं सुसूक्ष्मंसर्वतोमुखमनिर्देश्यममृतमस्ति तदिदं निष्कलं रूपम ।।४।।
अथास्य या सहजास्त्यविद्या मूलप्रकृतिर्माया लोहितशुक्लकृष्णातया सहायवान् देवः कृष्णपिङ्गलो महेश्वर ईष्टे तदिदमस्य सकलं रूपम् ।।५।।
अथैष ज्ञानमयेन तपसा चीयमानोऽकामयत बहुस्यां प्रजायेयेतिअथैतस्मात्तप्यमानात्सत्यकामात्त्रीण्यक्षराण्या-जायन्ततिस्रो व्याहृतयस्त्रिपदा गायत्री त्रयो वेदास्त्रयो देवास्त्रयो वर्णास्त्रयोऽग्नयश्च जायन्तेयोऽसै देवो भगवान्सर्वैश्वर्यसंपन्नः सर्वव्यापी सर्वभूतानां हृदये संनिविष्टो मायावीमायया क्रीडति स ब्रह्मा स विष्णुः स रुद्रः स इन्द्रः स सर्वे देवाः सर्वाणि भूतानि स एव दक्षिणतः स एवाधस्तात्स एवोपरिष्टात्स एव सर्वम् अथास्य देवस्यात्मशक्तेरात्मक्रीडस्य भक्तानुकम्पिनो

दत्तात्रेयरूपा सुरूपातनूरवासा इन्दीवरदलप्रख्या
चतुर्बाहुरघोरापापकाशिनीतदिदमस्य सकलनिष्कलं रूपम् ॥६॥

atha hainaṃ śāṇḍilyo'rthavaṇaṃ papraccha yadekamakṣaraṃ niṣkriyaṃ śivaṃ sanmātraṃ paraṃbrahmatasmātkathamidaṃ viṣvaṃ jāyate kathaṃ sthīyate kathamasmillīyate tanme saṃśayaṃ chettumarhasīti (1)
sa hovācātharvā satyaṃ śāṇḍilya parabrahma niṣkriyam akṣaramiti athāpyasyārūpasya brahmaṇastrīṇi rūpāni bhavanti sakalaṃ niṣkalaṃ sakalaniṣkalaṃ ceti (2-3)
yatsatyaṃ vijñānamānandaṃ niṣkriyaṃ nirañjanaṃ sarva-gataṃ susūkṣmaṃ sarvatomukhamanirdeśyamamṛtam-astitadidaṃ niṣkalaṃ rūpam (4)
athāsya yā sahajāstyavidyā mūlaprakṛtirmāyā lohitaśukla-kṛṣṇā tayā sahāyavān devaḥ kṛṣṇapiṅgalo maheśvara īṣṭetadidamasya sakalaṃ rūpam (5)
athaiṣa jñānamayena tapasā cīyamāno'kāmayata bahusyāṃ prajāyayetiathaitasmāttapyamānātsatyakāmāttrīṇyakṣarāṇy ājāyantatisro vyāhṛtayastripadā gāyatrī trayo vedāstrayo devāstrayovarṇāstrayo'gnayaśca jāyanteyo'sai devo bhagavānsarvaiśvaryasaṃpannaḥ sarvavyāpīsarvabhūtānāṃ hṛdaye saṃniviṣṭo māyāvī māyayā krīdatisa brahmā sa viṣṇuḥ sa rudraḥ sa indraḥ sa sarve devāḥsarvāṇi bhūtāni sa eva purastātsa eva paścātsa evottarataḥsa eva dakṣiṇataḥ sa evādhastātsa evopariṣṭātsa eva sarvamathāsya devasyātmaśakterātmakrīḍasya bhaktānukampino-dattātreyarūpā surūpā tanūravāsā indīvaradalaprakhyācaturbāhuraghorāpāpakāśinītad-idamasya sakalaniṣkalaṃ rūpam (6)

Vocabulary

atha śāṇḍilyaḥ: then Śāṇḍilya; *papraccha*: asked; *arthavaṇam*: Arthavan; *tasmāt yad*: from him who; *ekam paraṃ brahma*: the one Supreme Brahman; *akṣaram*: imperishable; *niṣkriyam*: actionless; *śivam*: auspicious; *sanmātram*: true essence; *katham*: how; *idam viṣvam*: this universe; *jāyate*: did take place; *katham sthīyate*: how does it endure; *katham līyate*: how is it absorbed; *iti chettum*: please remove; *tat saṃśayam*: this doubt; *me*: for me; *arhasi*: o Noble One.

atharvā uvāca ha: Atharvan replied thus; *śāṇḍilya* o Śāṇḍilya; *parabrahma iti*: Supreme Brahman is; *satyam*: truth; *niṣkriya akṣaram*: imperishable and actionless; *atha brahmaṇaḥ*: then from Brahman; *āpyasya-arūpasya*: beyond form; *trīṇi rūpāni bhavanti*: three forms emerged; *sakalam*: with parts; *niṣkalam*: without parts; *ca sakala-niṣkalam*: and with and without parts; *yat asti*: that which is; *satyam*: true; *vijñānam-ānandam*: wise and blissful; *niṣkriyam*: without action; *nirañjanam*: without blemish; *sarvagatam*: omnipresent; *susūkṣmam*: subtle; *sarvataḥ-mukham*: with faces in every direction; *anirdeśyam-amṛtam*: undefinable and immortal; *tad-idam niṣkalam rūpam*: that [is] the form without parts; *yāḥ*: she who; *sahaja-asti*: ori-ginates; *asya*: from him; *avidyā*: *avidyā*, spiritual ignorance; *mūlaprakṛtiḥ-māyā*: source of nature and illusive power; *lohita-śukla-kṛṣṇā*: red, white and black; *īṣṭe*: is ruled by; *devaḥ maheśvaraḥ*: Divine Maheśvara; *kṛṣṇa-piṅgalaḥ*: black and yellow; *sahāyavān tayā*: accompanied by her; *tad-idam-asya*: this is his; *rūpam sakalam*: form with parts.

atha eṣa: then he; *jñānamayena*: by his divine wisdom; *cīya-mānaḥ tapasā*: by increase of willpower; *akāmayata*: without restraint of desire; *iti*: said; *prajāyeya*: let me bring forth; *bahusyām*: let me be many; *atha etasmāt ājāyanta*: then from him were born; *tapya-mānāt*: from the will of purity; *satya-kāmāt*: desire for truth; *trīṇi akṣarāṇi*: three letters; *tisraḥ vyāhṛtayaḥ*: three worlds; *trayaḥ gāyatrī*: three-footed Gāyatrī; *trayaḥ vedāḥ*: three vedas; *trayaḥ devāḥ*: three devas; *trayaḥ varṇāḥ*: three *varṇas*; *trayaḥ agnayaḥ*: three fires; *jāyante*: arose; *devaḥ bhagavān*: Divine Lord; *yaḥ saṃpannaḥ*: who is endowed with; *sarva-eśvarya*: all powers; *sarva-vyāpī*: all pervading; *saṃniviṣṭaḥ*: enveloped; *hṛdaye*:in the heart; *sarva-bhū-tānām*: of all beings; *māyāvī*: Lord of *māyā*; *krīḍati māyayā*: plays through *māyā*; *sa brahmā*: he is Brahmā; *sa viṣṇuḥ*: he is Viṣṇu; *sa rudraḥ*: he is Rudra; *sa indraḥ*: he is Indra; *sa sarve devāḥ*: he is all Divine Beings; *sarvāṇi bhūtāni*: all the elements; *sa purastāt*: he is in front; *sa paścāt*: he is behind; *sa uttarataḥ*: he is north; *sa dakṣiṇataḥ*: he is south; *sa adhastāt*: he is below; *sa upariṣṭāt*: he is above; *sa eva sarvam*: indeed he is all; *dattātreya-rūpā*: form of [him-self as] Dattātreya; *ātma-krīḍasya*: who amuses himself; *śakteḥ*: as Śakti; *bhakta-anukampinaḥ*: compassionate to his devotees; *surūpā*: wise; *tanūḥ-avāsā*: not abiding in the body; *indīvara-dala-prakhyā*: splendid as the petal of a blue lotus; *catuḥ-bāhuḥ*: with four arms; *aghora*: benign; *kāśinī*: shining; *apāpa*: purely; *tadidamasya*: this is his; *rūpam sakalaniṣkalam*: form with and without parts.

Translation
Then Śāṇḍilya asked Atharvan: "From him who is the one Supreme Brahman, imperishable, actionless, auspicious, the true essence, how did this universe take birth? How does it endure? How is it absorbed? Please remove this doubt for me, o Noble One."

Atharvan replied thus: "O Śāṇḍilya, the Supreme Brahman is truth, imperishable and actionless. Then, from Brahman, [who is] beyond form, three forms emerged, with parts, without parts and both with and without parts. That which is true, wise and blissful, without action, without blemish, omnipresent, subtle, with faces in every direction, undefinable and immortal, that [is] the form without parts. She who originates from Him [as] avidyā, the source of nature and the illusive power, [which is] red, white and black, is ruled by the Divine Maheśvara [who is] black and yellow, [and] accompanied by her. This is the form with parts.

Then He, by his divine wisdom, increase of willpower

without restraint of desire, said: 'let me bring forth, let me be many'. Then from Him were born, from the will of purity [and] desire for truth, the three letters. The three worlds, the three-footed Gāyatrī, the three Vedas, the three devas, the three varṇas and the three fires arose. The Divine Lord, who is endowed with all powers, all pervading, enveloped in the heart of all beings [and] the Lord of māyā, plays through māyā. He is Brahmā; Heis Viṣṇu; He is Rudra; He is Indra; He is all Divine Beings; [He is] all the elements; He is in front; He is behind; He is north; He is south; He is below; He is above; indeed He is all. The form of [himself as] Dattātreya, who amuses himself as Śakti, compassionate to his devotees, wise, not abiding in the body, splendid as the petal of a blue lotus, with four arms, benign [and] shining purely, this is his form with and without parts."

Commentary

Śāṇḍilya now asked Atharvan how did the formless Supreme Brahman create a universe of forms. Atharvan, once more describing the pure qualities of Brahman, answered thus.

"From Brahman came three types of form: with parts, without parts, and both with and without parts. The forms without parts have ten divine qualities, including 'faces in every direction' (meaning 'omniscient').

The forms with parts are the forms of nature. *Cūdāmani Upaniṣad* relates the colours red, white and black to the AUM mantra: 'The A sound form, which is rajasic and red, has been called the consciousness of Brahma. Similarly, the U sound form, which is sattwic and white, is called Viṣṇu. Like this, it has been said that the M sound form, which is tamasic and black, is called Rudra'.[25] 'She who originates from Him' refers to *prakṛti*, nature, (literally 'made from above'), who is in the state of *avidyā*, the form of *māyā*, the illusive power, which casts a veil over her original source. Maheśvara, the

Great Lord Śiva, who has the power of destruction or transformation, rules prakṛti.

Brahman, through the qualities of divine wisdom and willpower, was able to fulfil a desire to produce many forms. The first form was the praṇava AUM. According to the *Mandukya Upaniṣad*, A represents the waking state of consciousness, U the dreaming state and M the state of deep sleep. From AUM came the three *vyāhṛtis* of earth, sky and heaven; and the three-footed Gāyatrī, whose first foot consists of the totality of earth, sky, and heaven, whose second foot consists of the Ṛg Veda, the Yajur Veda, and the Sama Veda, and whose third foot consists of prāṇa, apāna and vyāna; and the three devas, the *Trimūrti* of Brahma, Viṣṇu and Maheśvara; and the three *varṇas* of Brahmana (priest), Kṣatriya (royal and warrior) and Vaiśya (trade); and the three fires of earth as fire, atmosphere as lightning, and sky as sun.

He is the source of all the gods, all divine beings, all the elements and is in all directions. He takes the form of Dattātreya, who plays in the world, in whom the Divine Light is visible, who has the body of a man, yet does not identify with this body. This is his form with and without parts.

Second Section

Verses 1 to 10: Names of Brahman

अथ हैनमथर्वाणं शाण्डिल्यः पप्रच्छ

भगवन्सन्मात्रं चिदानन्दैकरसं कस्मादुच्यते परं ब्रह्मेति ।

स होवाचाथर्वा यस्माच्च बृहति बृंहयति च सर्वं तस्मादुच्यते

परंब्रह्मेति ।।१-२।।

अथ कस्मादुच्यते आत्मेति ।यस्मात्सर्वमाप्नोति सर्वमादत्ते

सर्वमत्ति च तस्मादुच्यते आत्मेति ।।३-४।।

अथ कस्मादुच्यते महेश्वर इति ।

यस्मान्महत ईशः शब्दध्वन्या चात्मशक्त्या च महत ईशते

तस्मादुच्यते महेश्वर इति ।।५-६।।

अथ कस्मादुच्यते दत्तात्रेय इति ।

यस्मात्सुदुश्चरं तपस्तप्यमानायात्रये पुत्रकामायातितरां तुष्टेन

भगवता ज्योतिर्मयेनात्मैवदत्तो

यस्माच्चानसूयायामात्रेतनयोऽभवत्तस्मादुच्यते

दत्तात्रेय इति ।।७-८।।

अथ योऽस्य निरुकतानि देव स सर्वं देव ।अथ यो ह वै

विद्ययैनं परमुपास्ते साऽहमिति स ब्रह्मविद्भवति ।।९-१०।।

atha hainamatharvāṇaṃ śāṇḍilyaḥ papraccha bhagavansanmātraṃcidānandaikarasaṃ kasmāducyate paraṃ brahmetisa hovācātharvā yasmācca bṛhati bṛṃhayati ca sarvaṃtasmāducyate paraṃbrahmeti (1-2)
atha kasmāducyate ātmetiyasmātsarvamāpnoti sarvamādatte sarvamatti ca tasmāducyate ātmeti (3-4)
atha kasmāducyate maheśvara itiyasmānmahata īśaḥ śabdadhvanyā cātmaśaktyā camahata īśate tasmāducyate maheśvara iti (5-6)

atha kasmāducyate dattātreya itiyasmātsuduścaraṃ tapastapyamānāyātraye putrakāmāyātitarāṃtuṣṭena bhagavatā jyotirmayenātmaiva dattoyasmāccānasūyāyāmātretanayo'bhavattasmāducyate dattātreya iti (7-8)
atha yo'sya niruktāni deva sa sarvaṃ devaatha yo ha vai vidyayainaṃ paramupāste sā'hamiti sa brahmavidbhavati (9-10)

Vocabulary
atha śāṇḍilyaḥ: then Śāṇḍilya; *papraccha*: asked; *arthavaṇam*: Arthavan; *bhagavan*: o Lord; *sanmātram*: true essence; *eka-rasam*: only delight; *cit-ānanda*: bliss of consciousness; *kasmāt-ucyate*: why is he called; *paraṃ brahmā*: Supreme Brahman.

atharvā uvāca ha: Atharvan replied thus; *yasmāt*: because; *bṛṃhayati*: He expands; *bṛhati*: heaven and earth; *ca sarvam*: and everything; *tasmāt-ucyate*: therefore He is called; *paraṃ brahmā*: Supreme Brahman; *kasmāt-ucyate ātmā*: why is he called Ātmā; *yasmāt āpnoti sarvam*: because He obtains everything; *sarvam-ādatte*: receives everything; *ca sarvam-atti*: and consumes everything; *tasmāt-ucyate ātmā*: therefore He is called Ātmā; *atha kasmāt-ucyate maheśvaraḥ iti*: then why is He called Maheśvara?; *yasmāt śabda-dhvanyā*: because by the sound of the words; *mahata īśaḥ*: Mahata Īśaḥ (Great Lord); *ca-ātma-śaktyā*: and by his own power; *mahata īśate*: mahata rules; *tasmāt-ucyate maheśvaraḥ*: therefore He is called Maheśvara; *atha kasmāt-ucyate dattātreya iti*: then why is He called Dattātreya?; *dattaḥ bhagavatā ātmā*: was given by the Lord himself; *jyotirmayena*: through His Divine Light; *yasmāt*: because; *tuṣṭenaḥ*: pleased; *atraye*: with Atri; *tapya-mānāyā*: who had purified by performing; *suduścaram tapaḥ*: very arduous austerities; *putrakā-māyāt*: desirous of sons; *ca tanayuḥ*: and for the son; *abhavat*: to have; *anasūyāyā-mātre*: Anasūyā as his mother; *tasmāt-ucyate dattātreyaḥ*: therefore he is called Dattātreya; *atha yaḥ*: now whoever; *asya devaḥ niruktāni*: this divine explanation; *sarvam devaḥ*: everything divine; *atha yaḥ enam param-upāste*: now whoever is devoted to the Supreme; *vidyayā*: with the knowledge; *aham iti saḥ*: I am He; *bhavati*: becomes; *brahma-vid*: knower of Brahman.

Translation

Then Śāṇḍilya asked Atharvan: "O Lord, He [who is] the True Essence, [whose] only delight [is] the bliss of consciousness - why is He called the Supreme Brahman?"

Atharvan replied thus: "Because He expands heaven and earth and everything [in it], therefore He is called the Supreme Brahman. Why is He called Ātmā? Because He obtains everything, receives everything and consumes everything, therefore He is called Ātmā. Then why is He called Maheśvara? Because by the sound of the words Mahata Īśaḥ, and by His own power, Mahata rules [everything]. Therefore He is called Maheśvara. Then why is He called Dattātreya? [Dattātreya] was given by the Lord himself through His Divine Light because He was pleased with Atri who had purified [himself] by performing very arduous austerities [as he was] desirous of sons and for the son to have Anasūyā as his mother. Therefore he is called Dattātreya. Now whoever [understands] this divine explanation [understands] everything divine. Now whoever is devoted to the Supreme with the knowledge that 'I Am He', becomes a knower of Brahman.

Commentary

Śāṇḍilya asked Atharvan why is that which is the true essence of all and which delights in the bliss of pure consciousness has the name of Supreme Brahman.

The name Brahman comes from the verb *barh*, to increase, expand. He is the eternal origin who is the cause and foundation of all existence. Brahman is called Supreme, because He is the Highest, the Absolute Reality, encompassing and transcending all other realities. He is called Ātmā, the pure consciousness in everything, including humans where it transcends the identity with the mind and body. He is called Maheśvara (Mahā Īśvara), the Great Lord, because He is Mahata Īśaḥ, the Great Divine Ruler of the world, who is all powerful. He is called Dattātreya, ('given by three'), because he was born through the power of the Divine Light as well as through his physical father, Atri and physical mother, Anasūyā.

Whoever has total devotion to Brahman, knowing that he or she is beyond the ego personality, attains realisation of the Self.

Verses 11 to 15: Dattātreya

अत्रैते श्लोका भवन्ति ।दत्तात्रेयं शिवं शन्तमिन्द्रनीभं प्रभुम्
।आत्ममायारतं देवमवधूतं दिगम्बरम् ।।११।।
भस्मोद्धूलितसर्वाङ्गं जटाजूटधरं विभुम ।चतुर्बाहुमुदाराङ्गं
प्रफुल्लकमलेक्षणम् ।।१२।।
ज्ञानयोगनिधिं विश्वगुरुं योगिजनप्रियम् ।भक्तानुकम्पिनं
सर्वसाक्षिणं सिद्धसेवितम् ।।१३।।
एवं यः सततं ध्यायेद्देवदेवं सनातनम् ।स मुक्तः सर्वपापेभ्यो
निःश्रेयसमवाप्नुयात् ।।१४।।
इत्यों सत्यमत्युपनिषद् ।।१५।।

atraite ślokā bhavantidattātreyaṃ śivaṃ śantamindranīlanibhaṃ prabhumātmamāyāratam devamavadhūtaṃ digambaram (11)
bhasmoddhūlitasarvāṅgaṃ jaṭājūṭadharaṃ vibhumcaturbāhumudārāṅgaṃ praphullakamalekṣaṇam (12)
jñānayoganidhiṃ viśvaguruṃ yogijanapriyambhaktānukampinaṃ sarvasākṣiṇaṃ siddhasevitam (13)
evaṃ yaḥ satataṃ dhyāyeddevadevaṃ sanātanamsa muktaḥ sarvapāpebhyo niḥśreyasamavāpnuyāt (14)
ityoṃ satyamityupaniṣad (15)

Vocabulary

atra bhavanti: here are; *ete ślokāḥ*: these verses; *yaḥ satatam dhyāyet*: whoever always meditates on; *evam*: thus; *sanātanam devamdevam dattātreyam*: eternal Lord of Lords Dattā-treya; *śivam*: benevolent; *śantam*: peaceful; *prabhum indra*: mighty Lord; *nīla-nibham*: like a sapphire; *ātma-māyā-ratam*: delights in his own māyā; *devam-avadhūtam*: Lord [who has] shaken off; *digambaram*: naked; *sarva-aṇgam*: whole body; *bhasma-uddhūlita*: smeared with ash; *jaṭājūṭa-dharam*: having long twisted tresses; *vibhum*: all-pervading; *udāra-aṅgam*: lofty body; *catuḥ-bāhum*: four arms; *ikṣanam*: eyes; *praphulla-kamala*: lotus in full bloom; *jñāna-yoga-nidhim*: store of jñāna and yoga; *viśva-gurum*: guru of all worlds; *yogijana-priyam*: dear to yogins; *bhakta-anukampinam*: compassionate to his devotees; *sarva-sākṣiṇam*: witness of all; *siddha-sevitam*: served by siddhas; *muktaḥ*: is freed; *sarva-pāpebhyaḥ*: from all sins; *avāpnuyāt*: attains; *niḥśreyasam*: ultimate bliss; *om iti satyam*: om is truth; *iti upaniṣad*: this [ends] the upaniṣad.

Translation
Here are these verses:

'Whoever always meditates thus on the eternal Lord of Lords, Dattātreya, [who is] benevolent, peaceful, a mighty Lord [who is] like a sapphire, [who] delights in his own māyā, the Lord [who has] shaken off [everything], naked, [whose] whole body is smeared with ash, having long twisted tresses, all-pervading, [whose] lofty body [has] four arms, [and] eyes [like] the lotus in full bloom, [who is] the store of jñāna and yoga, the guru of all worlds, dear to yogins, compassionate to his devotees, the witness of all [and] served by siddhas, is freed from all sins [and] attains ultimate bliss.'

Om is Truth."

Commentary
The first verse of *Yoga Darśana Upaniṣad* describes Dattātreya thus: 'The great yogin, Dattātreya, [is] the blessed one [who] promotes the welfare of all living beings. The four-armed great Viṣṇu initiated [him] into the brilliance of yoga'.[26]

Dattātreya is regarded as an *avatāra*, or direct incarnation of the *Trimūrti*, combining all the divine qualities of *Brahma* (lord of creation), *Viṣṇu* (lord of sustenance), and *Śiva* (lord of dissolution) in one divine or supreme being. The name

Dattātreya is a combination of two words: *datta*, meaning 'that which is given' and *atreya*, referring to the rishi and seer Atri, who was his physical father. His mother was Anasūya, who had all the powers and knowledge of yoga, due to her flawless character and high morals.

These verses describe Dattātreya as the eternal Lord of Lords, who is benign, peaceful, compassionate and powerful, all divine qualities. He is like a sapphire, its blue symbolising celestial hope and faith, bringing protection and spiritual insight, and a symbol of power, compassion and wisdom. He loves to play in māyā, the material world, yet not attached to it, so goes about naked. His body is smeared with ash, indicating purity and renunciation. The flow of his long air represents vāyu or prāṇa. It is matted, representing restraint of desires. His four arms represent the four directions, and his eyes the beauty and wisdom of the lotus which grows in and above muddy water. He is the embodiment of jñāna and yoga, beloved by yogins, and is the guru of everyone in all places. He has attained the ultimate bliss of pure consciousness.

Dattātreya is still worshipped today in South India as a divine manifestation and many legends confirm his spiritual origin. Being a human vessel for the qualities of the three gods, Brahma, Viṣṇu and Śiva, he is said to be the blessed one, who promotes the welfare of all living beings.

This [ends] the Upaniṣad.

APPENDICES

A. Notes

1. Feuerstein, Georg and Kak, Subhash and Frawley, David *In Search of the Cradle of Civilization* (Quest Books, Illinois, USA 2001) p.20
2. *Bhagavad Gita* Srinivas Fine Arts Ltd (nightingale.co.in 2009) Ch.14. Verses 11-14
3. *Talks with Ramana Maharishi* (V.S. Ramanan, Sri Ramanasraman, 10th edition, Tiruvannamalai 2000)
4. Feuerstein, Georg *The Yoga Tradition* (Hohm Press, Prescott, Arizona, 2001) p.245
5. *ibidem* p.147
6. Swami Sivananda *Bliss Divine* (Divine Life Society 2004) p.2
7. *ibidem* p.4
8. Feuerstein, Georg *The Philosophy, History and Literature of Yoga* (Yoga Research and Education Center, Manton California USA 2003) p.635
9. Feuerstein, Georg *The Yoga Tradition* (Hohm Press, Prescott, Arizona USA 2001) p.245
10. *Bhagavad Gita* Srinivas Fine Arts Ltd (nightingale.co.in 2009) p.315
11. *ibidem* p.312
12. Feuerstein, Georg *The Philosophy, History and Literature of Yoga* (Yoga Research and Education Center, Manton California USA 2003) p.636
13. Feuerstein, Georg *The Philosophy, History and Literature of Yoga* (Yoga Research and Education Center, Manton California USA 2003) p.636
14. Swami Muktibodhananda Saraswati *Hatha Yoga Pradipika* (Bihar School of Yoga,Munger, Bihar, India 1998) Vs.113, p.387
15. Avalon, Arthur *The Serpent Power* (Dover Publications, New York, USA 1974) p.111
16. Feuerstein, Georg *The Encyclopedia of Yoga and Tantra* (Shambala Publications, Boulder, USA 2011) p.225
17. *ibidem* p.118 *dvādaśānta* (ending *'anta'* at the twelfth *'dvādaśa' [digit]):* 'an esoteric psychoenergetic centre (*cakra*) that, according to some schools of Shaiva Yoga, is said to be situated twelve digits above the head. It is commonly equated with the *sahasrāra cakra.'*

18. *ibidem* p.371 *tāraka*: world of light or 'wisdom born of discernment' (*viveka-ja-jñāna*)'
19. Avalon, Arthur *The Serpent Power* (Dover Publications, New York, USA 1974) p.9
20. Sri Aurobindo *Vedic Symbolism* (Lotus Press, Twin Lakes, Wisconsin 1992) p.90
21. Levacy, William *Vedic Astrology Simply Put* (Hay House, Carlsbad, California USA 2007) p.14
22. Feuerstein, Georg *The Yoga Tradition* (Hohm Press, Prescott, Arizona USA 2001) p.275
23. Swami Satyadharma Saraswati *Yoga Darshana Upanishad* (2018) pp.206-207 (translated by Ruth Perini)
24. *ibidem* pp.214-215
25. Swami Satyadharma Saraswati *Yoga Chudamani Upanishad* (Yoga Publications Trust, Munger Bihar, India 2003) pp.188-190
26. Swami Satyadharma Saraswati *Yoga Darshana Upanishad* (2018) Vs. 1, p.19 (translated by Ruth Perini)

B. References

Aiyar, N.K. *Thirty Minor Upanishads* (Parimal Publications, Delhi, India 2009)

Avalon, Arthur *The Serpent Power* (Dover Publications, New York, USA 1974)

Bhagavad Gita Srinivas Fine Arts Ltd (nightingale.co.in 2009)

Feuerstein, Georg and Kak, Subhash and Frawley, David. *In Search of the Cradle of Civilization* (Quest Books, Illinois USA 2001)

Feuerstein, Georg *The Encyclopedia of Yoga and Tantra* (Shambala Publications, Boulder, Colorado USA 2011)

Feuerstein, Georg *The Philosophy, History and Literature of Yoga* (Yoga Research and Education Center, Manton, California USA 2003)

Feuerstein, Georg *The Yoga-Sūtra of Patañjali* (Inner Traditions International, Rochester Vermont USA 1989

Feuerstein, Georg. *The Yoga Tradition* (Hohm Press, Prescott, Arizona USA 2001

Frawley, David. *Gods, Sages and Kings* (Passage Press, Salt Lake City, Utah USA 1991)

Swami Satyadharma Saraswati *Yoga Chudamani Upanishad* (Yoga Publications Trust, Munger, Bihar, India 2003)

Swami Satyadharma Saraswati *Yoga Darshana Upanishad* (2018)

Swami Muktibodhananda Saraswati *Hatha Yoga Pradipika* (Bihar School of Yoga, Munger, Bihar, India 1998)

Swami Satyananda Saraswati *Asana Pranayama Mudra Bandha* (Bihar Yoga Bharati, Munger, Bihar, India 1996)

Swami Sivananda *Bliss Divine* (Divine Life Society 2004)

Talks with ***Ramana Maharishi*** (V.S. Ramanan, Sri Ramanasraman, 10th edition, Tiruvannamalai 2000)

C. Pronunciation Guide

a	n<u>u</u>t
ā	f<u>a</u>ther
i	b<u>i</u>t
ī	kn<u>ee</u>
u	h<u>oo</u>k
ū	s<u>ue</u>
ṛ	h<u>ur</u>t
e	n<u>e</u>t
ai	t<u>i</u>me
o	g<u>o</u>t
au	h<u>ou</u>se
ṃ	hu<u>m</u>
ḥ	<u>h</u> + preceding vowel
k	papri<u>k</u>a
kh	in<u>k h</u>orn
g	a<u>g</u>o
gh	bi<u>g h</u>ut
ṅ	a<u>n</u>ger
c	<u>ch</u>at
ch	mu<u>ch h</u>arm
j	<u>j</u>og
jh	ra<u>j h</u>ouse
ñ	e<u>n</u>gine
ṭ	borsch<u>t</u>
ṭh	borsch<u>t h</u>ome
ḍ	fresh <u>d</u>ill
ḍh	flushe<u>d h</u>eart
ṇ	rai<u>n</u>y
t	<u>t</u>arp
th	scou<u>t h</u>all
d	mo<u>d</u>ern
dh	mu<u>d h</u>ut
n	ba<u>n</u>al
p	<u>p</u>apa

ph	top half
b	maybe
bh	mob hall
m	chroma
y	young
r	merit
l	alas
v	lava
ś	shin
ṣ	sunshine
h	hut

D. Sanskrit Text

शाण्डिल्योपनिषत्प्रोक्तयमाद्यष्टाङ्गयोगिनः ।यद्वाधाद्यान्ति कैवल्यं स रामो मे पर गतिः ।।ॐ भद्रं कर्णेभिः शान्तिः ।।

प्रथमोऽध्यायः

प्रथमः खण्डः

शाण्डिल्यो ह वा अथर्वाणं पप्रच्छात्मलाभोपायभूतमष्टाङ्गयोगमनुब्रूहीति ।स होवाचाथर्वा यमनियमासनप्राणायामप्रत्याहारधारणाधानसमधयोऽष्टाङ्गानि ।तत्र दश यमाः । तथा नियमाः । असनानयष्टौ । त्रयः प्राणायामाः । पञ्च प्रत्याहाराः ।तथा धारणा । द्विप्रकारं ध्यानम् । समाधिस्त्वेकरूपः ।तत्राहिंसासत्यास्तयब्रह्मचर्यदयार्जवक्षामाधृतिमिताहारशौचानि चेति यमा दश ।तत्राहिंसा नाम मनोवाक्कायकर्मभिः सर्वभूतेषु सर्वदाऽक्लेशजननम् ।सत्यं नाम मनोवाक्कायकर्मभिर्भूतहितयथर्थाभिभाषणम् । अस्तेयं नाम मनोवाक्कायवर्मभिः परद्रव्येषु निःस्पृहता ।ब्रह्मचर्य नाम सर्वावस्थासु मनोवाक्कायवर्मभिः सर्वत्र मैथुनत्यागः ।दया नाम सर्वभूतेषु सर्वत्रानुग्रहः ।आर्जवं नाम मनोवाक्कायकर्मणां विहिताविहितेषु जनेषु निवृत्तौ वा एकरूपत्वम् ।क्षमा नाम प्रियाप्रियेषु सर्वेषु ताडनपूजनेषु सहनम् ।धृतिर्नामार्थहानौ स्वेष्टबन्धुवियोगे तत्प्राप्तौ सर्वत्र चेतःस्थापनम् ।मिताहारो नाम चतुर्थांशावशेषकसुस्निग्धमधुराहारः ।शौचं नाम द्विविधं

बाह्यमान्तरं चेति । तत्र मृच्चलाभ्यां बाह्यम् ।मनःशुद्धिरान्तरम् । तदध्यात्मविद्यया लभ्यम् ।।१।।

द्वितीयः खण्ड:

तपः सन्तोषास्तिक्यदानेश्वरपूजनसिद्धान्तश्रवणह्रीमतिजपव्रतानि दश नियमाः ।तत्र तपो नाम विध्युक्तकृच्छ्रचान्द्रायणादिभिः शरीरशोषणम् ।संतोषो नाम यदृच्छालाभसंतुष्टिः । आस्तिक्यं नाम वेदोक्तधर्माधर्मेषु विश्वासः ।दानं नाम न्यायार्जितस्य धनधान्यादेः श्रद्धयार्थिभ्यः प्रदानम् ।ईश्वरपूजनं नाम प्रसन्नस्वभावेन यथाशक्ति विष्णुरुद्रादिपूजनम् ।सिद्धान्तश्रवणं नाम वेदान्तार्थविचारः । ह्रीर्नाम वेदलौकिकमार्गकुत्सितकर्मणि लज्जा ।मतिर्नाम वेदविहितकर्ममार्गेषु श्रद्धा । जपो नाम विधिवद्गुरूपदिष्ट वेदाविरुद्धमन्त्राभ्यासः ।तद् द्विविधं वाचिकं मानसं चेति । मानसं तु मनसा ध्यानयुक्तं मे ।वाचिकं द्विविधमुच्चैरुपां शुभेदेन । उच्चैरुच्चारणं यथोक्त फलम् ।उपांशु सहस्रगुणम् । मानसं कोटिगुणम् ।व्रतं नाम वेदोक्तविधिनिषेधानुष्ठाननैयत्यम् ।।१।।

तृतीयः खण्ड:

स्वस्तिकगोमुखपद्मवीरसिंहभद्रमुक्तमयूराख्यान्यासनान्यष्टै । स्वस्तिकं नाम जानूर्वोरन्तरे सम्यक्कृत्वा पादतले उभे ।

ऋजुकायः समासीनः स्वस्तिकं तत्प्रचक्षते ।।१।।
सव्ये दक्षिणगुल्फं तु पृष्ठपार्श्वे नियोजयेत् ।
दक्षिणेऽपि तथा सव्यं गोमुखं गोमुखं यथा ।।२।।
अङ्गुष्ठेन निबधिन्याद्धस्ताभ्यां व्युत्क्रमेण च ।
ऊर्वोरुपरि शाण्डिल्य कृत्वा पादतले उभे ।पद्मासनं
भवेदेतत्सर्वेषामपि पूजितम् ।।३।।

एकं पादमथैकस्मिन्विन्यस्योरुणि संस्थितः ।
इतरस्मिंस्तथा चोरुं वीरासनमुदीरितम् ।।४।।
दक्षिणं सव्यगुल्फेन दक्षिणेन तथेतरम् ।
हस्तौ च जान्वोः संस्थाप्य स्वाङ्गुलीश्च प्रसार्य च ।।५।।
व्यात्तवक्त्रं निरीक्षेत नासाग्रं सुसमाहितः ।
सिंहासनं भवेदेतत्पूजितं योगिभिः सदा ।।६।।
योनिं वामेन संपीद्य मेढ्रादुपरि दक्षिणम् ।
भ्रूमध्ये च मनोलक्ष्यं सिद्धासनमिदं भवेत् ।।७।।

गुल्फौ तु वृषणस्याधः सीवन्याः पार्श्वयोः क्षिपेत् ।
पादपापार्श्वे तु पाणिभ्यां दृढं बद्धा सुनिश्चलम् ।
भद्रासनं भवेदेतत्सर्वव्याधिविषापहम् ।।८।।
संपीड्य सीविनीं सूक्ष्मां गुल्फेनैव तु सव्यतः ।
सव्यं दक्षिणगुल्फेन मुक्तासनमुदीरितम् ।।९।।
अवष्टभ्य धरां सम्यक्तलाभ्यां तु करद्वयोः ।
हस्तयोः कूर्परै चापि स्थापयेन्नाभिपार्श्वयोः ।।१०।।
समुन्नतशिरः पादो दण्डवद्व्योम्नि संस्थितः ।

मयूरासनमेतत्तु सर्वपापप्रणाशनम् ।।११।।
शरीरान्तर्गताः सर्वे रोगा विनश्यन्ति ।विषाणि जीर्णानि ।।१२।।
येन केनासनेन सुखधारणं भवत्यशक्तस्तत्समाचरेत् ।।१३।।
येनासनं विजितं जगत्त्रयं तेन विजितं भवति ।।१४।।
यमनियमासनाभ्यासयुक्तः पुरुषः प्राणायामं चरेत् ।
येन नाड्यः शुद्धा भवन्ति ।।१५।।

चतुर्थः खण्ड:

अथ हैनमथर्वाणं शाण्डिल्यः पप्रच्छ केनोपायेन नाड्यः
शुद्धाः स्यूः ।
नाड्यः कतिसंख्याकाः । तासामुत्पक्तिः कीदृशी ।
तासु कति वायवस्तिष्ठन्ति । तेषां कानि स्थानानि ।
तत्कर्माणि कानि ।
देहे यानि यानि विज्ञातव्यानि तत्सर्वं मे ब्रूहीति ।।१।।

स होवाचाथर्वाः अथेदं शरीरं षण्णवत्यङ्गुलात्मकं भवति ।
शरीरात्प्राणो द्वादशाङ्गुलाधिको भवति ।।२।।
शरीरस्थं प्राणमग्निना सह योगाभ्यासेन समन्यूनं वा यः
करोति स योगिपुङ्गवो भवति ।।३।।
देहमध्ये शिखिस्थानं त्रिकोणं तप्तजाम्बूनदप्रभं मनुष्याणाम ।
चतुष्पदां चतुरश्रम् । विहङ्गानां वृत्ताकारम् ।
तन्मध्ये शुभा तन्वी पावकी शिखा तिष्ठति ।।४।।
गुदाद्द्व्यङ्गुलादूर्ध्वं मेढ्राद्द्व्यङ्गुलादधो देहमध्यं मनुष्याणां
भवति ।चतुष्पदां हृन्मध्यम् । विहगानां तुन्दमध्यम् ।५।

देहमध्यं नवाङ्गुलं चतुरङ्गुलमुत्सेधायतमण्डाकृति ।।५।।
तन्मध्ये नाभिः । तत्र द्वादशारयुतं चक्रम् ।तच्च मध्ये पुण्यपापप्रचोदितो जीवो भ्रमति ।।६।।
तन्तुपञ्जरमध्यस्थलूतिका यथा भ्रमति तथा चासौ तत्र प्राणाश्चरति ।देहेऽस्मिञ्जीवः प्राणारूढो भवेत् ।।७।।

नाभेस्तिर्यगाध ऊर्ध्वं कुण्डलिनीस्थानम ।
अष्टप्रकृतिरूपाऽष्टधा कुण्डलीकृता कुण्डलिनी शक्तिर्भवति ।
यथावद्वायुसंचारं जलान्नादीनि परितः स्कन्धपार्श्वेषु निरुध्यैनं मुखेनैव समावेष्ट्य ब्रह्मरन्ध्रं योगकाले चापानेनाग्निना च स्फुरति ।हृदयाकाशो महोज्ज्वला ज्ञानरूपा भवति ।।८।।

मध्यस्थकुण्डलिनीमाश्रित्य मुख्या नाड्यश्चतुर्दश भवन्ति ।
इडा पिङ्गला सुषुम्ना सरस्वती वारुणी पूषा हस्तिजिह्वा यशस्विनी विश्वोदरी कुहूः शङ्खिनी पयस्विनी अलम्बुसा गान्धारीति नाड्यश्चतुर्दश भवन्ति ।।९।।
तत्र सुषुम्ना विश्वधारिणी मोक्षमार्गेति चाचक्षते ।
गुदस्य पृष्ठभागे वीणादण्डाश्रिता मूर्धपर्यन्तं विज्ञेया व्यक्ता सूक्ष्मा वैष्णवी भवति ।।१०।।
सुषुम्नायाः सव्यभागे इडा तिष्ठति । दक्षिणभागे पिङ्गला ।
इडायां चन्द्रश्चरति । पिङ्गलायां रविः । तमोरूपश्चन्द्रः ।
रजोरूपो रविः । विषभागो रविः ।अमृतभागश्चन्द्रमाः ।
तावेव सर्वकालं धत्तः । सुषुम्ना कालभोक्तृ भवति ।
सुषुम्नापृष्ठपार्श्वयोः सरस्वतीकुहू भवतः ।

यशस्विनीकुहूमध्ये वारुणी प्रतिष्ठिता भवति ।
पूषासरस्वतीमध्ये पयस्विनी भवति ।
कन्दमध्येऽलम्बुसा भवति ।
सुषुम्ना पूर्वपूर्वभागे मेढ्रान्तं कुहूर्भवति ।
कुण्डलिन्या अधश्चोर्ध्वं वरुणी सर्वगामिनी भवति ।
यशस्विनी सौम्या च पादाङ्गुष्ठान्तमिष्यते ।
पिङ्गला चोर्ध्वगा याम्यनासान्तं भवति ।
पिङ्गलायाः पृष्ठतो याम्यनेत्रान्तं पूषा भवति ।
याम्यकर्णान्तं यशस्विनी भवति ।
जिह्वाया ऊर्ध्वान्तं सरस्वती भवति ।
आसव्यकर्णान्तमूर्ध्वगा शङ्खिनी भवति ।
इडापृष्ठभागात्सव्यनेत्रान्तगा गान्धारी भवति
।पायुमूलादधोर्ध्वगाऽलम्बुसा भवात ।
एतासु चतुर्दशसु नाडीष्वन्या नाड्यः संभवन्ति ।
तास्वन्यास्तास्वन्या भवन्तीति विज्ञेयाः । यथाऽश्वत्थादिपत्रं सिराभिर्व्याप्तमेवं शरिरं नाडीभिर्व्याप्तम ।।११।।

प्राणापानसमानोदानव्याना नागकूर्मकृकरदेवदत्तधनञ्जय एते दश वायवः सर्वासु नाडीषु चरन्ति ।।१२।।
आस्यनासिकाणठनाभिपादाङ्गुष्ठद्वयकुण्डल्यदश्चोर्ध्वभागेषु प्राणाः संचरति ।
श्रोत्राक्षिकटिगुल्फघ्राणगलस्फिग्देशेषु व्यानः संचरति ।गुदमेढ्रोरुजानूदरतृषणकटिजङ्घानाभिगुदातन्यागारेष्वपानः संचरति । सर्वसंधिस्थ उदानः ।

पादहस्तयोरपि सर्वगात्रेषु सर्वव्यापी समानः ।
भुक्तान्नरसादिकं गात्रेऽग्निना सह व्यापयन्द्विसप्ततिसहस्रेषु नाडीमार्गेषु चरन्समानवातग्निना सह साङ्गोपाङ्गकलेवरं व्याप्नोति ।
नागादिवायवः पञ्च त्वगस्थ्यादिसंभवाः ।
तुन्दस्थं जलमन्नं च रसादिषु समीरितं तुन्दमध्यगतः प्राणस्तानि पृथक्कुर्यात् ।
अग्नेरुपरि जलं स्थाप्य जलोपर्यन्नादीनि संस्थाप्य स्वयमपानं संप्राप्य तेनैव सह मारुतः प्रयाति देहमध्यगतं ज्वलनम् ।
वायुना पालितो वह्निरपानेन शनैर्देहमध्ये ज्वलाति ।
ज्वलनो ज्वालाभिः प्राणेन कोष्ठमध्यगतं जलमत्युष्णमकरोत् ।
जलोपरि समर्पितव्यञ्जनसंयुक्तमन्नं वह्निसंयुक्तवारिणा तप्नमकरोत् ।
तेन स्वेदमूत्रजलरक्तवीर्यरूपरसपुरीषादिकं प्राणः पृथक्कुर्यात् ।समानवायुना सह सर्वासु नाडीषु रसं व्यापयञ्छ्वासरुपेण देहे वायुश्चरति ।
नवभिर्व्योमरन्ध्रैः शरीरस्य वायवः कुर्वन्ति विण्मूत्रादिविसर्जनम् ।
निश्वासोच्छ्वासकासश्च प्राणकर्मोच्यते ।
विण्मूत्रादिविसर्जनमपानवायुकर्म ।हानोपादानचेष्टादि व्यानकर्म ।
देहस्योन्नयनादिकमुदानकर्म ।शरीरपोषणादिकं समानकर्म ।
उद्गारादि नागकर्म । निमीलनादि कूर्मकर्म ।
क्षुत्करणं कृकरकर्म । तन्द्रा देवदत्तकर्म ।
श्लेष्मादि धनञ्जयकर्म ।।१३।।

एवं नाडीस्थानं वायुस्थानं तत्कर्म च सम्यग्ज्ञात्वा नाडीसंशोधनं कुर्यात् ।।१४।।

पंचमः खण्डः

यमनियमयुतः पुरुषः सर्वसङ्गविवर्जितः कृतविद्यः सत्यधर्मरतो जितक्रोधो गुरुशुश्रूषानिरतः पितृमातृविधेयःस्वाश्रमोक्तसदाचारविद्वच्छिक्षितः फलमूलोदकान्वितं तपोवनं प्राप्य रम्यदेशे ब्रह्मघोषसमन्वितेस्वधर्मनिरतब्रह्मवित्समावृते फलमूलपुष्पवारिभिः सुषंपूर्णे देवायतने नदीतीरे ग्रामे नगरे वापिसुशोभनमठं नात्युच्चनीचायतमल्पद्वारं गोमयादिलिप्तं सर्वरक्षासमन्वितं कृत्वा तत्र वेदान्तश्रवणंकुर्वन्योगं समारभेत् ।।१।।

आदौ विनायकं संपूज्य स्वेष्टदेवतां नत्वा पूर्वोक्तासने स्थित्वा प्राङ्मुख उदङ्मुखो वापि मृद्वासनेषुजितासनगतो विद्वान्समग्रीवशिरोनासाग्रदृग्भ्रूमध्ये शशभृद्विम्बं पश्यन्नेत्राभ्याममृतं पिबेत् ।
द्वादशमात्रया इडया वायुमापूर्योदरे स्थितं ज्वालावलीयुतं रेफबिन्दुयुक्तमग्निमण्डलयुतं ध्यायेद्रेचयेत्पिङ्गलया ।
पुनः पिङ्गलयाऽपूर्व कुम्भित्वा रेचयेदिडया ।।२।।
त्रिचतुस्त्रिचतुःसप्तत्रितुर्मासपर्यन्तं त्रिसंधिषु तदन्तरालेषु च षट कृत्व आचरेन्नाडीशुद्धिर्भवति ।
ततः शरीरे लघुदीप्तिवह्निवृद्धिनादाभिव्यक्तिर्भवति ।।३।।

षष्ठ: खण्ड:

प्राणापानसमायोग: प्राणायामो भवति ।
रेचकपूरककुम्भकभेदेन स त्रिविधः ।ते वर्णात्मकाः ।
तस्मात्प्रणव एव प्राणायामः ।।१-२।।

पद्मादयासनस्थः पुमान्नासाग्रे
शशभृद्बिम्बज्योत्स्नाजालवतानिताकारमूर्तोरक्ताङ्गी हंसवाहिनी
दण्डहस्ता बाला गायत्री भवति ।
उकारमूर्तिः श्वेताङ्गी ताक्ष्र्यवाहिनी युवती चक्रहस्ता सावित्री
भवति ।मकारमूर्तिः कृष्णाङ्गी वृषभवाहिनी वृद्धा त्रिशूलधारिणी
सरस्वती भवति ।।३।।
अकारादित्रयाणां सर्वकारणमेकाक्षरं परंज्योतिः प्रणवं
भवतीति ।।४।।

ध्यायेत इडया बाह्याद्वायुमापूर्य षोडशमात्राभिरकारं
चिन्तयन्पूरितं वायुं चतुःषष्तिमात्राभिःकुम्भयित्वोकारं
ध्यायन्पूरितं पिङ्गलया दवात्रिंशन्मात्रया मकारमूत्रिध्यानेनैवं
क्रमेण पुनः पुन: कुर्यात् ।।५।।

सप्तमः खण्ड:

अथासनदृढो योगी वशी मितहिताशनः सुषुम्नानाडीस्थमल-
शोषार्थं योगी बद्ध्वपद्मासनो वायुं चन्द्रेणापूर्ययथाशक्ति
कुम्भयित्वा सूर्येण रेचित्वा पुनः सूर्येणापूर्य कुमभयित्वा

चन्द्रेण विरेच्य यया त्यजेत्तया संपूर्य धारयेत् ।
तदेते श्लोका भवन्तिप्राणं प्रागिडया पिबेन्नियमितं भूयोऽन्यया
रेचयेत्पीत्वा पिङ्गलया समीरणमथो बद्ध्वा त्यजेद्वामया ।
सूर्याचन्द्रमसोरनेन विधिनाऽभ्यासं सदा तन्वतां शुद्धा
नाडिगणा भवन्ति यमिनां मासान्नयादूर्ध्वतः ।।१।।

प्रातर्मध्यन्दिने सायमर्धरात्रे तु कुम्भकान्शनैरशीतिपर्यन्तं
चतुर्वारं समभ्यसेत् ।।२।।
कनीयसि भवेत्स्वेदः कम्पो भवति मध्यमे ।उत्तिष्ठत्युत्तमे
प्राणरोधे पद्मासनं भवेत् ।।३।।
जलेन श्रमजातेन गात्रमर्दनमाचरेत् ।दृढता लगुता चापि तस्य
गात्रस्य जायते ।।४।।
अभ्यासकाले प्रथमं शस्तं क्षीराज्यभोजनम् ।ततोऽभ्यासे
स्थिरीभूते न तावन्नियमग्रहः ।।५।।
यथा सिंहो गजो व्याघ्रो भवेद्वश्यः शनैःशनैः ।तथैव सेवितो
वायुरन्यथा हन्ति साधकम् ।।६।।

युक्तंयुक्तं त्यजेद्वायुं युक्तंयुक्तं च पूरयेत् ।युक्तंयुक्तं च
बन्धीयादेवं सिद्धिमवाप्नुयात् ।।७।।
यथेष्टधारणाद्वायोरनलस्य प्रदीपनम् ।
नादाभिव्यक्तिरारोग्यं जायते नाडीशोधनात् ।।८।।
विधिवत्प्राणसंयामैर्नाडीचक्रे विशोधिते ।सुषुम्नावदनं भित्त्वा
सुखाद्विशति मारुतः ।।९।।
मारुते मध्यसंचारे मनःस्थैर्यं प्रजायते ।यो मनः सुस्थिरो भावः

सैवावस्था मनोन्मनी ।।१०।।
पूरकान्ते तु कर्तव्यो बन्धो जालन्धराभिधः ।
कुम्भकान्ते रेचकादौ कर्तव्यस्तूड्डियाणकः ।।११।।
अधस्तात्कुञ्चनेनाशु कण्ठसंकोचने कृते ।मध्ये पश्चिमतानेन स्यात्प्राणो ब्रह्मनाडिगः ।।१२।।
अपानमूर्ध्वमुत्थाप्य प्राणं कण्ठादधो नयन् ।
योगी जराविनिर्मुक्तः षोडशो वयसा भवेत् ।।१३।।

सुखासनस्थो दक्षनाड्या बहि:स्थं पवनं समाकृष्याकेशमानखाग्रं कुम्भयित्वा सव्यनाड्या रेचयेत् ।तेन कपालशोधनं वातनाडीगतसर्वरोगसर्वविनाशनं भवति ।।१३-१।।
हृदयादिकण्ठपर्यन्तं सस्वनं नासाभ्यां शनैः पवनमाकृष्य यथाशक्ति कुम्भयित्वा इडया विरेच्य गच्छंस्तिष्ठनकुर्यात ।
तेन श्लेष्महरं जठराग्निवर्धनं भवति ।।१३-२।।
वक्त्रेण सीत्कारपूर्वकं वायुं गृहीत्वा यथाशक्ति कुम्भयित्वा नासाभ्यां रेचयेत् ।
तेन क्षुत्तृष्णालस्यनिद्रा न जायन्ते ।।१३-३।।
जिह्वया वायुं गृहीत्वा यथाशक्ति कुम्भयित्वा नासाभ्यां रेचयेत् ।
तेन गुल्मप्लीहज्वरपित्तक्षुधादीनि नश्यन्ति ।।१३-४।।

अथ कुम्भकः । स द्विविधः सहितः केवलश्चेति ।
रेचकपूरकयुक्तः सहितः । तद्विवर्जितः केवलः ।
केवलसिद्धिपर्यन्तं सहितमभ्यसेत् ।
केवलकुम्भके सिद्धे त्रिषु लोकेषु न तस्य दुर्लभं भवति ।

केवलकुम्भकात्कुण्डलिनीबोधो जयते ।।१३-५।।
ततः कृशवपुः प्रसन्नवदनो निर्मललोचनोऽभिव्यक्तनादो
निर्मुक्तरोगजालो जितबिन्दुः पट्वग्निर्भवति ।।१३-६।।

अन्तर्लक्ष्यं बहिर्दृष्टर्निमेषोन्मेषवर्जिता ।एषा सा वैष्णवी मुद्रा
सर्वतन्त्रेषु गोपिता ।।१४।।
अन्तर्लक्ष्यविलीनचित्तपवनो योगी सदा वर्तते दृष्ट्या
निश्चलतारया बहिरधः पश्यन्नपश्यन्नपि ।
मुद्रेयं खलु खेचरी भवति सा लक्ष्यैकताना शिवा
शून्याशून्यविवर्जितं स्फुरति सा तत्त्वं सदं वैष्णवी ।।१५।।
अर्धोन्मीलितलोचनः स्थिरमना नासाग्रदत्तेक्षणश्चन्द्रार्कावपि
लीनतामुपनयन्निष्पन्दभावोत्तरम् ।
ज्योतीरूपमशेषहृयरहितं देदीप्यमानं परं तत्त्वं तत्परमस्ति
वस्तुविषयं शाण्डल्य विद्धीह तत् ।।१६।।

तारं ज्योतिषि संयोज्य किंचिदुन्नमयन्भ्रुवै ।पूर्वाभ्यासस्य
मार्गोऽयमुन्मनीकारकः क्षणात् ।।१७।।
तस्मात्खेचरीमुद्रामभ्यसेत् । तत उन्मनी भवति ।
ततो योगनिद्रा भवति । लब्धयोगनिद्रस्य योगिनः कालो
नास्ति ।।१७-१।।
शक्तिमध्ये मनः कृत्वा शक्तिं मानसमध्यगाम् ।मनसा मन
आलोक्य शाणडिल्य त्वं सुखी भव ।।१८।।
खमध्ये कुरु चात्मानमात्ममध्ये च खं कुरु ।
सर्वं च खमयं कृत्वा न किंचिदपि चिन्तय ।।१९।।

बाह्यचिन्ता न कर्तव्या तथैवान्तरचिन्तका ।सर्वचिन्तां परित्यज्य चिन्मात्रपरमो भव ।।२०।।

कर्पूरमनले यद्वत्सैन्धवं सलिले यथा ।तथा च लीयमानं सन्मनस्तत्त्वे विलीयते ।।२१।।

ज्ञेयं सर्वप्रतीतं च तज्ज्ञानं मन उच्यते ।ज्ञानं ज्ञेयं समं नष्टं नान्यः पन्था द्वितीयकः ।।२२।।

ज्ञेयवस्तुपरित्यागाद्विलयं याति मानसम् ।मानसे विलयं याते कैवल्यमवशिष्यते ।।२३।।

द्वै क्रमौ चित्तनाशस्य योगो ज्ञानं मुनिश्वर ।योगस्तद्वत्तिरोधो हि ज्ञानं सम्यगवेक्षणम् ।।२४।।

तस्मिन्निरोधते नूनमुशान्तं मनो भवेत् ।मनः स्पन्दोपशान्त्यायं संसारः प्रविलीयते ।।२५।।

सूर्यालोकपरिस्पन्दशान्तौ व्यवहृतिर्यथा ।शास्त्रसज्जनसंपर्कवैराग्यासयोगतः ।।२६।।

अनास्थायां कृतास्थायां पूर्वं संसारवृत्तिषु ।यथाभिवाच्छितध्यानाच्चिरमेकतयोहितात् ।।२७।।

एकतत्त्वदृढाभ्यासात्प्राणस्पन्दो निरुध्यते ।पूरकाद्यनिलायामादृढाभ्यासादखेदजात् ।।२८।।

एकान्तध्यानयोगाच्च मनःस्पन्दो निरुध्यते ।ओङ्कारोच्चारणप्रान्तशब्दतत्त्वानुभावनात् ।सुषुप्ते संविदा ज्ञाते प्राणस्पन्दो निरुध्यते ।।२९।।

तालुमूलगतां यत्नाज्जिह्वयाक्रम्य घण्टिकाम् ।ऊर्ध्वरन्ध्रं गते

प्राणे प्राणस्पन्दो निरुध्यते ॥३०॥

प्राणे गलितसंवित्तौ तालूर्ध्वं द्वादशान्तगे ।अभ्यासादूर्ध्वरन्ध्रेण प्राणस्पन्दो निरुध्यते ॥३१॥

द्वादशाङ्गुलपर्यन्ते नासाग्रे विमलेऽम्बरे ।
संविद्दृशि प्रशाम्यन्त्यां प्राणस्पन्दो निरुध्यते ॥३२॥

भ्रूमध्ये तारकालोकशान्तावन्तमुपागते ।चितनैकतने बद्ध्वे प्राणस्पन्दो निरुध्यते ॥३३॥

ओमित्येव यदुद्भूतं ज्ञानं ज्ञेयात्मकं शिवम् ।
असंस्पृष्टविकल्पांशं प्राणस्पन्दो निरुध्यते ॥३४॥

चिरकालं हृदेकान्तव्योमसंवेदनान्मुने ।
अवासनमनोध्यानात्प्राणस्पन्दो निरुध्यते ॥३५॥

एभिः क्रमैस्तथान्यैश्च नानासंकल्पकल्पितैः ।
नानादेशिकवक्त्रस्थैः प्राणस्पन्दो निरुध्यते ॥३६॥

आकुञ्चनेन कुण्डलिन्याः कवाटमुद्धात्य मोक्षद्वारं विभेदयेत् ॥३६ ख॥

येन मार्गेण गन्तव्यं तद्द्वारं मुखेनाच्छाद्य प्रसुप्ता ।
कुण्डलिनी कुटिलाकारा सर्पवद्वेष्टिता भवति ॥३६ ग॥

साशक्तिर्येन चालिता स्यत्स तु मुक्ते भवति ।सा कुण्डलिनी कण्ठोर्ध्वभागे सुप्ता चेद्योगिनां मुक्तये भवति ।
बन्धनायाधो मूढानाम ॥३६ घ।

इडादिमार्गद्वयं विहाय सुषुम्नामार्गेणागच्छेत्तद्विष्णोः परमं पदम् ॥३६ ङ॥

मरुदभ्यसनं सर्वं मनोयुक्तं समभ्यसेत् ।

इतरत्र न कर्तव्या मनोवृत्तिर्मनीषिना ।।३७।।
दिवा न पूजयेद्विष्णुं रात्रौ नैव प्रपूजयेत् ।
सततं पूजयेद्विष्णुं दिवारात्रं न पूजयेत् ।।३८।।

सुषिरा ज्ञानजनकः पञ्चस्रोतः समन्वितःतिष्ठते खेचरी मुद्रा त्वं हि शाण्डिल्य तां भज ।।३९।।
सव्यदक्षिणनाडीस्थो मध्ये चरति मारुतः ।तिष्ठते खेचरी मुद्रा तस्मिन्स्थाने नसंशयः ।।४०।।
इडापिङ्गलयोर्मध्य शून्यं चैवानिलं ग्रसेत् ।
तिष्ठतति खेचरी मुद्रा तत्र सत्यं प्रतिष्थम् ।।४१।।
सोमसूर्यद्वयोर्मध्ये निरालम्बतले पुनः ।
संस्थिता व्योमचक्रे सा मुद्रा नाम्ना च खेचरी ।।४२ क।।
छेदनचालनदोहैः कलां परां जिह्वां
कृत्वा दृष्टिं भ्रूमध्ये स्थाप्य कपालकुहरे जिह्वा विपरीतगा यदा भवति तदा खेचरी मुद्रा जायते ।
जिह्वा चित्तं च खे चरति तेनोर्ध्वजिह्वः पुमानमृतो भवति ।।४२ ख।।
वामपादमूलेन योनिं संपीड्य दिक्षनपादं प्रसार्य तंकराभ्यां धृत्वा नासाभ्यां वायुमापूर्य कण्ठबन्धं समारोप्योर्ध्वतो वायुं धारयेत् । तेन सर्वक्लेशहानिः ।ततः पीयूषमिव विषं जीर्यते ।
क्षयगुल्मगुदावर्तजीर्नत्वगादिदेषा नश्यन्ति ।एष प्राणजयोपायः सर्वमृत्यूपघातकः ।।४२ घ।।

बाह्यात्प्राणं समाकृष्य पूरयित्वोदरे स्थितम् ।

नाभिमध्ये च नासाग्रे पादाङ्गुष्ठे च यत्नतः ।।४३।।
धारयेन्मनसा प्राणं सन्ध्याकालेषु वा सदा ।
सर्वरोगविनिर्मुक्तो भवेद्योगी गतक्लमः ।।४४ क।।
नासाग्रे वायुविजयं भवाति । नाभिमध्ये सर्वरोगविनाशः
।पादाङ्गुष्ठधारणाच्छरीरलघुता भवति ।।४४ ख।।
रसनाद्वायुमाकृष्य यः पिबेत्सततं नरः ।
श्रमदाहौ तु न स्यातां नश्यन्ति व्याधयस्तथा ।।४५।।
सन्ध्ययोर्ब्राह्मणः काले वायुमाकृष्य यः पिबेत् ।
त्रिमासात्तस्य कल्याणी जायते वाक् सरस्वती ।।४६।।
एवं षण्मासाभ्यासात्सर्वरोगङिवृत्तिः ।
जिह्वया वायुमानीय जिह्वामूले निरोधयेत् ।
यः पिबेदमृतं विद्वान्सकलं भद्रमश्नुते ।।४७।।
आत्मन्यात्मानमिड्या धारयित्वा भ्रुवोऽन्तरे ।
विभेद्य त्रिदशाहारं व्याधिस्थोऽपि विमुच्यते ।।४८।।
नाडीभ्यां वायुमारोप्य नाभौ तुन्दस्य पार्श्वयोः ।
घटिकैकां वहेद्यस्तु व्याधिभिः स विमुच्यते ।।४९।।
मासमेकं त्रिसन्ध्यं तु जिह्वयारोप्य मारुतम् ।
विभेद्य त्रिदशाहारं धारयेत्तुन्दमध्यमे ।।५०।।
ज्वराः सर्वऽपि नश्यन्ति विषाणि विविधानि च ।
मुहूर्तमपि यो नित्यं नासाग्रे मनसा सह ।
सर्वं तरति पाप्मानं तस्य जन्मशतार्जितम् ।।५१।।
तारसंयमात्सकलविषयज्ञानं भवति । नासाग्रे
चित्तसंयमादिन्द्रलोकज्ञानम् ।तदधश्चित्तसंयमादग्निलोकज्ञानम् ।
चक्षुषि चित्तसंयमात्सर्वलोकज्ञानम् ।

श्रोत्र चित्तस्य संयमाद्यमलोकज्ञानम् ।
तत्पार्श्वे संयमान्निरृति लोकज्ञानम् ।पृष्ठभागे
संयमाद्वरुणलोकज्ञानम् । वामकर्णे संयमाद्वायुलोकज्ञानम् ।
कण्ठे संयमात्सोमलोकज्ञानम् ।
वामचक्षुषि संयमाच्छिवलोकज्ञानम् ।
मूर्ध्नि संयमाद्ब्रह्मलोकज्ञानम् ।
पादाधोभागे संयमादतललोकज्ञानम् ।
पादे संयमाद्वितललोकज्ञानम्लोकज्ञानम् । पादसन्धौ
संयमान्नितललोकज्ञानम् ।जङ्घे संयमातसुतललोकज्ञानम् ।
जानौ संयमान्महातललोकज्ञानम् ।
ऊरौ चित्तसंयमाद्रसातललोकज्ञानम् ।
कटलौ चित्तसंयमात्तलातललोकज्ञानम् ।
नाभौ चित्तसंयमाद्भूलोकज्ञानम् ।
कुक्षौ संयमाद्भुवर्लोकज्ञानम् ।
हृदि चित्तस्य संयमात्स्वर्लोकज्ञानम् । हृदयोर्ध्वभागे
चित्तसंयमान्महर्लोकज्ञानम् ।कण्ठे चित्तसंयमाज्जनोलोकज्ञानम् ।
भ्रूमध्ये चित्तसंयमात्तपोलोकज्ञानम् ।
मूर्ध्नि चित्तसंयमात्सत्यलोकज्ञानम् ।५२।

धर्माधर्मसंयमादतीतानागतज्ञानम् ।तत्तज्जन्तुध्वनौ
चित्तसंयमात्सर्वजन्तुरुतज्ञानम् ।संचितकर्मणि
चित्तसंयमात्पूर्वजातिज्ञानम् ।परचित्ते चित्तसंयमात्परचित्तज्ञानम्
।कायरूपे चित्तसंयमादन्यादृश्यरूपम् ।
बले चित्तसंयमाद्धनुमादिबलम् ।

सूर्ये चित्तसंयमाद्भुवनज्ञानम्।चन्द्रे चित्तसंयमात्ताराव्यूहज्ञानम् ।
ध्रुवे तद्गतिदर्शनम् । स्वार्थसंयमात्पुरुषज्ञानम् ।
नाभिचक्रे कायव्यूहज्ञानम् ।कण्ठकूपे क्षुत्पिपासानिवृत्तिः ।
कूर्मनाड्यां स्थैर्यम् । तारे सिद्धदर्शनम् ।
कायाकाशसंयमादाकाशगमनम् ।
तत्तत्स्थाने संयमात्तत्तत्सिद्धयो भवति ।।५२ ।।

अष्टमः खण्डः

अथ प्रत्याहारः ।
स पञ्चविधः विषयेषु विचरतामिन्द्रियाणां बलादाहरणं प्रत्याहारः ।
यद्यत्पश्यति तत्सर्वमात्मेति प्रत्याहारः ।
नित्यविहितकर्मफलत्यागः प्रत्याहारः ।
सर्वविषयपराङ्मुखत्वं प्रत्याहारः ।
अष्टादशसु मर्मस्थानेषु क्रमाद्धारणं प्रत्याहारः ।।१।।
पादाङ्गुष्ठगुल्फजङ्घाजानूरुपायुमेढ्रनाभिहृदयकण्ठ-
कूपतालुनासाक्षिभ्रूमध्यललाटमूर्ध्नि स्थानानि ।
तेषु क्रमादारोहावरोहक्रमेण प्रत्याहरेत् ।।२।।

नवमः खण्डः

अथ धाराणा ।सा त्रिविधा आत्मनि मनोधारणं दहराकाशे
बाह्याकाशधारणंपृथिव्यप्तेजोवाय्वाकाशेषु पञ्चमूर्तिधारनं
चेति ।।१।।

दशमः खण्डः

अथ ध्यानम् ।तदद्विविधं सगुणं निर्गुणं चेति ।
सगुणं मूर्तिध्यानम् । निर्गुणमात्मयाथात्म्यम् ।।१।।

एकादशः खण्डः

अथ समाधिः ।जीवात्मपरमात्मैक्यावस्था त्रिपुटारहितापरमानन्दस्वरूपा शुद्धचैतन्यात्मिका भवति ।।१।।

द्वितीयोऽध्यायः

अथ ह शाण्डिल्यो ह व वै ब्रह्मऋषिश्चतुर्षु वेदेषु ब्रह्मविद्यामलभमानः किं नामेत्यथर्वणंभगवन्तमुपसन्नः पप्रच्छाधीहि भगवन् ब्रह्मविद्यां येन श्रेयोऽवाप्स्यामिति ।।१।।
स होवाचाथर्वा शाण्डिल्य सत्यं विज्ञानमनन्तं ब्रह्मा ।।२।।
यस्मिन्निदमोतं च प्रोतं च ।यस्मिन्निदं सं च विचैति सर्वं यस्मिन्विज्ञाते सर्वमिदं विज्ञातं भवति ।तदपाणिपादमचक्षुःश्रोत्रमजिह्वमशरीरमग्राह्यमनिर्देश्यम् ।।३।।
यतो वाचो निवर्तन्ते अप्राप्य मनसा सह ।यत्केवलं ज्ञानगम्यम् । प्रज्ञा च यस्मात्प्रसृता पुराणी । यदेकमद्वितीयम् ।आकाशवत्सर्वगतं सुसूक्ष्मं निरञ्जनं निष्क्रयं सन्मात्रं चिदानन्दैकरसं शिवं प्रशान्तममृतं तत्परं च ब्रह्म । तत्त्वमसि तज्ज्ञानेन हि विजानीहि ।।४।।
य एको देव आत्मशक्तिप्रधानः सर्वज्ञः सर्वेश्वरः सर्वभूतान्तरा-

त्मा सर्वभूताधिवासः सर्वभूतनिगूढो भूतयोनिर्योगैकगम्यः ।
यश्च विश्वं सृजति विश्वं बिभर्ति विश्वं भुङ्क्ते स आत्मा ।
आत्मनि तं तं लोकं विजानिहि ।।५।।मा
शोचीरात्मविज्ञानी शोकस्यान्तं गमिष्यसि ।।६।।

तृतीयो"ध्याय:

प्रथमः खण्ड:

अथ हैनं शाण्डिल्योऽथर्वणं पप्रच्छ यदेकमक्षरं निष्क्रियं शिवं सन्मात्रं परंब्रह्मतस्मात्कथमिदं विष्वं जायते कथं स्थीयते कथमस्मिल्लीयतेतन्मे संशयं छेत्तुमर्हसीति ।।१।।

स होवाचाथर्वा सत्यं शाण्डिल्य परब्रह्म निष्क्रियमक्षरमितिअथाप्यस्यारूपस्य ब्यह्मणस्त्रीणि रूपानि भवन्ति सकलं निष्कलं सकलनिष्कलं चेति ।।२-३।।

यत्सत्यं विज्ञानमानन्दं निष्क्रियं निरञ्जनं सर्वगतं सुसूक्ष्मंसर्वतोमुखमनिर्देश्यममृतमस्ति तदिदं निष्कलं रूपम ।।४।।

अथास्य या सहजास्त्यविद्या मूलप्रकृतिर्माया लोहित-शुक्लकृष्णा तया सहायवान् देवः कृष्णपिङ्गलो महेश्वर ईष्टेतदिदमस्य सकलं रूपम् ।।५।।

अथैष ज्ञानमयेन तपसा चीयमानोऽकामयत बहुस्यां प्रजायेयेतिअथैतस्मात्तप्यमानात्सत्यकामात्त्रीण्यक्षराण्याजाय-न्ततिस्रो व्याहृतयस्त्रिपदा गायत्री त्रयो वेदास्त्रयो देवास्त्रयो वर्णास्त्रयोऽग्नयश्च जायन्तेयोऽसै देवो भगवान्सर्वैश्वर्यसंपन्नः

सर्वव्यापी सर्वभूतानां हृदये संनिविष्टो मायावीमायया क्रीडति स ब्रह्मा स विष्णुः स रुद्रः स इन्द्रः स सर्वे देवाः सर्वाणि भूतानि स एव दक्षिणतः स एवाधस्तात्स एवोपरिष्टात्स एव सर्वम् अथास्य देवस्यात्मशक्तेरात्मक्रीडस्य भक्तानुकम्पिनो दत्तात्रेयरूपा सुरूपातनूरवासा इन्दीवरदलप्रख्या चतुर्बाहुरघोरापापकाशिनीतदिदमस्य सकलनिष्कलं रूपम् ।।६।।

द्वितीयः खण्डः

अथ हैनमथर्वाणं शाण्डिल्यः पप्रच्छ भगवन्सन्मात्रं चिदानन्दैकरसं कस्मादुच्यते परं ब्रह्मेति ।स होवाचाथर्वा यस्माच्च बृहति बृंहयति च सर्वं तस्मादुच्यते परंब्रह्मेति ।।१-२।।
अथ कस्मादुच्यते आत्मेति ।यस्मात्सर्वमाप्नोति सर्वमादत्ते सर्वमत्ति च तस्मादुच्यते आत्मेति ।।३-४।।
अथ कस्मादुच्यते महेश्वर इति ।यस्मान्महत ईशः शब्दध्वन्या चात्मशक्त्या च महत ईशते तस्मादुच्यते महेश्वर इति ।।५-६।।
अथ कस्मादुच्यते दत्तात्रेय इति ।यस्मात्सुदुश्चरं तपस्तप्यमानायात्रये पुत्रकामायातितरां तुष्टेन भगवता ज्योतिर्मयेनात्मैवदत्तो यस्माच्चानसूयायामात्रेतनयोऽभवत्तस्मादुच्यते दत्तात्रेय इति ।।७-८।।
अथ योऽस्य निरुकतानि देव स सर्वं देव ।अथ यो ह वै विद्ययैनं परमुपास्ते साऽहमिति स ब्रह्मविद्भवति ।।९-१०।।

अत्रैते श्लोका भवन्ति ।दत्तात्रेयं शिवं शन्तमिन्द्रनीभं प्रभुम्
।आत्ममायारतं देवमवधूतं दिगम्बरम् ।।११।।
भस्मोद्धूलितसर्वाङ्गं जटाजूटधरं विभुम ।चतुर्बाहुमुदाराङ्गं
प्रफुल्लकमलेक्षणम् ।।१२।।
ज्ञानयोगनिधिं विश्वगुरुं योगिजनप्रियम् ।भक्तानुकम्पिनं
सर्वसाक्षिणं सिद्धसेवितम् ।।१३।।
एवं यः सततं ध्यायेद्देवदेवं सनातनम् ।स मुक्तः
सर्वपापेभ्यो निःश्रेयसमवाप्नुयात् ।।१४।।
इत्यों सत्यमत्युपनिषद् ।।१५।।

E. Continuous Translation

Opening Invocation

Śāṇḍilya Upaniṣad describes the eightfold path of the yogins, beginning with *yama.* Just as they ascend to liberation, so Rāma is my supreme refuge. Om, may we hear [that which is] auspicious. Peace.

Chapter One

First Section

1.

Śāṇḍilya himself did ask Atharvan: "[Please] impart [to me] the eight limbs [of] yoga, being the means of attaining the ātmā."Atharvan did respond thus: "The eight limbs [of yoga are] *yama, niyama, āsana, prāṇāyama, pratyāhāra, dhāraṇā, dhyāna* [and] *samādhi.* There [are] ten yamas, likewise [ten] niyamas, eight āsanas, three kinds of prāṇāyama, five [of] pratyāhāra, [and] also [of] dhāraṇā. Dhyāna [has] two kinds, but samādhi [has only] one.There [are] ten yamas: *ahiṃsā, satya, asteya, brahmacarya, dayā, ārjava, kṣamā, dhṛti, mitāhāra* and *śauca.*Non-violence (called *ahiṃsā*) [is] always the cause [of] non-suffering to all living beings through the actions of mind, speech [or] body. Truth (called *satya*) [is] speaking [that which is] beneficial and suitable for living beings through the actions of mind, speech [or] body. Honesty (called *asteyam*) [is] not craving for the goods of others through the actions of mind, speech [or] body. Continence (called *brahmacarya*) is always forsaking sexual intercourse in all conditions through the actions of mind, speech [or] body. Compassion (called *dayā*) [is] treating kindly all creatures everywhere. Straightforwardness (called *ārjava*) [is] maintaining steadiness and equanimity of mind, speech [and] body in the accomplishment or non-accomplishment of actions. Patience (called *kṣamā*) [is] enduring everything pleasant [and] unpleasant, [such as] respect [or] insult. Firmness (called *dhṛti*) is always preserving (firmness of mind) whether one has wealth or poverty, or separated from dear ones or relatives. A moderate, balanced diet (called *mitāhāra*) [is] the taking of good, [naturally] oily [and] sweet food, leaving a quarter [of the stomach] empty. And it is said cleanliness (called *śauca*) [is] of two kinds: external [and] internal. Of these, external is cleaning with water; internal [is] purification [of] the mind. This [is] to be obtained through knowledge of the inner self.

Second Section

1.

The ten niyamas [are]: *tapas, santoṣa, āstikya, dāna, īśvarapūjana, hrīḥ, mati, japa* [and] *vrata.*Of these, austerity (called *tapas*) [is] destroying [attachment to] the body through [penances such as] *kṛcchra* [and] *cāndrāyaṇa* etc as expressed in the precepts. Contentment (called *santoṣa*) [is] acceptance of whatever happens [and] whatever loss. Piety (called *āstikya*) [is] faith in the rules of right [and] wrong as described in the Vedas. Donation (called *dāna*) [is] giving with faith corn [and] money acquired honestly to those in need. Worship of the Lord (called *īśvarapūjana*) [is] worshipping Viṣṇu, Rudra etc with one's pure inherent nature to the utmost of one's power. Listening to sacred teachings (called *siddhāntaśravaṇam*) [is] reflecting on the meaning of Vedānta. Shame (called *hrīḥ*) [is being] ashamed of actions [which are] despicable according to the way of the Vedas. Understanding (called *mati*) [is] faith in the paths of action prescribed by the Vedas. Mantra repetition (called *japa*) [is] constant practice of the mantra [into which one is] duly initiated by the guru, [and which is] not contrary to the Vedas. It [is] of two kinds, spoken and mental. Now the mental is connected with meditation by the mind. The spoken [has] two different kinds, loud and low. The loud pronunciation [gives] the reward as stated [in the Vedas]. The low [gives rewards of] a thousand kinds, the mental ten million kinds. A vow (called *vrata*) [is] the obligatory practice of the precepts [and] prohibitions stated in the Vedas.

Third Section

1 to 3.

The eight *āsanas* are called *svastika* (auspicious), *gomukha* (cow-face), *padma* (lotus), *vīra* (hero), *siṃha* (lion), *bhadra* (gracious), *mukta* (liberated) [and] *mayūra* (peacock). Sitting with the body straight, placing both knees exactly parallel with both soles of the feet, this is called *svastika*, the auspicious [pose]. Placing the right ankle on the left beside the back, and then the left on the right is thus *gomukha*, the cow-face [pose]. O Śāṇḍilya, *padmāsana* is placing both soles of the feet up-ward on the thighs, and with big toes turned up, held by the hands. This is honoured by all.

4 to 7.

Placing one foot on one [opposite] thigh and then the other [foot] under its [opposite] thigh is called *vīrāsana,* the hero pose. Placing together the right ankle with the left one and the left at the right (i.e. crossing the ankles), the hands on the knees and the fingers extended, the mouth opened wide, gazing intently at the tip of the nose, this is *siṃhāsana*, the lion pose, forever honoured by the yogis. Pressing the erineum with the left [heel], the right one above the genitals [and] fixing the mind on the eye-brow centre, this is *siddhāsana,* accomplished pose.

8 to 12.

Now putting the ankles under the testes beside the perineum, knees out to the sides, held firmly [and] stable with the hands, this is *bhadrāsana,* the gracious pose, the antidote to all disease. Pressing the right side [of] the soft perineum with the [left] heel, then the left [side] with the right heel is called *muktāsana,* the liberated pose. Holding tightly the soles [of the feet] together with the two palms [of the hands], and placing the elbows against the sides of the navel, both hands [on the ground], head raised, legs straight in the air, then this [is] *māyūrāsana*, the peacock pose, remover of all obstructions. [Then] all diseases [which] have entered the body are destroyed; the poisons are digested.

13 to 15.
Whoever is unable [to do] this [posture] should practise thoroughly whichever postures [one can] hold comfortably. Thus one [who] has mastery over *āsana* [has] mastery over the three worlds. The person established in yama, niyama [and] āsana practice should perform *prāṇāyāma.* Thus the *nāḍīs* become purified.

Fourth Section
1.
Now Śāṇḍilya asked Lord Atharvan: "By what means might the nāḍīs be purified? How many nāḍīs are there in number? How do they arise? Which vital airs are located in them? Which are their seats? What are their actions? Please tell me all that which is to be known in the body."

2 to 5a.
Now Atharvan replied: "This body consists of ninety-six digits [in length]. Prāṇa extends twelve digits beyond the body. Whoever with regular yoga practice makes the prāṇa in the body equal to or not less than the fire [in it], he becomes the best of yogis. In humans, the region of fire, [which is] triangular [and as] radiant [as] molten gold, [is] in the middle of the body. In four-footed animals, [it is] quadrangular. In birds [it is] round. In its centre is situated the auspicious, subtle, purifying flame. Two digits above the anus [and] two digits below the sexual organ is the centre of the body in humans. In four-footed animals, [it is] the centre of the heart. In birds, [it is] the centre of the abdomen.

5b to 7.

Nine digits [from] the centre of the body [and] four digits [in] width and length [is] an oval. In its middle [is] the navel. There [is] a cakra with twelve spokes, and in its midst the *jīva* wanders, impelled by its good and bad [actions]. Just as a spider wanders among the threads of a web, so that prāṇa roams about there. In this body, the jīva is carried by prāṇa.

8.

Lying below the navel [and] above [it is] the seat of the kuṇḍalinī. Kuṇḍalinī śakti has the form [of] eight *prakṛtis* (elements of nature), making eightfold coils. The movement of the vital air duly controls the food and water all around beside the *skandha*. She covers with her mouth [the way to] the *brahma-randhra*, and breaks forth at the time of yoga by the fire of *apāna*. A great blaze in the form of wisdom appears in the heart space.

9 to 11.

Having recourse to kuṇḍalinī located in the centre, are fourteen main nāḍīs. The fourteen nāḍīs are thus: *iḍā piṅgalā suṣumnā sarasvatī vāruṇī pūṣā hastijihvā yaśasvinī viśvodarī kuhūḥ śaṅkhinī payasvinī alambusā gāndhārī.* Among them, suṣumnā is declared the sustainer of the universe, and thus the way to liberation. Dwelling in the spinal column from the back of the anus right up to the crown of the head, she is regarded as the manifest, subtle power of Viṣṇu.

On the left of suṣumnā is located iḍā, on the right [is] piṅgalā. The moon moves in iḍā, the sun in piṅgalā. The moon [has] the nature of *tamas*, the sun of *rajas.* The sun [has] the share of poison, the moon nectar. They both determine all time. Suṣumnā is the consumer of time.

Sarasvatī and kuhū are at the back and to the side of suṣumnā [respectively]. Vāruṇī is situated between yaśasvinī and kuhū. Payasvinī is between pūṣā and sarasvatī. Yaśasvinī is between gāndhārī and sarasvatī. Alambusā is in the centre of the navel. Kuhū is in front of suṣumnā up to the genital organ. Vāruṇī goes everywhere, below and above kuṇḍalinī, and auspicious yaśasvinī leads to the tip of the big toes, and piṅgalā goes upwards to the right nostril.

Pūṣā is behind piṅgalā [and goes] up to the right eye. Yaśasvinī goes up to the right ear. Sarasvatī goes to the upper side of the tongue. Śaṅkhinī goes upwards to the left ear. Gāndhārī goes from behind iḍā to the left eye. Alambusā goes downwards and upwards from the base of the anus.

From these fourteen nāḍīs, other nāḍīs arise. From these others arise, and from these others; thus they should be known. Just as the leaf [of] the holy fig tree and others is pervaded with veins, so the body is pervaded with nāḍīs.

12 to 14.
Prāṇa, apāna, samāna, udāna, vyāna, nāga, kūrma, kṛkara, devadatta, dhanañjaya: these ten vital airs move in all the nāḍīs. Prāṇa moves through the face, nostrils, throat, navel, two big toes [and] in the lower and upper parts of the kuṇḍalī. Vyāna moves in the areas [of] the ears, eyes, loins, ankles, nose, throat and buttocks. Apāna moves in the anus, genitals, thighs, knees, stomach, testicles, hips, calves, navel, [and] the anus in the abode of fire. Udāna is in all the joints as well as the feet and hands. Samāna spreads everywhere through all the limbs. Causing first the food and drink consumed to pervade the body together with the fire, [and] moving through the seventy two thousand nāḍīs, the vital air [of] samāna with its fire permeates the confluence [of] the divisions [of] the body. The five vāyus, nāga and others, enter the skin and bones etc.

The prāṇa there, having gone to the centre of the navel, sepa rates the water and food situated around the navel, stirring [them] in the fluids etc. Having placed the water above the fire [and] put together the food etc upon the water, arriving at the apāna itself, the vital air goes forth with it right to the centre of the body, feeding the fire with energy [so that] it burns more and more brightly in the centre of the body. The fire, with its flames, makes the water, [which] has gone through prāṇa to the centre of the bowels, very hot. The fire, together with the water, heats the food and condiments placed above the water. Then prāṇa separates the sweat, urine, water, blood, semen, faeces and others [in] the form of fluid.

The prāṇa, together with samāna vāyu, causing the fluid to spread in all the nāḍīs, moves in the body in the form of breath. The vāyus discharge the faeces and urine etc through the nine openings of the body [into] the air [outside]. It is said the action of prāṇa [is] coughing, inhalation and exhala-tion. The action of apāna vāyu [is] discharging faeces and urine. The action of vyāna [is] giving, taking and moving. The action of udāna [is] the straightening of the body. The action of samāna [is] nourishing the body. The action of nāga [is] vomiting. The action of kūrma [is] closing [and opening] the eyelids. The action of kṛkara [is] the causing of hunger. The action of devadatta [is] lassitude. The action of dhanañjaya [is] phlegm.

Thus, having a complete knowledge of the seat of the nāḍīs [and] of the vāyus and their actions, one should undertake the purification of the nāḍīs.

Fifth Section

1.

The person [who] practises the yamas and niyamas, avoids all company, has completed his studies, delights in truth and righteousness, has overcome anger, rejoices in serving his guru, obedient to [his] father and mother, has been educated in wise [and] virtuous conduct [and] instructed in his stage of life, [then] arrives at a sacred grove replete with fruit, roots and water in a pleasing spot resounding with sacred chants

[and] protected by knowers of Brahma intent on their own dharma, [then] builds a beautiful monastery either in a temple with plenty of fruits, roots, flowers and streams, or on a river bank or in a village or town, possessing every protection [and which has] a closed small door, [is] neither [too] high nor low, [and is] smeared first with cow-dung. There, listening to Vedānta, he should begin to practise yoga.

2 to 3.
Firstly, having paid homage to Vināyaka [and] bowed to his Iṣṭa-Devata, [then] remaining in a posture described before, facing either east or north, the posture perfected on soft seats, the wise person, neck and head aligned, gazing at the nosetip, observing the sphere supporting the hare at the eyebrow centre, drinks the nectar through his eyes. Inhaling the air through iḍā for twelve mātrās, he should meditate on the ring of fire situated in the abdomen as encircled with flames, as well as on the point of the letter 'raṃ', [and then] exhale through piṅgalā. Again, inhaling through piṅgalā [and] retaining [the breath], he should exhale through iḍā.

For twenty-one up to twenty-eight months, having practised six [times] at the three *sandhyās* and in the intervals, he should practise purification of the nāḍīs. Then, when the body becomes light and bright, the inner fire increases [and] the inner sound is expressed.

Sixth Section
1 to 2.
Prāṇāyāma is the union of prāṇa and apāna, with a division of three kinds: exhalation, inhalation and retention. They consist of a [particular] group of letters. Thus prāṇāyāma is praṇava.

3 to 4.
Seated in the lotus or other posture, a person [should visualise] on the nosetip Gāyatrī, a girl [of] the colour of Indian madder, surrounded by a web [of] rays from the disk [of] the

moon [and] borne by a swan, a mace [in] her hand, she is the form [of] the sound A. Sāvitrī, a young woman [of] the colour white, a discus in [her] hand, mounted on a *garuḍa*, is the form of the sound U. Sarasvatī, an old woman [of] the colour black,holding a trident [and] mounted on a bull, is the form [of] the sound M. Thus the supreme light, the praṇava Om, is the one sound [which is] the cause of all three, beginning with the sound A.

5.
Having inhaled the external air through iḍā for sixteen mātrās, one should meditate on the sound A. Retaining the inhaled air for sixty-four mātrās [at the same time] meditating on the sound U, [one should then exhale] the inhaled [air] through piṅgalā for thirty-two mātrās, meditating on the form of the sound M. One should do [this] again and again in the [same] order.

Seventh Section

1.
Now, firm in the posture [and] established in perfect [self]-control, the yogin, fixed in padmāsana, should, in order to remove impurities from suṣumnā and the nāḍīs, inhale the air through the left nostril, hold [it] as long as one is able, then exhale through the right. Again, inhaling through the right nostril, holding it, exhaling through the left, then inhaling that through which he exhales, one should hold [it]. These verses are thus: First one should draw the breath in through iḍā as prescribed, then exhale through the other [nostril]. Then inhaling the air through piṅgalā, retaining [it], one exhales through the left. [For those who] have self-control, continually [and] forever practising through this method [of] sun and moon, all the nāḍīs are purified in one month or more.2 to 6.One should practise retention of the breath slowly up to eighty times early morning, midday, evening [and] midnight for four weeks. When there is, [seated in] padmāsana, suppression of the breath, in the beginning there

is perspiration, in the middle [stage] there is trembling [and] finally levitation. One should massage the body when perspiration is produced, and then this body becomes firm and light. Early in the time of practice, an excellent food is milk and ghee. If one has not yet become Firm in the practice, one should adhere to this rule. Just as the lion, elephant [and] tiger can be gradually tamed, likewise the breath can be managed, otherwise it kills the aspirant.

7 to 13.
One should inhale the air properly, exhale properly and with proper retention. Thus one will attain success. Just by the holding of the two breaths in the approved way [and] by purification of the nāḍīs, the fanning of the fire, clarity of inner sounds [and] good health are produced. When the nāḍīs and cakras have been purified through appropriate suspension of the breath, the breath, having broken into suṣumnā, spreads joyfully [up it]. When the air moves up the middle, the mind becomes steady. The mind, having become stable, [is] now in a state [of] mindlessness. The contraction named *jālandhara* is to be done after inhaling. Then, after retaining and exhaling, *uḍḍiyāna bandha* is to be done. When the throat is contracted and immediately closed below, the prāṇa moves up *brahma nāḍī* in the middle of the back. Having caused apāna to rise upwards [and] drawn the prāṇa down from the throat, the yogin, freed from old age, becomes like a sixteen year old youth.

13.1 to 13.4.
Seated in a comfortable posture, drawing the air from outside through the right nāḍī [and] retaining [it from] the top [of] the hair [to] the toe-nails, one should exhale through the left nāḍī. Through this, the brain is purified [and] every disease [which] has gone into the vāta nāḍī is destroyed. Having slowly drawn in the vital air noisily through the nostrils from the heart up to the throat, retained it as long as one is able, exhaled through iḍā, one should go and rest. Thus this

removes phlegm [and] hunger, stimulating digestion.

Having first taken in the air with a hissing sound through the mouth, [and] retained it as long as one is able, one should exhale through both nostrils. Hence, hunger, thirst, idleness [and] sleep do not arise. Having taken in the air through the tongue, [and] having retained it as long as one is able, one should exhale through both nostrils. Thereby diseases of the spleen, fever, bile and hunger are destroyed.

13.5 to 13.6.
Now kumbhaka is of two kinds, *sahita* and *kevala*. Sahita is connected with inhalation and exhalation. That [which] excludes [these is] kevala. Until [there is] perfection in kevala, one should practise sahita. If [there is] perfection in kevala kumbhaka, there is nothing difficult to attain in the three worlds. Through kevala kumbhaka comes knowledge of kuṇḍalinī. Then, [when the yogin is] lean in body, serene of countenance, bright-eyed, the inner sounds distinct, freed from the web of disease [and his] seed subdued, the fire becomes intense.

14 to 16.
[Concentration on] an inner object while looking outside with out closing or opening the eyelids, this is *vaiṣṇavī mudrā,* con cealed in all the tantras. Mind and breath immersed in the inner object, the yogin, seeing, yet not seeing, [what is] outside and below, remains continually intent on looking with motionless pupils.

Now this is khecarī mudrā. It has one sense object [as its] goal, [which is] auspicious. The true seat of Viṣṇu, [which is] neither void nor non-void, shines brightly. With eyes half-closed [and] a firm mind, eyes fixed on the nose-tip, becoming absorbed in the sun and moon, then in an immoveable state, [the yogin] is of the form of light free from all externals, [and is] radiant, the Supreme Truth, the

Absolute Reality. Know this, o Śāṇḍilya!

17 to 23.
Having merged the sound in the light, raising the brows a little, this [is] the way of former practice [and] immediately brings forth *unmanī*. Thus one should practise khecarī mudrā. Then there is *unmanī*. Then there is *yoga nidrā*. [For] yogins who have attained deep relaxation, time does not exist. Having put the mind in the midst of *śakti*, śakti going into the midst of the mind, observing the mind with the mind, o Śāṇḍilya, may you be happy! Place the ātman within the ether, and the ether within the ātman, and having made everything ether, do not think of anything else. External thoughts are not to be had, likewise internal thoughts. Having renounced all thoughts, become the highest measure of thought. Just as for instance camphor becomes absorbed in fire and salt in water, so the mind is absorbed in its true nature. [That which] is called mind is knowing all that is past and [all that] is to be known. [When] knowledge of past and future [is] equally lost, [there is] no other second path. By abandoning future knowledge [of] objects, the mind goes into dissolution. When the mind goes into dissolution, there remains only *kaivalya*.

24 to 27.
The two ways of destruction of *citta* [are] yoga and jñāna, o excellent Sage. Thus yoga controls [it], and jñāna [gives] correct understanding. So when [thinking] is thus prevented, the mind becomes calm. Through the interruption of activity, the illusory mind becomes dissolved. As when the action of maintaining the light of the sun has ceased, so by means of yoga practice, keeping virtuous company, sacred teachings, detachment [from sensory pleasures], [and] indifference to the mental influences of the illusory world, previously contemplated, then one by one, through meditation for a long time, the desires are borne away.

28 to 36.

The movement of prāṇa is controlled by consistent yoga practice on the one essential nature. By holding the breath, first inhaling, by firm practice [which] does not cause fatigue, and by solitary deep meditation, the activity of the mind is restrained. Through direct experience of the true essential nature of the sound [at] the extremity [of] the enunciation of Aum [and] when consciousness is known in deep sleep, the movement of prāṇa is controlled. [When] the passage at the root of the palate, [like] a small bell, is closed by the tongue with effort, [and] the prāṅa enters the upper aperture, the move-ment of prāṇa is controlled. When consciousness is merged with prāṇa, [and] when through yoga practice, [prāṇa goes] through the upper aperture into the *dvādaśānta* above the palate, the movement of prāṇa is controlled. When the eye of consciousness, becoming calm, [can see] in the clear ether up to twelve digits from the nosetip, the movements of prāṇa cease. When many thoughts arise, bound up [in the mind], they are finally extinguished in the world of *tāraka* at the eyebrow centre [and] the movements of prāṇa cease. When the know-ledge in the form of that which is to be known [is] auspicious,untouched by the oscillations throughout [the mind] and,and, brows raised, is just Aum, then the movements of prāṇa have ceased. By being conscious for a long time of the space within the heart, o Sage, [and] meditating on the mind free from impressions, the movements of prāṇa cease. Thus by these methods and many others [which] come to mind [and] by the connection with the appearance of many guides, the movements of prāṇa cease.

36kha to 38.

Having opened up by contraction the doorway to kuṇḍalinī, one can break through the door [to] liberation. Having covered with her mouth that door through which one enters, the kuṇḍalinī, coiled up like a snake in spiral form, is sleeping. The one who causes this *śakti* to move is liberated.

If the kuṇḍalinī sleeps in the upper part of the neck of the yogins, they will be liberated. [If she sleeps] in the lower [part], [there is] bondage of the ignorant. Moving away from the two paths of *īḍa* [and *piṅgalā*], she will go up through the path of *suṣumnā* to that supreme seat of Viṣṇu. One should always practise controlling the breath with concentration on the mind. The activity of the mind is not to be placed elsewhere by the wise person. One should not worship Viṣṇu by day only, nor worship [him] by night [only]. One should worship Viṣṇu continually, not [only] by day and night.

39 to 42gha.
The opening generating wisdom possesses five canals. Here abides khecarī mudrā. Practise it, o Śāṇḍilya! When one rests in khecarī mudrā, the vital air, having been in the left and right nāḍīs, flows [and] remains in the middle [nāḍī]. [About this] there is no doubt. One should swallow the air in the void between iḍā and piṅgalā. There khecarī mudrā is located, the seat of truth. Again, that mudrā, khecarī by name, is situated in *ākāśa* cakra in the unsupported part between the sun and the moon.

Having made the tongue another digit [in length] by an incision, shaking and milking [it], fixing the gaze at the eyebrow centre [and] when the tongue is reversed into the hole of the skull, then [this] becomes khecarī mudrā. [When] *citta* moves with the tongue in the ākāśa, then the person [whose] tongue is raised up becomes immortal. Pressing the perineum with the left heel, stretching out the right leg, grasping it [the right foot] with both hands [and] inhaling the air through the nostrils, one should hold the throat lock, raising the air upwards.

Thus every affliction is destroyed. Then poison is digested like nectar. The problems of consumption, the spleen, turning up of the anus, old age and skin etc are removed. This is the way to conquer prāṇa, overcoming every [type of] death.

Pressing the left heel in the area of the perineum, placing the right foot on the left thigh, inhaling the vital air, resting the chin on the chest, contracting the perineum, [then] holding one's own ātman within the mind as long as possible, one can realise [it].

43 to 51.

Having inhaled the prāṇa from outside [and] filled the place in the stomach [with it], one should hold [it] with the mind in the centre of the navel and at the nosetip and with great effort at the toes at the times of sunrise and sunset or at all times. The yogin becomes refreshed and freed from all disease. [With the prāṇa] at the nosetip, the vital air is mastered; at the centre of the navel, all diseases are destroyed. By holding [it] at the toes, the body becomes light. The person who always drinks the air inhaled through the tongue, does not have fatigue and fever. Then, he who, having inhaled the air, drinks [it], mouth open, at dawn, dusk and at the time of Brahma, within three months his speech is born from the auspicious Sarasvatī. Thus after six months' practice, all disease has disappeared. Having brought in the air through the tongue, he should retain [it] at the root of the tongue. The wise one who drinks [this] nectar gains every benefit.

Holding the ātman in the ātman at the eyebrow centre, [having inhaled] through iḍā, [and] pierced it thirty times, even a very sick person is freed [from disease]. He who having inhaled the air through the nāḍīs, holds it for twenty-four minutes in the navel [and] both sides of the belly, then he is freed from disease. Inhaling through the tongue for one month at sunrise, noon and sunset [and] pierced thirty times, he should hold the vital air in the middle of the navel, and several poisons as well as all fevers are destroyed. Whoever holds [the vital air] regularly together with the mind at the nosetip even for a short time, [destroys] every wrongdoing committed by him during one hundred births.

52a.

Through concentration on Tāra, one gains knowledge of all subjects. By holding the mind at the nosetip, one gains knowledge of the Indra world. By holding the mind below that, one gains knowledge of the Agni world. By holding the mind in the eye, one gains knowledge of all worlds; in the ear, knowledge of the Yama world; beside it, knowledge of the Nirṛti world; at the back [of the ear] knowledge of the Varuṇa world; in the left ear, knowledge of the Vāyu world; in the throat, knowledge of the Soma world; in the left eye, knowledge of the Śiva world; in the head, knowledge of the Brahma world; in the soles of the feet, knowledge of the Atala world; in the feet, knowledge of the Vitala world; in the ankles, knowledge of the Nitala world; in the calves, knowledge of the Sutala world; in the knees, knowledge of the Mahātala world; in the thighs, knowledge of the Rasātala world; in the loins, knowledge of the Talātala world; in the navel, knowledge of Bhūrloka; in the belly, knowledge of Bhruvarloka; in the heart, knowledge of the Suvar world; in the place above the heart, knowledge of the Mahar world; in the throat, knowledge of the Jana world; in the eyebrow centre, knowledge of the Tapa world; in the head, knowledge of the Satya world.

52b.

By constraint on what is right and wrong, one knows the past and future. By holding the mind on the sound of this and that creature, one can know the cry of all creatures. By constraint on the mind on past karmas, one has knowledge previous births. By constraint on the mind of another, one can know the thoughts of others. By constraint on the form of the body, the form [of] other [objects] can be seen. By constraint on strength, the strength of Hanumān and others [can be attained]. By constraint on the sun, one can know the cosmos. By constraint on the moon, one can know the formation of the fixed stars. [By constraint on] the pole star, one has insight into its movement. By constraint on one's own Self, [one gains] knowledge of pure consciousness; at the cakra at the navel, [one gains] knowledge [of oneself as] a group of bodies; at the well of the throat, freedom from hunger and thirst; in the *kūrma nāḍī* [in the well of the throat], steadiness [of concentration]; in the pupil of the eye, the sight [of] the perfected ones. By constraint on the *ākāśa* in the body, one moves in the ākāśa. Thus, whoever [can practise] constraint in any place, becomes a seer.

Eighth Section

1 to 2.

Now *pratyāhāra*: it [is] of five kinds. Pratyāhāra [is] the withdrawal [of the mind] from the power of the sense organs moving in the objects of the senses. Whatever ones sees is all ātman: this is pratyāhāra. Renouncing the fruits of actions performed daily [is] pratyāhāra. Turning away from all sense objects of the outer world [is] pratyāhāra. Concentration on eighteen parts of the body in the [following] order [is] pratyāhāra. The feet, big toes, ankles, calves, knees, thighs, anus, penis, navel, heart, well of the throat, palate, nose, eyes, eyebrow centre, forehead and head [are their] locations. One should withdraw from these gradually, in ascending and descending order.

Ninth Section

1.

Now *dhāraṇā*: it [is] of three kinds: thus, holding the mind in the *ātman*, contemplating the external *ākāśa* in the small ākāśa, and concentrating on the five forms [of the elements]: earth, water, fire, air and ether.

Tenth Section

1.

Now *dhyānam*: so this [is] of two kinds, *saguṇa* and *nirguṇa*. Saguṇa [is] meditation on a form, whereas nirguṇa [is meditation on] one's own Self.

Eleventh Section

1.

Now *samādhi* [is] the union of the individual self [with] the cosmic Self, free from the threefold state. It is [of] the nature of supreme bliss, based on pure consciousness.

Chapter Two

1 to 6.

Now the Brahma-Ṛṣi Śāṇḍilya, not obtaining the knowledge of Brahman in the four Vedas, respectfully approached the Lord Atharvan [and with this] desire asked: "O Lord, by what means can I obtain the knowledge of Brahman, [who is] supreme?"

Atharvan replied: "Śāṇḍilya, Brahman [is] truth, wisdom [and] infinity, in which all this is woven and pervaded by, and in which all this is manifested and in which all [that] is known is all understood. It [is] without hands and feet, without eyes and ears, without tongue, without body, [and is] unattainable and indescribable. Since [Brahman] cannot be reached, speech together with mind must turn back. This pure consciousness is attainable through jñāna, from which ancient wisdom came forth. That which is one and non-dual, moves in everything within ākāśa, [is] subtle, without blemish, invaluable, the true essence, [whose] only delight [is] the bliss of consciousness, auspicious; calm and immortal, supreme, that [is] Brahman. That thou art. That you realise through jñāna.

He who [is] the one Divine Being, the cause of the power of the ātman, the omniscient, the lord of all, the inner Self of all beings, who dwells in all beings, hidden in all beings, the source of [all] beings, accessible only by yoga, and who creates the universe, maintains the universe [and] consumes the universe - he is Ātmā. Know all worlds in the ātman. Do not grieve, knower of the Self. You will reach the end of sorrow."

Chapter Three
First Section
1 to 6.
Then Śāṇḍilya asked Atharvan: "From him who is the one Supreme Brahman, imperishable, actionless, auspicious, the true essence, how did this universe take birth? How does it endure? How is it absorbed? Please remove this doubt for me, o Noble One."

Atharvan replied thus: "O Śāṇḍilya, the Supreme Brahman is truth, imperishable and actionless. Then, from Brahman [who is] beyond form, three forms emerged, with parts, without parts and both with and without parts. That which is true, wise and blissful, without action, without blemish, omnipresent, subtle, with faces in every direction, undefinable and immortal, that [is] the form without parts. She who originates from Him [as] *avidyā*, the source of nature and the illusive power, [which is] red, white and black, is ruled by the Divine Maheśvara [who is] black and yellow, [and] accompanied by her. This is the form with parts.

Then He, by his divine wisdom, increase of willpower, without restraint of desire, said: 'let me bring forth, let me be many'. Then, from Him were born, from the will of purity [and] desire for truth, the three letters. The three worlds, the three-footed Gāyatrī, the three Vedas, the three devas, the three *varṇas* and the three fires arose. The Divine Lord, who is endowed with all powers, all pervading, enveloped in the heart of all beings [and] the Lord of *māyā,* plays through *māyā*. He is Brahmā; He is Viṣṇu; He is Rudra; He is Indra; He is all Divine Beings; [He is] all the elements; He is in front; He is behind; He is north; He is south; He is below; He is above; indeed He is all. The form of [himself as] Dattātreya, who amuses himself as Śakti, compassionate to his devotees, wise, not abiding in the body, splendid as the petal of a blue lotus, with four arms, benign [and] shining purely, this is his form with and without parts."

Second Section

1 to 10.

Then Śāṇḍilya asked Atharvan: "O Lord, He [who is] the True Essence, [whose] only delight [is] the bliss of consciousness - why is He called the Supreme Brahman?"

Atharvan replied thus: "Because He expands heaven and earth and everything [in it], therefore He is called the Supreme Brahman. Why is He called Ātmā? Because He obtains everything, receives everything and consumes everything, therefore He is called Ātmā. Then why is He called Maheśvara? Because by the sound of the words Mahata Īśaḥ, and by His own power, Mahata rules [everything]. Therefore He is called Maheśvara. Then why is He called Dattātreya? [Dattātreya] was given by the Lord himself through His Divine Light because He was pleased with Atri who had purified [himself] by performing very arduous austerities [as he was] desirous of sons and for the son to have Anasūyā as his mother. Therefore he is called Dattātreya. Now whoever [understands] this divine explanation [understands] everything divine. Now whoever is devoted to the Supreme with the knowledge that 'I Am He', becomes a knower of Brahman.

11 to 15.

Here are these verses:

'Whoever always meditates thus on the eternal Lord of Lords, Dattātreya, [who is] benevolent, peaceful, a mighty Lord [who is] like a sapphire, [who] delights in his own māyā, the Lord [who has] shaken off [everything], naked, [whose] whole body is smeared with ash, having long twisted tresses, all-pervading, [whose] lofty body [has] four arms, [and] eyes [like] the lotus in full bloom, [who is] the store of jñāna and yoga, the guru of all worlds, dear to yogins, compassionate to his devotees, the witness of all [and] served by siddhas, is freed from all sins [and] attains ultimate bliss.'

Om is Truth."

This [ends] the Upaniṣad.

F. Swami Satyadharma

On 12th June 2019 on the Central Coast of New South Wales, Australia, our beloved Swami Satyadharma left her body. It was on the day of Ganga Dussehra, celebrating the descent to Earth of the goddess Ganga, Ganga the mother providing nourishment to all her children.

Dedications in her commentaries on the Yoga Upanishads have been to all spiritual aspirants. Swami Satyadharma's life was dedicated for over forty years to providing spiritual nourishment and bringing the light of yoga to all those who attended her programs throughout the world.

Swami Satyadharma was born in 1946 to a middle-class family in Connecticut, USA. She was the youngest of three and lived surrounded by nature and animals. She recognised the spiritual energy of nature, and was never attracted to big cities.

In search of purpose and spiritual guidance she travelled for years throughout Europe, Africa and Asia, where she met many enlightened masters. She spent two years in Nepal studying with Tibetan Buddhist lamas. She was an accomplished musician of the flute and guitar, and spent two years at the University of Bengal studying the sitar. In Java, Indonesia she first studied batik, and then took part in a meditation program in one of the Javanese mystical schools. Her teacher was a *mahasiddha* who was 'breathtaking, awe-inspiring, transformative'. He specifically singled her out and said 'you have a future if you go and study earnestly, and after a long time you will attain an elevated consciousness as a yoga teacher, and you'll spend the later part of your life travelling internationally, and you'll teach the highest level yoga teachings'. She was directed by the master to go to Mungher, Bihar, India, where she would meet a great teacher, Swami Satyananda, a disciple of Swami Sivananda. There she stayed for thirty-five years.At the age of 28, she was initiated by Swami Satyananda into *pūrṇa sannyasa* (full renunciation), a Dashnami order connected with the Advaita Vedanta tradition established by Adi Shankaracharya to protect, preserve and propagate spiritual knowledge. She absorbed the teachings and worked hard for the ashram for the first twenty years she spent there.

Then she edited books written by Swami Satyananda and, under his guidance, travelled the world teaching a range of different spiritual courses on the Yogic Scriptures. And teach she did in Australia, USA, Canada, India, Nepal, Tibet, China, Japan, Korea, Columbia, Greece, Germany, Hungary, Bulgaria, France, Italy, Indonesia, New Zealand. In all those countries she was invited to come back time and time again. She had a great ability to teach. Her vast knowledge of the ancient scriptures was amazing. It just flowed from her. When she taught it was like she stepped into another zone, where she spoke with profound insight. That is why, if Swami Satyadharma was running a course, people would sign up regardless of the topic. Her deep understanding of yoga was reflected in the numerous topics she taught.

Her later years were devoted to writing commentaries on the Yoga Upanishads, including *Yoga Tattwa, Yoga Darshana, Yoga Kundali, Nadabindu* and *Dhyanabindu Upanishads*.

Swami Satyadharma's Programs, Retreats and Lectures
Programs
Awakening Kundalini, Meditations from the Tantras, Dancing with Divine, Atma Darshan, Intuition, Guru Tattwa, Shiva Sutras, Mantra Yantra and Mandala, Ashram Life, Sadhana, Chakra Meditation, Spiritual Life.

***Deepening Sadhana* Retreats**
Kriya Yoga, Tattwa Shuddhi, Chakra Shuddhi, Prana Vidya and Mahavidya Sadhana.

Lectures

During the years she lived in Australia, she gave many satsangs and lectures to students enrolled in Yogic Studies courses. Topics included Origins of Yoga, Samkhya Tantra & Vedanta, Yoga Sutras, Koshas, Chakras, Gunas, Bhagavad Gita, SWAN Theory, Raja Yoga, Gyan Yoga, Bhakti Yoga, Karma Yoga, Hatha Yoga, Upanishads, Pranava, Shiva Shakti, Mantra & Nada, Mantra Yoga, Nada Yoga, Mudra & Bandha,Shatkarmas, Kundalini Yoga, Swara Yoga, Prana & Pranayama, Pratyahara, Theory & Practice of Antar Mouna, Yoga Psychology, Yoga Philosophy, Yoga in India, Yoga Ecology, Yoga History, Path of the Rishis, Yamas & Niyamas, Yoga & Religion, Meditation, Yoga Nidra, Addiction,Purpose in Life, Grief, Body-Mind Therapy, Opening the Heart, Perception, Models of Mind, Mind & Consciousness, Mind Management and Living Consciously.

I was privileged to have worked with Swami Satyadharma for nine years. Her unlimited love and teachings will live on well into the future.

Om Tat Sat

Srimukti

G. Author's Note

I started working with Swami Satyadharma early in 2010, collating teachings on Bhakti Yoga, Rāja Yoga and Jñāna Yoga. At that time I had a yoga studio in Sydney, Australia, where I would occasionally invite senior teachers to give weekend programs. Swami Satyadharma had agreed to give a program on *Prāṇa Prāṇāyama Prāṇa Vidyā*. As usual with her programs, it was booked out well in advance. In 2011 she gave a program on *Managing the Mind through Meditation* and in 2014 *Yoga of the Heart* at a time when she was very supportive to me as my husband was ill in hospital.

Our working relationship and friendship developed over the nine years I worked with her on the teachings project and later as translator of the Yoga Upanishads on which she wrote commentaries. She had asked me what I was going to do with the Sanskrit I had studied. "Look for something to translate, I suppose," I said. "I've got something for you to translate: the Yoga Upanishads, there are only twenty-one of them," she said as if the matter had been settled. The project was unique because there were no other published commentaries on the Yoga Upanishads, except for *Chudamani Upanishad* which she'd completed in Bihar in 2003.Later she told me she had made a *sankalpa* before she moved to Australia that she would find a translator here.

Together we collaborated on the *Yoga Tattwa, Yoga Darshana, Yoga Kundali, Nadabindu* and *Dhyanabindu Upanishads.* Wherever we were, at her home, on a bushwalk or at a beach, we would have long talks about the work we were doing together. She wanted us to work on *Shandilya Upanishad* next, so I hope my commentary has done her justice.

For many years I was a teacher of yoga and meditation. Already a linguist, having graduated in French, Italian and Japanese from the Universities of Sydney and Queensland, Australia, I undertook four years of studies in Sanskrit at the Australian National University (ANU) with Dr McComas Taylor. I was invited to join the Golden Key International Society for outstanding academic achievement, having gained High Distinctions throughout my Sanskrit studies.

Ruth Perini (Srimukti)
26th June 2020
yoga.upanishads@yahoo.com.

www.ingramcontent.com/pod-product-compliance
Lightning Source LLC
Chambersburg PA
CBHW070252010526
44107CB00056B/2435
9780648910701